Immigration and social cohesion in the Republic of Ireland

MANCHESTER
1824

Manchester University Press

Immigration and social cohesion in the Republic of Ireland

BRYAN FANNING

Manchester University Press
Manchester and New York

distributed exclusively in the USA by Palgrave Macmillan

Copyright © Bryan Fanning 2011

The right of Bryan Fanning to be identified as the author of this work has been asserted by him in accordance with the Copyright, Designs and Patents Act 1988.

Published by Manchester University Press
Oxford Road, Manchester M13 9NR, UK
and Room 400, 175 Fifth Avenue, New York, NY 10010, USA
www.manchesteruniversitypress.co.uk

Distributed exclusively in the USA by
Palgrave Macmillan, 175 Fifth Avenue, New York,
NY 10010, USA

Distributed exclusively in Canada by
UBC Press, University of British Columbia, 2029 West Mall,
Vancouver, BC, Canada V6T 1Z2

British Library Cataloguing-in-Publication Data
A catalogue record for this book is available from the British Library

Library of Congress Cataloging-in-Publication Data applied for

ISBN 978 0 7190 8478 2 *hardback*
     978 0 7190 8479 9 *paperback*

First published 2011

The publisher has no responsibility for the persistence or accuracy of URLs for external or any third-party internet websites referred to in this book, and does not guarantee that any content on such websites is, or will remain, accurate or appropriate.

Typeset in Minion Pro by
Koinonia, Manchester
Printed and bound in Great Britain by
CPI Antony Rowe Ltd, Chippenham, Wiltshire

Contents

List of figures

Acknowledgements

First and foremost I wish to thank Dr Neil O'Boyle, my colleague on the Integration and Social Change research project funded by the Irish Research Council for the Humanities and Social Sciences (IRCHSS). A number of chapters in this book draw on our research modules on immigrant civic and political participation and the role of quantitative demographic data in understanding immigrant socio-spatial segregation and social exclusion. I also must acknowledge the contributions of other academic collaborators on various reports and articles produced as part of the Integration and Social Change programme: Professor Tony Fahey, Professor Jo Shaw, Dr Kevin Howard and Trutz Hasse. This book stands on the shoulders of the many immigrants, community activists, researchers and academics who have spoken and written about the experiences of immigrants in Irish society. In particular, I drew on qualitative research undertaken by the Migrants Rights Centre Ireland, journalism and commentary from *Metro Éireann*, quantitative research undertaken by the Economic and Social Research Institute and analyses of immigration and social change published in *Translocations*, the journal that I co-edit with Professor Ronaldo Munck (www.translocations.ie). I wish to particularly thank the eighteen immigrant candidates we interviewed in advance of the 2009 local elections for their insights. Thanks also to Viola De Bucchianico, Rafal Jaros and Kirsty Hanifin, respectively the integration officers for Fianna Fáil, Fine Gael and the Labour Party, and to Niamh Nestor for the support they gave to our research on immigrant political participation. I also received important assistance from the Immigrant Council of Ireland, in particular from Fidele Mutwarasibo. At University College Dublin, Dr Sean L'Estrange gave wise counsel on the structure of the book and was a sceptical sounding board. I also wish in particular to thank Professor Brian Nolan and Dr Ronnie Moore. Conversations with students, in particular Ann Kinsella, Esther Onolememen and Tutu Olaitan, influenced my analysis. The School of Applied Social Science provided a supportive environment for my research and my family, Joan, Caitriona, Eilis and Ellie, put up with me. This book is dedicated to Professor Gabriel Kiely in acknowledgement of his encouragement and example over the years.

List of abbreviations and Irish terms

AkiDwa	Akina Dada wa Africa (African Women's Organisation)
ASC	Africa Solidarity Centre / Africa Centre
CBP	*Common Basic Principles for Immigrant Integration in the European Union*
D15	Dublin 15
Dáil	Parliament, lower house
DEIS	Delivering Equality of Opportunity in Schools
DICP	Dublin Inner City Partnership
DJELR	Department of Justice, Equality and Law Reform
DWS	*The Developmental Welfare State*
ED	electoral district
ELS	English Language Support
ESRI	Economic and Social Research Institute
EU-10	The new 2004 European Union member states
FAS	Foras Áiseanna Saothair (Irish state employment training agency)
Gardai Síochána	Irish Police
HRC	Habitual Residence Condition
ICI	Immigrant Council of Ireland
IoD	Index of Dissimilarity
MRCI	Migrants Rights Centre Ireland
NASC	Cork immigrant support group
NESC	National Economic and Social Council
NCCRI	National Consultative Committee on Racism and Interculturalism
Oireachtas	Parliament, both houses
PPS	Personal Public Service number
Taoiseach	Prime Minister
VRC	Vincentian Refugee Centre
WBCFN	well-being of children, families and neighbourhoods

1

Identities and capabilities

Irish Society is fundamentally and irrevocably multicultural by nature. A new dimension in our planning which focuses on integrating our immigrant population is required. (*National Development Plan 2007–2013*, p. 266)

This book was envisaged as both sequel to and expansion on themes addressed in two earlier volumes published by Manchester University Press. The aim of *Racism and Social Change in the Republic of Ireland* (2002) was to draw attention to the exclusionary potential of the legacies of monocultural nation building during the nineteenth and twentieth centuries. It combined a historical focus on the marginalisation of Jewish, Protestant and Traveller minorities with case studies addressing the specific mechanics of exclusion in specific post-independence settings. These included examinations of the politics of spatial exclusions encountered by Travellers in County Clare, overt discrimination against Jewish refugees before, during and after the Holocaust and analyses of responses to asylum seekers and other migrants. *Immigration and Social Change in the Republic of Ireland* (2007) sought to bring together a growing body of research on the experiences of the new communities by Irish and immigrant academics. It captured a period of rapid demographic change between 1997 and 2005, with chapters on economy, law, social policy and politics and on the experiences of a number of immigrant communities.

Immigration and Social Cohesion in the Republic of Ireland draws on a rapidly growing body of research on the experiences of immigrants and responses to immigrants. It examines Irish debates about integration locating them against the European Union and post-9/11 Western liberal perspectives that have come to frame policy and media debates about the consequences of immigration. It makes a necessary distinction between such ideological and normative debates and empirical knowledge and knowledge gaps about the challenges of integration in particular contexts. Normative understandings of concepts and issues are crucial because dominant understandings tend to mould choices. Normatively, integration refers to the process by which immigrants become accepted into a society, both as individuals and as groups.[1]

However it comes to be defined, the implicit assumption is that some degree of conformity represents 'successful' integration.[2] But conformity to what? Sociological, political science and social policy vantage points posit overlapping rules of belonging. The first is preoccupied with understanding social reproduction, how society changes from one generation to the next in terms of values, culture and beliefs and the relationships between this changing social structure and individual agency. Here, it is not just identity rules of belonging that matter but the capabilities that contribute to successful adaptation within the host society. Overlapping aspects of these are captured by concepts such as habitus (sociology), acculturation (psychology) and capabilities (economics and social policy), the characteristics, dispositions, skills and forms of knowledge understood to foster integration; these can change over time as well as differ from place to place. As such, the integration of immigrants and the social inclusion of existing citizens, to whom such rules of belonging also pertain, must hit a moving target. In considering what this might be in the Irish case, Chapter 2 addresses the following question: why did a country adept at squeezing out surplus family members since the Famine, one that defined itself as monocultural, one that found it difficult to accommodate its small Jewish, Protestant and Traveller minorities, somehow embrace large-scale immigration?

The focus of this book is predominantly on the role of social policy rather than symbolic politics in promoting or impeding integration. A core argument is that integration debates and goals cannot be meaningfully detached from the social inclusion goals understood to apply to Irish citizens. The conversations about integration conducted from different angles in different chapters are variously framed in conceptual debates about social capital, cultural capital, human capital and human capability. Wherever possible the focus is on specific case studies; here I draw on the recent work of a large number of other researchers as well as specific research on immigration, well-being and social inclusion and immigrant participation in Irish politics. The aim, wherever possible, is to consider the experiences of immigrants in concrete situations. Much of the analysis concerns specific barriers encountered by immigrants that might be understood to undermine their integration into Irish society.

One aim of this empirical approach is to sidestep, insofar as this is practical, the sterile contributions of symbolic postures; here I have in mind the post-9/11 'narrative of crisis' which to some extent has come to frame Irish media commentary.[3] In Gavan Titley and Alana Lentin's summary:

> The notion that multiculturalism is in crisis is a predominant feature of the post-9/11 world and has become a pronounced aspect of public debate across Western Europe. A broadly shared narrative of crisis has emerged that perceives a range of states emerging from a period of failed experimentation that emphasized difference over commonality, cultural particularity over social cohesion, and a default relativism at the expense of shared liberal/universal/national values.[4]

Such perspectives present integration as being about public sphere politics, culture (protecting the former against the latter) and social cohesion (opposing 'too much diversity' as distinct from wider social and economic dislocations). Faced with complex social problems, the political temptation to reach for symbolic proxies can be strong. In France, for example, the challenges of addressing immigrant social exclusion are profound but French integration politics became fixated on the symbolic issue of prohibiting the headscarf in the public sphere. By liberal and feminist criteria the ban claimed to emancipate Muslim girls, but it hardly addressed the material exclusions experienced by Muslims in France. As put by Emmanuel Terray in 'Headscarf Hysteria', a 2004 analysis French symbolic politics,

> During the past year in France the headscarf issue has fulfilled the role of fictive problem very neatly. To be credible, the hysterical substitution must satisfy certain conditions. Firstly, it must bear some manifest relation to the actual problems it is called upon to replace, so that in speaking of it one can have the sense that one is grappling with them – although without ever needing to do so explicitly. The headscarf is worn by Muslim girls, nearly all of whom come from immigrant families; at a stroke it invokes – genie like – the problems of cultural exclusion and gender inequality.[5]

Somehow the fact that 1,200 or so Muslim girls sought to wear a headscarf to school (Terray found that this number had remained constant for several years prior to 2004, yet more than 4 million Muslims live in France) transmogrified into a 'great national debate', whilst sidelining how these people typically lived in neighbourhoods with unemployment rates of 30 to 40 percent.[6]

When a handful of Muslim girls sought permission to wear a hijab as part of their school uniform the Irish media smelled controversy; one prominent journalist, Kevin Myers, sought actively to promote headscarf hysteria.[7] Myers took vitriolic issue with a press statement by the Minister of State for Integration, Conor Lenihan, advocating tolerance: 'For those that wear the hijab, it's an issue of modesty. It's not so long since Irishwomen wore headscarves to church, so we have to respect that.'[8] In September 2007 the principal of Gorey Community School in County Wexford sought guidelines from the Department of Education on the wearing of the hijab by Muslim schoolgirls. The issue had also exercised the local Gaelic Athletic Association club (Naomh Enna), which decided to allow the girls to wear hijabs underneath their protective helmets when playing camogie (the women's equivalent of the sport of hurling). Groups such as the Joint Management Body for Secondary Schools and the Management Association of Catholic Secondary Schools advised schools not to make an issue of school uniform rules where these conflict with a child's religion.[9] When asked to comment in May 2008, the Minister of Education, Batt O'Keefe, said he did not regard questions about the Muslim veil as a serious issue in Ireland.[10] Yet none of this apparent tolerance should be taken to exempt Ireland from wider Western cultural presumptions about integration and social cohesion.

The cultural politics of integration

With slight variation in different Western countries, the liberal narrative of progress included extension of the franchise, female suffrage, adopting ideals of universal human rights, decriminalisation of homosexuality, influential feminist challenges to gender inequality, contestation of racism, focus on the rights of people with disabilities and, most recently, legal recognition of same-sex relationships. The intersection of post-9/11 'clash of civilisation' responses to Islam and antipathy to multiculturalism within liberal democracies highlights the extent to which the public sphere is understood as a cultural sphere in its own right, one idealised in terms of secular values and individual personal autonomy and history of progress. Here, as always, the role of out-groups in communal self-definition is important. Examples include not only perceived external threats to liberal values but also 'enemies within', who are seen to undermine individual freedom, undermine progressive political gains or intellectually turn back the clock on the Enlightenment.

However, ethnocentric liberalism is not solely defined against Christian or Muslim 'fundamentalism'. Sociologists have emphasised how modernity reconfigured social cohesion from what Ferdinand Tönnies called *Gemeinschaft* to *Gesellschaft* or what Emile Durkheim similarly referred to as a shift from mechanistic solidarity to an organic solidarity of interdependence.[11] Simply put, modernity produced shifts in dominant cultural identities and nation-state rules of belonging, not just through the modernisation of culture but also through ontological displacement. For all that nation-states venerate their pasts, they may find little room for real ancestors, as is evident from the marginal status of 'indigenous' remaindered out-groups whose beliefs, cultural practices and norms present them as out of step with dominant current ones.[12] How and to what extent such modernisation shaped Irish responses to immigration is considered in Chapter 2.

Archetypically, ethnocentric liberalism will tend to be directed at three kinds of out-groups: the Muslim communities taken to offer proof that multiculturalism does not work, largely because they are ontologically at odds with the West; Christian religious 'fundamentalists', also seen to challenge the gains of the Enlightenment; and some remaindered indigenous minorities living 'at odds' with modernity. One Irish example of the latter has been the increasing mobilisation of ethnocentric liberal intolerance towards Travellers. In each case cleavages relate to ontology and habitus rather than phenotype or linguistic culture, though out-groups may also be racialised.

Some of the political consequences of such cleavages had been anticipated by Richard Rorty during the later 1980s.[13] Rorty depicted Western liberalism as a socio-political culture that has come to make openness to other cultures central to its self-image. Liberalism so defined is presented as an *ethnos* which prides itself on its suspicion of ethnocentrism.[14] Yet its moral self-confidence unravels when it encounters the dilemma of being intolerant or intolerance. Rorty's challenge was directed at anxious 'wet liberals' who tied themselves in knots worrying about whether they were forcing their values on non-Western cultures. He made the case for intolerance of tolerance of intolerance, or as he put it, 'anti-anti-ethnocentricism'.[15] Rorty's intellectual vantage point is the pragmatist philosophy of Charles Sanders Pierce and William James.[16] Pierce interpreted beliefs as rules or habits of action.[17] Their usefulness lies in how they help those who hold them, as habits of action, or as will to power, or as good software, rather than whether or not particular beliefs are true. It is by no means important whether beliefs represent a true picture of reality; they are unlikely to do so in any case; Rorty described his own perspective as anti-representationalist.[18] Drawing on the early pragmatists, he depicted knowledge itself as ethnocentric; our only useful notions of 'true' and 'real' and 'good' are those extrapolated from our normative practices and our beliefs.[19]

But this pragmatic account of truth should not be confused with relativism. Relativism suggests three things for Rorty, the first two of which can be readily dismissed by a pragmatist. There is view that every belief is as good as another. The second is to maintain that 'true' is an equivocal term with as many meanings as there are procedures for justification. The third is an ethnocentric pragmatist view that there is nothing to be said for either truth or rationality other than that they offer descriptions of the familiar procedures of justification that are used by a given society, namely one's own.[20] The choice then, for liberals (or anyone else), is whether to privilege to one's own community or to pretend an impossible tolerance for every other group:

> I have been arguing that we pragmatists should grasp the ethnocentric horn of this dilemma. We should say that we must, in practice, privilege our own group, even though there can be no noncircular justification for doing so ... We Western liberal intellectuals should accept the fact that we have to start from where we are, and this means that there are lots of views which we cannot take seriously.[21]

Rorty emphasised that the core values of liberalism were hardly *a priori* truths; they were recent parochial cultural developments worth fighting to preserve (to those who value them), but ones unlikely to be universally accepted.[22] In Barry Allen's summary, Rorty condoned ethnocentrism where the ethnos at the centre was a liberal democratic society. Without liberalism, ethnocentrism would be awful: '*Our* ethnocentrism is different from other kinds.'[23]

Nevertheless there are overlaps and continuities between ethnocentric liberalism and past Western colonial racism.[24] Distinctions made in the nineteenth

century between superior and inferior races were part of a broader Enlightenment discourse of progress within the West. Ontological shifts occurred within
Western racism whereby, as Adam Lively put it, old wine poured into new
bottles.[25] The discrediting of religious and scientific 'proofs' of racism shifted
the emphasis towards claims about cultural inferiority; these continue to find
acceptance to a lesser or greater extent within mainstream Western politics.
To some extent there are commonalities between such cultural racialisation
and what is referred to here as ethnocentric liberalism; both *are* predicated
upon notions of cultural superiority and inferiority. The differences lie in the
nature and dynamics of licence for intolerance that ethnocentric liberalism
confers upon progressive Western politics and intellectual life. Politically and
intellectually, the civil war is with 'liberal-culturalism', a term that covers both
multicultural and liberal-nationalist endorsements for accommodating of
plural cultural identities within liberal-democratic states.[26]

Since 9/11 and the Bradford riots, much has been written about the
potential dangers of cultural conflicts to social cohesion; the dominant
ethnocentric liberal perspective has emphasised the dangers of multiculturalism and promoted more coercive regulation of culture within the public
sphere. In this context the hitherto much criticised idea of assimilation makes
something of a comeback. Rogers Brubaker tellingly described assimilation
(except in France) as a 'contaminated' term associated with the past failures
of nativist responses to immigration, 'morally and politically repugnant'
state policies that sought to assimilate people against their will: 'Abundant
historical and comparative evidence, moreover, suggests that they rarely
work, and they are indeed more likely to strengthen than erode difference by
provoking a reactive mobilisation against such assimilatory pressures.'[27] But
anti-racist critiques of multiculturalism have also emphasised policy failure.[28]
Brian Turner has argued that British multiculturalism was defined by British
liberalism (what Rorty calls liberal-culturalism); this permitted the 'benign
neglect' of minorities. In explaining this, Turner draws on Isaiah Berlin's two
concepts of liberty, the distinction between negative and positive conceptions
of liberty; immigrants were generally accorded the former but were often
denied the latter.[29]

As defined by Berlin, negative freedom was 'freedom from'; it existed until
someone encroached upon it, examples being freedoms of expression, worship
or assembly. Positive freedoms, Berlin emphasised, depended on access to the
means to achieve them: 'if a man is too poor to afford something on which
there is no legal ban – a loaf of bread, a journey round the world, recourse to
the law courts – he is as little free to have it as he would be if it were forbidden
to him by law.'[30] Berlin understood freedom as the capability of individuals
to realise their own ends. Yet individual capabilities are influenced by factors
outside of individual control. So too are the aspirations of individuals shaped

by the society or culture of which they were part. From this perspective the ability of immigrants to integrate (however this is defined) depends on the means to do so as well as upon the desire to do so.

Such means, various case studies in this book suggest, include individual capabilities, human capital, social capital and cultural capital. At a societal level the means of fostering integration necessarily include the contestation of racism and discrimination and the use of social policy to promote the social and economic inclusion of immigrants. A key problem is that some immigrants face deliberate barriers to their integration (lesser rights and entitlements that undermine their positive freedom to integrate) as well as various inadvertent institutional barriers. These, as Chapter 3 emphasises, are often put in place in the name of social cohesion; the Irish governance of immigration which overshadows predominant approaches to integration is predicated on security definitions of social cohesion that perceive any change resulting from immigration as unsettlement. The underlying presumptions are not too different from those of Robert Putnam, who has argued that immigration by its very nature undermines social cohesion; as he memorably put it, host communities will tend to 'hunker down'.[31]

Positive freedom, capabilities and personal capital

The approach of this book has been to draw wherever possible on the experiences of immigrants in considering the factors that facilitate or impede their integration. Analysis of these in Chapter 5 and Chapter 7 draws upon Amartya Sen's concept of capabilities. It also draws on equivalent understandings amongst sociologists and psychologists of how individual skills, dispositions and attributes confer the ability to participate in particular organisational or societal contexts. From Sen's capabilities perspective, freedom depends on the options a person has in deciding what kind of life to lead as well as the presence or absence of coercion. Much the same might be said about their opportunities to integrate. Some immigrants have considerably lesser rights or poorer options than many Irish citizens. They make choices about where to live and work, to live apart from children and family or not, but often not under circumstances of their choosing.

The basic capabilities of any immigrant (or indeed anyone else) include various kinds of knowledge in addition to human capital. The potential benefits of human capital may be undermined by language barriers or by a lack of meaningful access to employment rights; such factors contribute to what economists call the immigrant penalty of lower incomes as compared to similarly qualified citizens within the labour market. Sen places considerable emphasis on how knowledge impediments, lesser rights or inadequate protection from discrimination translate into capabilities deficits.

Capabilities define aspects of a person's abilities to function in terms of what she manages to do or be. What a person can do with a bundle of commodities, such as the food she has to eat, depends on physical factors such as metabolism, age, gender and health. But humans do not merely perform well or poorly as biological machines. They make choices based on the information they have access to and can understand. Functioning, from Sen's perspective, refers to the use a person makes of the commodities at her command.[32] As he puts it with an audience of economists in mind:

> If education makes a person more efficient in commodity production, then this is clearly an enhancement of human capital. This can add to the value of production in the economy and also to the income of the person who has been educated. But even with the same level of income, a person may benefit from education, in reading, communicating, arguing, in being able to choose in a more informed way, in being taken more seriously by others and so on.[33]

Capabilities might be defined as the attributes that a person has at her disposal to realise her own ends. Like human capital or incomes, their practical value comes from what they help people to achieve.[34] Sen is critical of overtly simplistic accounts of human motivations proposed by economists that ignore 'all other motivations other than the pursuit of self-interest'.[35] He argues that 'so-called rational choice theory' actually takes the rationality out of choice; it ignores the conditions, contexts and individual capabilities which inform the actual choices open to people. To this effect he repeatedly quotes Adam Smith against the neo-liberal economists who claim to be his disciples. The influence of Smith on Sen's understanding of capabilities is suggested by the following quote from *The Wealth of Nations*:

> The difference between the most dissimilar characters, between a philosopher and common street porter, for example, seems to arise not so much from nature as from habit, custom and education. When they come into the world, and for the first six or eight years of their existence, they were, perhaps, very much alike, and neither their parents nor play-fellows could perceive any remarkable difference.[36]

Somewhat similarly, social research on well-being and living conditions emphasises a range of factors other than material conditions. In Brian Nolan's summary of Swedish 'level of living' welfare research (which has much in common with Sen's capabilities approach) these include 'knowledge, mental and physical energy and social relationships, through which an individual can control and consciously direct his living conditions'.[37]

Futhermore some degree of overlap can be identified between capabilities and some forms of individual social or cultural capital. One of the case studies examined in Chapter 5 considers the role of what Robert Putnam calls bonding social capital. Putnam argues that bonding social capital can undermine wider social cohesion. The Chapter 5 case study illustrates how immigrants who cannot speak English or who lack the capabilities to interact independently in the host society may be exploited by co-ethnics who, in effect, charge for brokering access to jobs and services. In such cases bonding social capital potentially impedes access to the wider Irish society. However, where immigrants possess the autonomy to engage independently in the wider society, where they can seek employment and access services in their own right, they may be less likely to experience bonding social capital as oppressive. Putnam places considerable importance on the integrating role of bridging social capital. He tends to measure this in terms of levels of participation rather than to focus on the skills and capabilities that engender such participation.

Pierre Bourdieu defines cultural capital as skills and dispositions that confer advantage on a person. Whilst capabilities are depicted as empowering (the power to achieve one's own ends) cultural capital is seen to be unequally distributed and to contribute to the intergenerational reproduction of inequalities.[38] Bourdieu uses the concept of habitus to describe how social structure becomes inscribed upon an individual. An individual's dispositions (how they perceive, behave, act, their 'feel for the game') are influenced by their experiences within the social structure (such as social class or educational background). Habitus, which in effect means habitual disposition, guides the choices individuals make; individual agency as such reflects the social milieu that individuals internalise as aspects of their personality. Bourdieu uses the term 'reproduction' to refer to the political, social and cultural processes that transmit the social structure and culture of a society over time. This includes the social policies and cultural mechanisms that transmit education and skills from one generation to the next. Cultural capital may be understood as a form of intellectual capital that affects the life chances of individuals even as it reproduces a specific social order. It confers status-enhancing forms of knowledge, norms and habits. The unequal distribution of cultural capital is seen to result in cultural hierarchies (defined in terms of socio-economic status as well as in terms of ethnic or religious divides) alongside material ones.[39] Much of this can be rendered in the language of Sen's capabilities approach, even if Sen the economist emphasises the potential of human agency to a greater extent than Bourdieu the determinist sociologist. Capabilities include habitual dispositions and forms of knowledge that structure the choices that people understand themselves as having. The case studies considered in Chapter 5 (Some immigrant lives) are examined from a capabilities perspective, but these could no less profitably be considered as an Irish equivalent to those examined by Bourdieu in his pioneering account of French immigrant lives in *The Weight of the World*.[40]

The capabilities approach and cultural capital perspectives find their equivalents in other social sciences. Both cultural capital and capabilities effects are suggested by child well-being research from a psychological perspective. This focuses on behavioural or cognitive attributes that also might be understood as capabilities deficits. For example, widely used methods of assessing child well-being (considered in Chapter 6) assess child psychological well-being by evaluating factors such as conduct, emotional symptoms, hyperactivity, peer problems and anti-social behaviour. To some extent such psychological well-being scores offer a proxy for cultural capital; children with serious difficulties patently lack many of the attributes that translate into educational advantage. But these disadvantages are hardly innate. Occupational therapy and special educational needs provision can play a crucial role in combating educational disadvantage. In Ireland, as elsewhere, comparatively low child well-being scores are disproportionately found in deprived communities. Yet Chapter 6 considers the findings of research on child well-being which suggests that some immigrant children fare better than long-standing inhabitants of these areas.

Capabilities, culture and empowerment

Some degree of caution is needed when moving from the use of such theories to explain how immigrants fare (as attempted in Chapter 5) to policy prescriptions. The attributes, skills and knowledge that count as capabilities depend on social context. The balance of capabilities that empower a person to flourish in one society may differ in another.[41] It is also the case that capabilities will be unequally distributed within a given society; capabilities are understood as conferring individual advantages; like individual social capital or cultural capital their value is relational. In other words, the advantages or opportunities these confer depend on the specific context. A charge can be levied that to speak of immigrant capabilities deficits is to be ethnocentric and that to insist on the acquisition of culturally specific capabilities is to advocate a degree of cultural assimilation. Certainly this would be the case where a zero-sum or essentialist definition of culture prevailed. Forms of education that impart new capabilities may also serve to acculturate recipients to new social circumstances. To some extent this is likely to be true of any empowering change of capabilities. Sen emphasises that culture is not a homogenous attribute; there can be great variations within any culture in terms of class, gender, profession, politics and even race; 'contemporary Iran has both conservative ayatollahs and radical dissidents just as America has room for born-again Christians and ardent nonbelievers'; within any culture there are a plethora of discordant voices and, in any case, culture does not stand still.[42] Chapter 5 argues that capabilities can usefully complement bonds with co-ethnics. Putnam distinguishes between bonding and bridging social capital; the implication is that the latter contributes to integration. A number of studies of immigrant culture considered in subsequent chapters suggest that bonds with co-ethnics or co-religionists can offer a staging post to wider participation in the host society. Strong immigrant religious or ethnic identities need not constitute a barrier to integration within the wider society if immigrants come to possess relevant capabilities and transferable cultural capital.

However, the host Irish society into which immigrants might integrate remains capable of raising ethnocentric barriers; the big example to date is the 2004 Referendum on Citizenship where Irish citizens voted by a four to one majority to remove the birthright to citizenship from the Irish-born children of immigrants. Capabilities in any quantity may not be able to overcome host-community ethnic nepotism, especially when the out-group cannot invoke citizenship rights and solidarities. Unless immigrants become Irish citizens in sufficient numbers to cognitively shift majority understandings of what it is to be Irish, the danger is always there that essentialist rules of belonging may trump any amount of capabilities. In another example of ethnic nepotism the Irish state has, for reasons considered in Chapter 3, imposed barriers to integration through the selective removal of some rights to welfare goods and services from some immigrants. These, as Chapter 7 explains, work to exclude immigrants from the remit of social inclusion programmes.

Yet, the cultural contexts against which immigrant capabilities must measure up to can hardly be reduced to some or other ethnic definition of belonging. Chapter 2 details the emergence of an Irish neo-liberal developmental modernity capable of discounting vulnerable and marginal Irish citizens whilst open to large-scale immigration. The 'rules of belonging', as inferred in reports advocating or describing economic development, seen as likely to confer social inclusion for citizens can be seen to shift over time. The main emphasis of such reports has been upon increasing levels of human capital, but a sociological analysis of these debates emphasises deeper underlying shifts in the habitual dispositions and capabilities required to flourish in Irish society. Ulrick Beck, Anthony Giddens and Stuart Lash (writing about changes within Western societies rather than immigrants) have variously emphasised an obligatory individual capacity for reflexive adaptation.[43] For its critics, the self-reflexive archetype became 'the ideal and privileged subject of neo-liberalism'.[44] As ever, the sociological and ideological debates become ones about individual agency and social structure, between claims about the potential for individual autonomy, and ones about the delimited contexts within which choices are exercised. Thinking of citizens rather than migrants, Paul Sweetman summarises the experience of reflexivity as one of self-regulation, self-surveillance and nervous self-scrutiny in a context of privatised risk and responsibility.[45] All this suggests that Westerners find rapid social change in their societies no less disconcerting than might immigrants cleaving to their traditions. If self-reflexivity was once billed as something new in such sociological theory, it has now, Matthew Adams suggests, become routinised as the habitual individual disposition of the times we live in.[46] Writing in 1992, Giddens suggested that: 'the self today is for everyone a reflexive project', which is to say that reflexivity has (or must) become habitual.[47] Both Giddens and Sen are preoccupied with the cognitive skills needed to adapt to changing social circumstances. To complain that the requirement to master these is oppressive is to misunderstand the bounded contexts within which people generally exert freedom. But it is also the case that changing societies create their own remaindered populations, those left behind because they were denied opportunities that others experienced as empowering. Nowhere is this so noticeable as in how education can reproduce intergenerational inequalities by literally leaving children behind. The potential for reflexivity and the opportunities to acquire capabilities (Adams uses the term 'reflexive capabilities') are unequally distributed.[48]

Whether the stakes are understood to be those depicted by Giddens or by Sen, citizens are no less candidates for integration than immigrants; they too must continually negotiate changing rules of belonging. As Ireland enters the second decade of the twenty-first century uncertainty about the future is the only certainty. Citizens and immigrants alike might be counselled to acquire flexible habits of mind as well as human capital. However, migrants who cannot demonstrate such qualities might be rejected out of hand. The example Christian Joppke gives is that of the Netherlands, where requirements that immigrants demonstrate 'autonomy' through labour market participation and learning the Dutch language have become increasingly coercive. In effect, they must learn Dutch before they are allowed in; individuals are required to invest in being able to fit into the host society in advance of being permitted to enter.[49] Many countries screen immigrants in such terms by restricting visas to skilled migrants. In the Irish case the ability to do so is restricted to non-EU migrants and this considerably explains the high levels of human capital such migrants possess. But, as Chapter 4 and Chapter 5 illustrate, the immigrant human capital advantage produced by such selection does not ensure integration even if this is defined solely in terms of labour market participation.

Various chapters examine institutional barriers to integration in the domains of education, social policy and politics and citizenship. In such domains different definitions of integration pertain, but these cumulatively suggest the need for holistic thinking about the attributes and rights that provide the opportunity structure for integration. Chapter 2 examines the 'nation-building' role of education in formation and reproduction of national identity. The education system has long been a crucial domain of cultural integration in this sense, but it is also, as considered in Chapter 6, a complex ecology within which social segregation can be enforced or contested. Both Chapter 4 and Chapter 6 consider the risks of the socio-spatial segregation of some immigrants in some relatively deprived areas. Some specific geographical areas feature prominently across different chapters, notably Dublin 15, which has featured in alarmist newspaper stories about 'white flight', in research about the experiences of African immigrant children in schools, but where also three African candidates contested the 2009 local government elections.

Collectively, the literatures on capabilities, social capital, cultural capital and psychological well-being emphasise the complexity of processes of social inclusion and exclusion. Together, this book argues, these can be taken to suggest (i) the value of defining integration in social policy terms as well as a political or economic issue; (ii) that emphasising the overlap between integration goals for immigrants and social inclusion goals for the host community (integration-as-social inclusion) offers a necessary empirical corrective to ideological debates which focus on multiculturalism and its discontents; and (iii) that integration-as-social inclusion cannot be reduced to economic participation but needs to take account of broader definitions of well-being and interdependency.

Notes

1 R. Penninx, 'Integration: The Role of Communities, Institutions, and the State' (2003). Available at: www.migrationinformation.org
2 H. Entzinger and R. Biezeveld, *Benchmarking in Immigrant Integration*, Report written for the European Commission, European Research Centre on Migration and Ethnic Relations (Rotterdam: ERCOMER, 2003), p. 8
3 G. Titley, 'Pleasing the Crisis: Anxiety and Recited Multiculturalism in European Communicative Space', in I.S. Moring (ed.), *Manufacturing Europe: Spaces of Democracy, Diversity and Communication* (Goteborg: Nordicom, 2010), p. 157
4 A. Lentin and G. Titley, *Questioning the European 'Crisis of Multiculturalism'* (2009). Available at: http://multiculturality.wordpress.com/about
5 E. Terray, 'Headscarf Hysteria', *New Left Review* (March 2004), 118–127
6 T.D. Keaton, *Muslim Girls and the Other France* (Bloomington, IN: Indiana University Press, 2006), p. 69
7 Kevin Myers, 'Shape Up or Ship Out Should Be Our Multicultural Message', *Irish Independent*, 5 June 2008
8 Cited in *ibid*.
9 K. Flynn 'Understanding Islam in Ireland', *Islam and Christian–Muslim Relations* 17.2 (2006), 223–238, p. 231
10 Shekina, Shakura and Shadia Egan were the daughters of a Gorey 'native' who had converted to Islam. 'State to Consider Muslim School-dress code', *Irish Independent*, 20 May 2008
11 F. Tönnies, *Community and Association* (London: Routledge and Kegan Paul, 1997); E. Durkheim, *The Division of Labour in Society* (London: Macmillan, 1984)
12 E. Gellner, *Culture, Identity and Politics* (Cambridge: Cambridge University Press, 1987), pp. 15–16
13 B. Fanning and T. Mooney, 'Pragmatism and Intolerance: Nietzsche and Rorty', *Philosophy and Social Criticism* 36 (2010), 735–755

14 R. Rorty, *Objectivism, Relativism and Truth* (New York: Cambridge University Press, 1991), p. 2

15 *Ibid.*, p. 203

16 The latter defined pragmatism as a philosophy with no dogmas, and no doctrine save its method. W. James, *Pragmatism* (Cambridge, MA: Harvard University Press, 1975), p. 317

17 Rorty, *Objectivity, Relativism and Truth*, p. 36

18 R. Rorty, *Philosophy and Social Hope* (London: Penguin, 1999) p. xxiv

19 Particularly on John Dewey, see B. Allen, 'What Was Epistemology?' in R.B. Brandom (ed.), *Rorty and His Critics* (London: Blackwell, 2002), p. 224, R. Rorty, *Philosophy and the Mirror of Nature* (Princeton, NJ: Princeton University Press, 1979), p. 337

20 Rorty, *Objectivity, Relativism and Truth*, p. 23

21 *Ibid.*, p. 29

22 *Ibid.*, pp. 208–209

23 Allen, 'What Was Epistemology?' p. 224

24 For example, in *On Liberty* John Stuart Mill defended colonialism in the West Indies, India and elsewhere, asserting that 'Despotism is a legitimate mode of government in dealing with barbarians, provided the end be their improvement and the means justified by actually effecting that end.' On the long-standing and troubled relationship between liberalism and multiculturalism see R. White, 'Liberalism and Multiculturalism: The Case of Mill', *The Journal of Value Inquiry* 37 (2003), 205–216, p. 205

25 A. Lively, *Masks: Blackness, Race and the Imagination* (London: Chatto and Windus, 1998), pp. 13–14

26 W. Kymlicka, *Politics in the Vernacular* (Oxford: Oxford University Press, 2001), pp. 47–48, C. Frost, 'Is Post-nationalism or Liberal-culturalism behind the Transformation of Irish Nationalism?' *Irish Political Studies* 21.3 (2006), 277–295, pp. 280–281

27 R. Brubaker, 'The Return of Assimilation? Changing Perspectives on Immigration and Its Sequels in France, Germany, and the United States', *Ethnic and Racial Studies* 24.4 (2001), 531–548, p. 533

28 Y. Alibhai-Brown, *After Multiculturalism* (London: The Foreign Policy Centre, 2000) p. 7

29 B.S. Turner, 'Citizenship and the Crisis of Multiculturalism', *Citizenship Studies* 10.5 (2006), 607–618, p. 614

30 I. Berlin 'Two Concepts of Liberty', in H. Hardy and R. Hausheer (eds) *The Proper Study of Mankind: An Anthology of Essays* (London: Pimlico, 1998), p. 194

31 R.D. Putnam, '*E Pluribus Unum*: Diversity and Community in the Twenty-first Century', *Scandinavian Political Studies* 30.2 (2006), 137–174

32 A. Sen, 'Capability and Well-being', in M. Nussbaum and A. Sen (eds), *The Quality of Life* (Oxford: Clarendon Press, 1993), pp. 30–53

33 A. Sen, 'Editorial: Human Capital and Human Capability', *World Development* 25.12 (1997) , 1959–1961, p. 1959

34 A. Sen, *The Idea of Justice* (London: Penguin, 2009) p. 226

35 *Ibid.*, p. 188

36 Adam Smith, *Wealth of Nations* (1776), pp. 28–29 cited in Sen, 'Human Capital and Human Capability', p. 1960

37 R. Erikson and R. Aberg (eds), *Welfare in Transition: Living Conditions in Sweden 1968–1981* (Oxford: Clarendon Press, 1987), cited in B. Nolan, 'Promoting the Well-being of Immigrant Youth', School of Applied Social Science, University College Dublin working paper, WP09/09, p. 3

38 P. Bourdieu 'The Social Space and the Genesis of Groups', *Theory and Society* 14.6 (1985), 723–444

39 P. Bourdieu *et al.*, *The Weight of the World: Social Suffering in Contemporary Society* (Cambridge: Polity Press, 1999), p. 186

40 *Ibid.*

41 Sen, *Idea of Justice*, p. 232

42 A. Sen, *Identity and Violence: The Illusion of Destiny* (London: Penguin, 2006), p. 112

43 See U. Beck, *Risk Society: Towards a New Modernity* (London: Sage, 1992) and various contributions to U. Beck, A. Giddens and S. Lash (eds), *Reflexive Modernization* (Cambridge: Polity Press 1994)

44 L. Adkins, *Revisions: Gender and Sexuality in Late Modernity* (Buckingham: Open University Press, 2002), p. 123

45 P. Sweetman, 'Twenty-first Century Dis-ease? Habitual Reflexivity and Reflexive Habitus', *Sociological Review* 51.4 (2003), 528–549

46 M. Adams, 'The Reflexive Self and Culture: A Critique', *British Journal of Sociology* 54.2 (2003), 221–238, p. 222

47 A. Giddens, *The Transformation of Intimacy* (Cambridge: Polity, 1992), p. 30

48 On the conceptual relationships between self-reflexivity, habitus and reflexive capabilities see M. Adams, 'Hybridizing Habitus and Reflexivity: Towards an Understanding of Contemporary Identity?' *Sociology* 40.3 (2006), 511–528, pp. 515–517

49 C. Joppke, 'Transformation of Immigrant Immigration: Civic Integration and Antidiscrimination in the Netherlands, France, and Germany', *World Politics*, 59 (January 2007), 243–273, p. 268

2

Integration into what?

They have declared their embarrassment in the face of simple-minded notions of nation, faith and fatherland; and have helped to erode these forces. But in the collapse all other 'isms', the market itself becomes the sole remaining ideology – and its idea of a Croatian or an Irish identity is Disneyesque in its naivety. (Declan Kiberd)

In 2004 the Republic of Ireland (hereafter Ireland) became one of just three European Union member states (along with the UK and Sweden) that agreed to allow unrestricted immigrants from the 10 new EU-accession states. Also in 2004, the Irish government introduced a referendum on citizenship. This was accompanied by a populist politics that emphasised distinctions between 'nationals' and 'non-nationals'. Some 80 percent of voters supported the removal of the constitutional birthright to Irish citizenship from the Irish-born children of migrants. But political populism in support of the referendum was mostly directed against formerly asylum-seeker African migrants and their children, not against immigration *per se*.[1] The contemporaneous government decision in 2004 to engineer rapid, large-scale immigration from within the EU barely caused a political ripple.

The change in policy in 2004 that allowed unfettered immigration from EU-accession countries had a dramatic demographic impact; between 1 May 2004 and 30 April 2005 some 85,114 workers from the new EU-10 were issued with PPS (national insurance) numbers, more than 10 times the number of new work permits granted to migrants from those countries in the preceding 12 months.[2] By 2005 Ireland's proportion of 10.4 percent foreign-born (as estimated by the OECD) exceeded that of the United Kingdom (8.3 percent) and was similar to those of countries with a longer history of immigration.[3] The 2006 Census identified some 610,000 or 14.7 percent of the total population (4,239,848) as born outside the Irish Republic and approximately 10 percent of the total population as 'non-Irish nationals'.[4]

My 2002 book, *Racism and Social Change in the Republic of Ireland*, posited that Ireland's history of antipathy towards indigenous Protestant, Jewish and Traveller communities would considerably inform Irish responses to immigration.[5] Why in the main this has not proved to be the case is one starting place of this chapter. Whilst the experiences of each differed, both Irish Protestants and Jews were marginalised by the dominant Catholic ethnonationalism. Studies of the former emphasise the role of sectarianism in a context where Irishness was defined in terms of Catholicism. Studies of the latter have emphasised sectarianism along with a tendency, in common with other European anti-Semitisms, to present the Jews as enemies of the nation-state. Prejudice towards Travellers, which deepened as Ireland developed, might be best explained in terms of the social and economic modernisation of Irish society.[6]

The very modernisation of belonging that threatened to displace Travellers and other Irish low on human capital is seen to have subsequently contributed to the acceptance of large-scale immigration. A 2006 National Economic and Social Council (NESC) report, *Managing Migration: A Social and Economic Analysis*, advocated large-scale and ongoing immigration as a means of sustaining economic growth.[7] In 2007 the Office of the Minister of State for Integration Policy published its first major report; *Migration Nation: Statement on Integration Strategy and Diversity Management* located the case for large-scale immigration explicitly within a developmental nation-building narrative:

> The important point for all Irish citizens to understand is that immigration is happening in Ireland because of enormous recent societal and economic improvement, beginning in the 1990s, but built on an opening to the world created by the late Sean Lemass as Taoiseach (Prime Minister) in the 1960s.[8]

The institutional narrative of Irish developmental modernisation has tended to focus on influential state-of-the-nation reports seen to exemplify emerging new political and economic orthodoxies. In positing the emergence of developmental rules of belonging, the focus of this chapter is upon shifting ideological, psychological and ontological *mentalités* identifiable within such reports and influential academic accounts of Irish modernisation.[9] *Economic Development* (1958)[10] became venerated as the foundation text, even if most of the ideas it presented as a new national project had been percolating for the best part of two decades within Irish academic circles.[11] The OECD/Irish Government report *Investment in Education* (1965) has been credited with jolting the focus of Irish education from character development and religious formation to one on economic development and the human capital needed for industrial development. The salience of developmental rules of belonging was exemplified by the 2005 NESC *Developmental Welfare State* (*DWS*) report. In *DWS* the developmental emphasis was upon choice, individual autonomy, enhanced individual opportunities, social conditions that would nurture and sustain individual adaptability, flexibility and risk-taking; a 'sustainable balance between dynamism and security'.[12] In this context it was unsurprising that the major statements since then about immigration and integration policy that are examined here have de-emphasised ethno-cultural rules of belonging.

From blocking coalitions to competitive corporatism

In answering the title question of his 2004 book *Preventing the Future: Why Was Ireland so Poor for so Long?* Tom Garvin emphasised the politics of overcoming protectionism and blocking coalitions. Garvin drew on Mancur Olson's thesis about the detrimental effects of established interest groups on economic growth.[13] Garvin emphasised the antipathy of 'free rider' members of Irish blocking-interest groups towards 'high riders', those deemed by their peers to be 'working too hard, too effectively or in ways that compete "unfairly" with conventional work practices'. Amongst the disparate possible 'high riders' listed by Garvin in an illustration of Olson's argument were class swots, scab workers, street traders, academics who publish far more than their colleagues, innovators and immigrant ethnic minorities seen to be taking 'our jobs'.[14]

Garvin's reference to immigrants is incidental but aptly recalls some experiences of migrants and ethnic minorities prior to the end of the 1950s, when the dismantling of tariff barriers began. In 1956 a cohort of Hungarian refugees was actively encouraged to settle in Ireland to mark Irish membership of the United Nations.[15] Although Article 17 of the UN Convention on the Rights of Refugees (1951), which Ireland had just ratified, conferred upon them a right to work, considerable efforts were made by the state to prevent the Hungarians seeking employment. The Department of Industry and Commerce proposed that in each case where refugees might be employed the relevant trade union should be consulted. In the face of difficulties in confronting such issues on a case-by-case basis, the Hungarians were confined to a former army barracks in Co. Limerick for quarantine periods. Illegal attempts were made to use the Gardai to restrict their movements.[16] In an earlier example, the Department of Industry and Commerce in 1937 opposed the entry of Jewish refugees because of the numbers of persons unemployed in the country.[17] Earlier again, the 1904 Limerick 'pogrom' succeeded because of an economic boycott against Jewish traders; the climate of the time was exemplified by an advertisement in the *Leader* by the Dublin Tailor's Co-Partnership urging customers to buy Irish and 'help stamp out Sweated, Jewish Labour, in the Tailoring Trade in Dublin'.[18]

Garvin argued that Olsonian sclerosis, Irish style, was partly caused by the ability of Irish industry and trade unions to preserve monopoly conditions.[19] Many of the losers became emigrants. Employment security and high wages for some, without the necessity of economic growth, became possible through an acceptance of emigration.[20] As claimed from an underdevelopment perspective by Raymond Crotty in 1980:

People made unemployed by trade unions forcing wage rates above the level at which people would be willing to work rather than remain unemployed, have not remained in Ireland. Neither have those made unemployed by the substitution of livestock for people. Emigration has given to Ireland, for over a century, conditions approximating to 'full employment' with no large pool of unemployed labour to form a source of competing non-unionised labour, working either as self -employed persons or for non-union firms. These virtually 'full employment' conditions brought about by mass emigration, have been fundamentally different from the normal conditions of massive, growing labour surpluses in the former capitalist colonies.[21]

As argued no less trenchantly by J.J. Lee from a developmental perspective in 1989, 'Few people anywhere have been as prepared to scatter their children around the world in order to preserve their own living standard.'[22] The invocation of Olson in the Irish case has been criticised for foregrounding just one factor (vested interests) out of many that might have impeded Irish economic development.[23] But taken as a description of *mentalité*, it depicts a sense of the deep-rooted exclusionary pressures that Garvin, Lee and Crotty variously represented as pathologies of Irish society.

Ultimately, Olsonian protectionism proved weak in the Irish case. When import substitution proved unable to sustain employment during the 1950s 'the resistance offered by Olson-type lobbies proved surprisingly weak'. In the face of an economic crisis, hard lessons trumped vested interests.[24] The significance of *Economic Development* was that it institutionalised the perspective that protectionism did not work. Key landmarks in the liberalisation of trade included the Anglo-Irish Free Trade Agreement in 1965 and EEC membership in 1973.[25] In an example of developmental *realpolitik*, a 1976 NESC report argued that if the foreign investment needed to provide new jobs were discouraged, Irish people would still have to work for foreign capital, but would be doing so outside of Ireland rather than at home.[26] The Irish developmental settlement occurred partly due to the co-option of erstwhile blocking coalitions within a competitive corporatist system of social partnership. Trade unions and employers repeatedly signed up to the pursuit of economic growth as a national project.[27] In this context, large-scale immigration later became justified within 'a national interest discourse' of economic growth.[28]

Developmental versus cultural reproduction

After Independence, the dominant sense of what it was to be Irish drew heavily on a nineteenth-century cultural 'revival' that had itself constituted a modernisation of belonging. Ernest Gellner's prerequisites for nationalism as a basis of social cohesion include mass literacy and school-inculcated culture, along with a codification of the past into a national history.[29] What is referred to as the 'Irish-Ireland' phase of political nation building persisted for several

decades after Independence. The Irish Free State became increasingly isolationist. Its education system was preoccupied with cultural (Irish language)
and religious (Catholicism) reproduction. Cultural nationalism generated
essentialist claims about Irish identity. The post-colonial Ireland it influenced was protectionist and isolationist. From the 1930s onwards, revisionist
historians contested many of the claims of essentialist nationalism.[30] To some
extent, historical revisionism itself was a proxy for a wider modernisation
of belonging. It formed part of a broader intellectual politics within which
both 'Irish-Ireland' cultural nationalism and Catholicism were challenged by
modernisation theories and presumptions.[31]

Parallel conflicts about the future of the Irish language were again predicated on conflicting readings of the Irish past. For example, Daniel Corkery, in
The Hidden Ireland (1925), influentially idealised the Gaelic past as a template
for the twentieth century.[32] Against this, Sean O'Faolain championed the utilitarian liberalism of Daniel O'Connell that had been de-emphasised by cultural
nationalists.[33] The nation-state, Michael Tierney observed, in a 1938 debate
on O'Connell's legacy, was a nineteenth-century invention that 'coincided
with the decay and gradual disappearance of the native ways of thought, life,
and expression.'[34] O'Connell's contribution to the modern Irish nation was,
Tierney argued, a philosophically utilitarian one that readily discarded the
Gaelic cultural legacy.[35] The English language and the ideas it communicated
became integral to the Irish nation.[36] Lee suggests that that linguistic utili-
tarianism flourished in the wake of the Famine because it was necessary for
effective emigration:

> A certain paradox was involved here. English was allegedly embraced as the
> reputed language of economic growth. When adequate growth failed to materi-
> alise, emigration became the alternative. Once again English was embraced as
> the reputed language of effective emigration. Thus both economic growth, and
> lack of economic growth, apparently encouraged the drift to English.[37]

From the 1950s the 'Irish-Ireland' nation-building project became contested
by a developmental modernising one, which came to emphasise economic
and human capital reproduction as utilitarian nation-building goals. Political
conflicts centred on the education system as a mechanism for cultural reproduction. *Investment in Education*[38] amounted to a paradigm shift whereby
a combined mercantile and human-capital paradigm broke with an earlier
dominant theocentric one. Within education policy, religious expertise,
epitomised by papal encyclicals and episcopal pronouncements, was displaced
from the 1960s onwards by World Bank and OECD reports.[39] A pre-develop-
mental 1954 Council for Education report depicted the role of schools in the
following terms:

The school exists to assist and supplement the work of parents in the rearing of children. Their first duty is to train their children to love and fear God. That duty becomes the first purpose of the primary school. It is fulfilled by the school through the religious and moral training of the child, through the teaching of good habits, through his instruction in the duties of citizenship and in his obligations to his parents and community – in short, through all that tends to the formation of a person of character, strong in his desire to fulfil the end of his creation.[40]

The political battles of Irish nation building were partly struggles over the means of control of social reproduction. Garvin emphasised how education expansion from the 1960s, in a context of weakening clerical control, reshaped culture and values. He cited 1981 attitudinal data that strongly correlated decline in traditional religious beliefs (the percentage who disagreed with the statement, 'There is only one true religion') with levels of educational attainment, by professional status and negatively correlated this decline by age. The younger the person, the better educated, the higher their socio-economic status, the less likely they were to cleave to traditional formulations of religious identity.[41] *Investment in Education* had replaced the theocratic expertise that dominated education policy with what Denis O'Sullivan referred to as a new 'mercantile' cultural trajectory. It emphasised that economic planning was incomplete without educational planning.[42] Human capital itself became understood as a key requirement for economic growth. *Investment in Education* made the case for educational reform to support the economic development objectives. It also argued that improved and extended educational facilities would 'help to equalise opportunities by enabling an increasing proportion of the community to develop their potentialities and raise their personal standards of living'.[43]

Forty years later, NESC recast the case for developmental education as one for developmental welfare. Effectively, it attributed to welfare goods and services a nation-building role that was previously the province of education. To a considerable extent *The Developmental Welfare State* echoed the late-1990s 'Third Way' critique of the welfare state advocated by Anthony Giddens and promoted politically by Tony Blair. In particular, *DWS* echoed the conception of an individualised risk society developed by Giddens from Ulrich Beck's account of 'reflexive modernity'.[44] What individuals needed in order to thrive under conditions of ongoing rapid social and economic change was the armour of self-reflexivity. For Giddens the role of the welfare state – redefined as a social investment state – was to support individual reflexivity in managing risks and hazards across the human life cycle.[45] As outlined in *DWS*: 'A fundamental standpoint from which to judge the adequacy and effectiveness of overall social protection is to assess the risks and hazards which the individual person in Irish society faces and the supports available to them at different stages of the lifecycle.' *DWS* portrayed a new individualist

Ireland that had broken with traditional understandings of security. There was, *DWS* argued, 'a stronger appreciation of the individual and of her/his life as something to be personally shaped'.[46] The autonomy to do so had primarily been depicted in human-capital terms in the policy reports that documented and advocated Irish economic modernisation. *DWS* implied that something more than education was needed; the flexible disposition it advocated was akin to the self-reflexivity that Giddens and others had commended some years earlier in the British case. In effect, self-reflexivity or reflexive capabilities were commended as necessary habitual individual dispositions.[47]

The modernising of belonging

Arguably, developmental nation building has undermined the political salience of essentialist representations of Irish identity. A lightly held sense of tradition aside – *Riverdance* rather than blood and soil nationalism – Irishness was to be equated with generic liberal democratic values and a surface-sameness of day-to-day life. As put by Taoiseach (Prime Minister) Bertie Ahern at the 2006 launch of *Managing Migration*:

> While it is no easy task to state clearly what it means to be Irish today, there are certain aspects of our community and Republic which, I believe, deserve respect and understandings from those who have come amongst us. That extends clearly, to the rule of law and the institutions and practices of constitutional democracy. It includes the characteristic features of community life in Ireland, including the unique place of the Irish language, Irish literature, music and folklore, and our religious and spiritual sense.[48]

The early developmentalists had emphasised the need for individuals to internalise new rules of belonging. A 1962 pro-EEC article by the iconoclastic Bishop William Philbin, who was cited by T.K. Whitaker in *Economic Development* as an influence, argued somewhat presciently that membership of the Common Market would jolt the Irish out of their complacency.[49] In 'The Irish and the New Europe' he enjoined the Irish to work as if their salvation depended on it, to understand that time was money, to strive for economic growth in a spirit of national corporatist cooperation and to respond competitively to the European Community as if jolted by national crises. The New Europe, as perceived somewhat presciently by Philbin, was a vehicle for economic competition. In 1964 Garret FitzGerald maintained that *Economic Development* and subsequent attempts at planning 'more than anything' provided a psychological basis for economic recovery, insofar as it helped to radically alter the unconscious attitude of many influential people and to make Ireland a growth-orientated community.[50] As claimed by Whitaker in 1961;

the psychological factor ... in my view is, and for long will remain, the most important factor of production in Ireland. This means that it is vital to sustain an atmosphere of enterprise and progress. In such an atmosphere we shall not allow ourselves to be over-awed by future difficulties or to fall into despondency by reason of temporary reverses and setbacks. If enterprise is welled to realism we can advance.[51]

Influenced by Whitaker, Lee argued (in the midst of the 1980s economic crisis) that post-Famine Ireland became dominated by a 'zero sum' mindset whereby people saw the advancement of others as only possible at their own expense. This was akin to the calculus of interests that Garvin defined in Olsonian terms. Lee's antidote to what he saw as 'prosperity-blocking fatalism' was a liberal mindset adept at enterprise.[52]

In the influential academic accounts, exemplified by *Preventing the Future*, modernisers came to triumph over a history of economic failure, emigration and cultural stagnation.[53] For critics of these, developmentalism proposed a simplistic and uncritical narrative of progress towards social liberalism, secularism, meritocracy and economic growth. Meritocracy was a taken-for-granted objective in the expansion of education, but what transpired within the new machinery of developmental social reproduction was often anything but.[54]

The *Report of the Commission on Itinerancy* (1963) warrants inclusion in the canon of Irish developmental texts. In starkly advocating the coercive assimilation of Travellers it suggested new, modern rules of belonging for all. Educational expansion and rising standards of living amongst the 'ordinary population' were deemed likely to increase social distance with Travellers and, by implication, between the former and other socio-economically marginal groups.[55] The Commission was set up at a time when Travellers had become displaced from the rural economy and were identified as an urban (and suburban) problem by the majority community. Its remit was to assimilate Travellers into the 'ordinary' population. The report emphasised that the rules of belonging of Irish society were being changed by 'the ever-rising standards of living of settled people' and the 'static, if not deteriorating, standards of itinerants'. It argued that 'the ever-growing disparity in relative social standards must render more difficult the mental adjustment which will be required of the settled people'.[56] This anticipated rise in intolerance towards Travellers would be worsened by their exclusion from education.

The Commission noted that high levels of illiteracy kept Travellers not only from entering vocational education but also from internalising the rules of belonging of a modernising society:[57] within *Investment in Education* much of the developmental emphasis fell upon relatively advantaged groups. In *DWS* emphasis on raising skill levels also tended to focus on the already employed and on those with higher levels of educational attainment.[58] These were seen to play a key role in securing the 'workforce quality that underpins a competitive, knowledge-based economy'.[59] All three reports traced an ontological modernisation of belonging that in policy documents and debates remaindered various Irish citizen as losers in the human capital, knowledge and reflexivity sweepstakes. In essence, these possessed capability deficits when it came to engaging successfully with the new social and economic order.

Investment in Education noted that some 82 percent of Irish-born UK residents had left school aged 15 or earlier. Those who emigrated during the 1950s and early 1960s were predominantly young, from agricultural backgrounds and from unskilled or semi-skilled labouring families. Even in the mid-1960s over two-thirds of recent male emigrants became manual workers.[60] During the 1970s return migrants were predominantly aged between 30 and 44 years. Available evidence suggests that just 28 percent of male returnees were unskilled manual workers. For those unable to improve their skills abroad, emigration was most likely a one-way ticket: 'Like their counterparts who had remained in Ireland throughout, those with minimal levels of skill or educational credential were able to improve their life chances and those who were not were consequently severely restricted.'[61]

Emigration itself came to be presented as developmental. The presumed flexibility of educated and skilled Irish migrants was valorised in 1980s debates about emigration. In a 1987 statement the Minister of Foreign Affairs, Brian Lenihan, offered two archetypical perspectives on Irish emigration, the first being an opinion that 'we could not all live on such a small island'. This recalled the 1958 Irish Banking Review commendation of emigration as 'a useful safety valve'.[62] The second was explicitly developmental:

> We regard emigrants as part of our global generation of Irish people. We should be proud of them. The more they hone their skills and talents in another environment, the more they develop a work ethnic in countries like Germany or the U.S., the better it can be applied to Ireland when they return.[63]

Such accounts, Jim McLaughlin argued, presented migration as an expression of agency and enterprise, 'conceptualising the "new wave" emigrant as a geographically mobile *homo economicus* logically moving between one labour market and the other, the embodiment of an Irish enterprise culture'. What McLaughlin called the radical openness of Irish society became a two-way street whereby both large-scale emigration and large-scale immigration could be presented as in the national economic interest.[64] The roots of this 'migration nation', Lee suggested, could be traced through a long history of utilitarian education for immigration. Lee observed that no other emigrant European people chose to abandon their language before immigrating.[65] In 2008 *Migration Nation* stated that English-language competence would be in the future one of the criteria for the admission of non-EU migrants.

Developmental immigration

In 2006 NESC published a cost-benefit analysis of immigration prepared on its behalf by the International Organisation on Migration (IOM). *Managing Migration in Ireland: A Social and Economic Analysis* was primarily focused on labour market policy. It strongly advocated ongoing immigration as a means of sustaining economic growth. The foreword of the report stated that 'immigration did not create the Irish economic miracle but, properly managed, migration can sustain Ireland's economic growth and generate many other benefits'.[66] *Managing Migration* argued that from the 1960s and 1970s government policies concerning trade liberalisation and foreign direct investment had begun to improve the domestic economic situation and hence, eventually, reversed the net loss of population due to migration. Weak economic performance during the 1980s was accompanied by a net outflow of migrants, a trend that was reversed in the mid-to-late 1990s. Economic growth during the 1990s saw the rapid expansion of the labour force from about 1.4 million in 1994 to just over 2 million in 2005. This increased labour demand was met initially by Irish nationals who had been previously unemployed or outside the labour market, by returning Irish migrants and, as these reduced as a proportion of in-migration, by non-Irish migrants; by 2004 Irish, returnees constituted less than 25 percent of total immigrants.[67] *Managing Migration* claimed that ongoing immigration was likely to make Irish society more resilient and adaptive:

> With Irish growth rates and employment projected in the near future to follow the impressive trend set during the last decade, migration will certainly remain a key feature allowing the labour market to react to changes in demand and further boosting Irish competitiveness. As such, Irish unemployment is expected to remain low, especially compared to other EU countries. This will be a significant advantage to Ireland in the expanded European Union.[68]

In effect, the report endorsed large-scale immigration whilst inferring that 'in the unlikely event of economic downturn' immigration levels could be controlled. However, the kind of measures suggested (limiting work visas to areas of labour market shortage) applied only to non-EU migrants.[69] With respect to these, *Managing Migration* endorsed selection criteria based on educational levels and skills. It noted that 'in Ireland as elsewhere', migrants were under-employed because of the failure of employers to recognise the educational and professional credentials of immigrants.[70]

NESC argued that, following the example of Canada and Australia in setting language and educational criteria for admission, this would result in significantly improved integration outcomes. Immigrants would be expected to 'invest' in these factors prior to applying for entry. This would 'shift the burdens of settlement (i.e. the cost of public and private integration programmes) from the host country back to the would-be-immigrants, and shifts the locus of adjustment from the country of destination back to the country of origin'.[71] In essence, it was proposed to accept where possible only those migrants with the capabilities to adhere to developmental criteria.

But government policy, as stated at the launch of *Managing Migration* by Bertie Ahern, was to source low-skilled workers from within the EU-25 and to limit low-skilled migrants from outside the EU.[72] *DWS* stated in 2005 that low-skilled immigrants were needed to fill large proportions of vacancies occurring in hotels, catering, factory production, childcare and other areas.[73] It claimed that because many immigrants did not face the same constraints as Ireland's jobless – for example, that more of them were single or without dependents – they would be more flexible than indigenous jobless. *DWS* acknowledged that immigrant competition for such jobs would benefit consumers (users of services provided by immigrants), but not long-standing Irish losers in the human-capital sweepstakes.[74] Such acknowledgements tacitly accepted the limits of a purely developmental welfare approach. The overall argument was that pushing the employment rate higher implied a focus on 'hitherto relatively neglected groups in the working-age population, the obstacles they face and the supports they need'.[75] However, it was admitted that from a utilitarian perspective the impetus to address the developmental needs of this residual rump was undermined by access to immigrant labour.

Both *Managing Migration* and *DWS* articulated a developmental national-interest case for migration, even if both underestimated the extent of immigrant human capital. Post-2004 high levels of immigrant 'quality' were not attributable to managed migration but, arguably, a somewhat unanticipated benefit, and from a developmental perspective all the more welcome as a result.

Yet, during late 2005 and into 2006 the possibility that trades unions might advocate anti-immigrant Olsonian barriers seemed considerable. On 9 December 2005 more than 100,000 union members demonstrated against Irish Ferries' plan to dismiss its 550 Irish employees and replace them with employees from Eastern Europe who would be paid a below-minimum-wage hourly rate of €3.60.[76] This dispute was resolved when the company agreed to pay no less than the Irish minimum wage to its all new Eastern European workforce. The issue of employment standards became one of the most contentious topics in the *Towards 2016* social partnership negotiations.[77]

The agreed solution was one that protected employment standards overall, rather than an Olsonian protection of Irish jobs for Irish workers. In 2005 and 2006 grassroots claims that Irish workers were being displaced by migrants tended not to be endorsed by trade union leaders and were rejected, for the most part, within the political mainstream. In an account of these debates David Begg, General Secretary of the Irish Congress of Trade Unions (ICTU), argued against the use of the emotive term 'displacement' ('it implies some fault on the part of immigrants'), whilst emphasising pressures to erode employment standards that could and should be addressed through regulation. These included direct replacement by lower-cost workers, outsourcing, off-shoring, use of temporary employment agency workers, bogus self-employment (mainly in construction) and bogus educational establishments which were really employment agencies. In Begg's 2008 analysis a degree of displacement had indeed occurred:

> The numbers of people who came to Ireland and their low expectations in terms of pay and their concentration, despite being highly qualified, in low paid sectors suggested potential for displacement. Yet, at an aggregate level there is no evidence for this. In the three years following enlargement 143,000 Irish people and 129,000 from the EU-10 secured employment.
>
> However, when you drill down into separate economic sectors and sub-sectors a more complex position is indicated. In the hotels and restaurants sector 18,000 new jobs were occupied by people from the EU-10 countries. Irish employment remained static. If this is not displacement, it does suggest that some degree of crowding out of Irish workers from the sector [has occurred].... The position in the manufacturing sector is more clear-cut. In the period under review people from the EU-10 countries filled 23,000 new jobs while 34,000 Irish people left the sector. In the food processing sub-sector the figures were 5000 and 9000 respectively.

The ICTU advocated securing employment standards for all workers whilst insulating the lower-skilled from the effects of an open labour market. Begg argued that part of the solution was to address blockages to immigrants getting jobs commensurate with their qualifications, 'which, on average, are higher than for the indigenous population'.[78] In September 2006 *Managing Migration* had cited estimates that if immigrants were in jobs that fully utilised their abilities, immigration would have increased by 3.3 percent in the five years to 2003, rather than the actual 2.3 percent.[79]

The Labour Party leader, Pat Rabbitte, on the other hand, advocated out-and-out protectionism. On 3 January 2006 Rabbitte called for a debate on the reintroduction of a work permit regime for migrant workers from the new EU states. His intervention was widely portrayed as 'political opportunism', 'appealing to the basest instincts' and as shifting the debate from one on exploitation of immigrant workers to one about protectionism. An *Irish Times* opinion poll (cited by Rabbitte) suggested that almost 80 percent of voters wanted a system of work permits to be reintroduced for citizens from the new EU-10 coming to Ireland.[80] The findings were that immigration restrictions on workers from the accession states appealed to some members of all the main political parties except the Progressive Democrats.

Arguably, the reintroduction of work permits advocated by Rabbitte was improbable from the onset. The main opposition parties, no less than those in government, were pro-Europe and had never opposed opening the Irish labour market to the new EU-10. Irish 'competitive corporatism' had bound the state, business and the trade unions to one another in the pursuit of economic growth even if there were cleavages between neo-liberal and regulatory developmentalists.[81] The unions, no less than the other social partners, had repeatedly signed up for a 'competitive corporatist' national project, rooted in a half century of developmental *mentalité* and policy formation.

Policy convergence and generic modernity

Drawing on an analysis of the Netherlands, France and Germany, Christian Joppke in 2007 emphasised a growing EU convergence of integration policy. A new European pro-immigration consensus had reversed three decades in which immigration was mostly unwanted.[82] Well into the 1990s the joint stance of European states was 'to sternly reject new labour migration'. During the 1990s refugee migration became explicitly politicised.[83] A resurgence of anti-immigrant political populism contributed to a 'Fortress Europe' harmonisation, whereby member states individually introduced harsh policies towards refugees. But alongside this, Joppke argues that a fundamental shift occurred whereby labour immigration was now presented as a 'permanent, even desirable feature of European societies', necessary to counter demographic decline and to preserve European competitiveness. Joppke's critique of EU harmonisation of integration policy depicts it as rooted in an influential cosmopolitan elite consensus, as well as in economic imperatives. The Europeanisation of civic integration policy is seen to occur though cultural standardisation no less than it does by legal mandate. Here, culture is defined apolitically in the bloodless language of policy-speak ('the soft force of best-practice emulation'), in contrast with European histories of blood-and-soil nationalist identity politics.[84]

Joppke does not argue that national difference in dealing with immigrants and ethnic minorities will disappear in Western Europe. But it is unlikely to be couched in grand 'national models' or philosophies of integration. He suggests that national difference will persist in two ways: 'trivially, as sheer contingency and history, which will never be the same in any two places', and in nation-state efforts 'sometimes to obstruct, but more often to accommodate and mould the new in the image of the past'.[85] Here, the declining influence of nation-building processes of modernisation, as influentially depicted by Ernest Gellner, is suggested.[86] Nation-building identity politics were portrayed as residual in the face of top-down EU-wide harmonisation. A key feature of EU integration norms is their presumed capacity to depoliticise integration by side-stepping thorny local histories of essentialist national identity. The new politics of immigration and integration charted by Joppke, with its emphasis on convergent legal and policy norms, is depicted as apolitical at the level of the nation-state. For example, as presented in the EU *Handbook on Integration for Policy Makers and Practitioners* (2007), the emphasis is on pragmatically redefining thorny questions of integration ends or goals into one about integration means or methods:

> What does integration mean? The question might be expected to trigger familiar debates about assimilation and multiculturalism, but participants at the technical seminars preparing the handbook hardly used these terms. As policy makers and practitioners working with immigrant integration on a daily basis they took a rather more practical approach, focusing on outcomes in terms of social and economic mobility, education, health, housing, social services, and societal participation.[87]

The *Handbook* emphasised the acquisition by migrants of competencies that would enable them to integrate. Language acquisition aside, what is required is the same kinds of human, social and cultural capital required of the overall population. For example, the *Handbook* called on 'each individual to engage in a process of lifelong learning' through 'continuous training and education'. It emphasised individualised empowerment through reflexive skills of 'learning to learn'.[88] In essence, it outlined a capabilities approach to integration.

Joppke's account of harmonisation is predominantly institutional. It instances the 2000 EU Race Directive, which requires that member states pass and implement laws against direct and indirect discrimination on the grounds of racial or ethnic origin. This protects non-EU immigrants as well as member-state citizens. Its remit encompasses education, employment, social protection, healthcare and access to vital goods and services such as housing and private insurance. A second instance of harmonisation is the 2003 Directive that extended the free-movement rights of EU citizens to non-EU residents. The third and most explicit indication of an EU integration project was the 2003 Council of the European Union-agreed non-binding *Common Basic Principles for Immigrant Integration in the European Union*.[89]

In Joppke's analysis, two different elements characterise the 'two way process' emphasised in the *Common Basic Principles (CBP)*. Civic integration rendered the individual responsible for her own integration. An accompanying emphasis on 'antidiscrimination' ('the liberalism of equal rights') at best retrospectively ameliorated inequalities resulting from the former:

> The emergent gestalt of contemporary European integration is a peculiar coexistence of civic integration and antidiscrimination policies. They are complementary in that they address different phases of the migration process – its initial (civic integration) or late phases (antidiscrimination). However both policies also exhibit countervailing, event contradictory dynamics. The logic of civic integration is to treat migrants as individuals who are depicted as responsible for their own integration; civic integration is an extension into the migration domain of

the austere neoliberalism that frames economic globalisation. The opposite logic of antidiscrimination is to depict migrants and their offspring as members of groups that are victimized by the majority society. There is thus reintroduced at the tail end of integration the ameliorative group logic that has been discarded at its beginning by the harsh individualization of civic integration.[90]

Joppke's concern was with the top-down diffusion of policy norms, influenced heavily by the Dutch rejection of multiculturalism and neo-liberal EU responses to globalisation, the latter exemplified by Lisbon Agenda goals of making the EU 'the most competitive and dynamic knowledge-based economy in the world'.[91]

As (until recently) an enthusiastic participant in the EU, Ireland has been open to the kinds of institutional harmonisation emphasised by Joppke. But Ireland's mass immigration-without-politics cannot be understood without considering the modernisation of belonging that changed the ground rules of being Irish. The convergence emphasised by Joppke concerned the means of harmonisation. This chapter suggests that there has also been a convergence of ends, by which is meant the kind of society into which integration might (or might not) occur as a political project. Here, modernisation theory as applied to the 'traditional' *Kulturnation* by Gellner and theories of reflexive modernity applied by Beck, Giddens and Urry to 'post-traditional' projects of social reproduction posit shifting integration ends.

Ideologically, the *CBP* presume the replacement of essential nationalism and multiculturalism by liberalism as a public-sphere value culture. An influential sociological literature emphasises the primacy of capabilities for social and economic self-integration, theorised in terms of reflexive modernity and neo-liberal individualism. Here, integration becomes defined sociologically in terms of autonomous individual capacity to flourish and individual responsibility to do so. Reflexivity, so understood, is something to be engineered as a political project, just as were the older mass identities of cultural nationalism.

Writing during a period of high emigration in the 1980s, Lee emphasised 'the psychic impact of emigration on those who stayed, the price paid by a society for the subterfuges to which it had to resort to preserve its self-respect while scattering its children'.[92] Lee's recurring depiction of Irish developmental modernity as an emotional experience as well as being about economics bears thinking about when seeking to explain current 'migration nation' rules of belonging. Developmental shifts in *mentalité* contributed to new implicit rules of belonging and assumptions that modern immigrants can be slotted easily into a modernised Ireland. In this context a developmental nation interest case for growth translated into large-scale immigration without politics. Here the economic-growth case for immigration prevailed. In this context any discussion of the need for protectionism, or even use of the term, was anathema. Arguably, the reasons for this had more to do with prevailing developmental *mentalité* than with disapproval of ethnocentrism. But again, a case could be made that developmental modernity had also undermined ethno-nationalist rules of belonging.

Arguably, what is being harmonised through the EU is not one single integration paradigm but a number of social, institutional and political ones. From a convergence perspective, harmonisation of integration exemplifies a new chapter in parallel modernisation of belonging within member states. The harmonisation of integration has emerged in a context of multiculturalism writ large, where the politics of incommensurability – the Europe of continual wars and, in Ireland, sectarian conflict predicated on the religious and political divisions of the Reformation – has been tamed, but by no means eliminated. As presented in the *CBP*, harmonisation preserves the linguistic claims to incommensurable national identities characteristic of essentialist nationalism. Ireland is something of an exception here, insofar as the nationalist Gaelic revival was only a partial success. English flourished after Independence for utilitarian reasons, a harbinger of the developmental nation-building project that began to displace cultural nationalism from the Irish rules of belonging, from the mid-twentieth century. EU integration norms posit a 'generic' modernisation of belonging. Insofar as the Irish case validates Joppke's harmonisation thesis, it does so because of an underlying cultural convergence characterised in the Irish case as developmental modernity.

But, as the post-boom economic crisis reveals, developmental modernity by no means constitutes an end of Irish history. The developmental case for large-scale immigration evaporated overnight. What remains, in essence, is the yet-to-be-assessed social cost of rapid and large-scale immigration as one of several challenges to social cohesion. As put by Declan Kiberd in an essay on some of these challenges from which this chapter's opening quotation is drawn: 'Things are often studied only when they start to go wrong. The end of things is the moment when we start to understand them.'[93] Many of the rules of belonging that transported Irish citizens and immigrants into their shared twenty-first-century Ireland may not apply in this new land.

Notes

1 B. Fanning and F. Mutwarasibo, 'Nationals/Non-nationals: Immigration, Citizenship and Politics in the Republic of Ireland,' *Ethnic and Racial Studies* 30.3 (2007), 439–460

2 National Economic and Social Council (NESC), *Managing Migration in Ireland: A Social and Economic Analysis* (Dublin: Stationery Office, 2005), p. 26

3 OECD data cited in *ibid.*, p. 25

4 Central Statistics Office, *2006 Census*, www.cso.ie

5 B. Fanning, *Racism and Social Change in the Republic of Ireland* (Manchester: Manchester University Press, 2002), pp. 30–58

6   A. Bhreatnach, *Becoming Conspicuous: Irish Travellers, Society and the State 1912–70* (Dublin: University College Dublin, 2007)

7   NESC, *Managing Migration*, p. xxi

8   Office of the Minister of Integration, *Migration Nation: Statement in Integration Strategy and Diversity Management* (Dublin: Stationery Office, 2008), p. 8

9   The term 'ontology' is used here to denote beliefs about the nature of reality that constitute social facts about the world.

10   Government of Ireland, *Economic Development* (Dublin: Stationery Office, 1958).

11   For example, in 1943 James Meenan's survey of Irish economic performance since Independence prefigured *Economic Development* as a sector-by-sector economic stocktaking exercise. In 1951 Roy Geary set out an extensive survey of Irish economic development since the Treaty. Geary, like Whitaker later addressed the economic and social consequences of emigration. J. Meenan, 'Irish Industry and Industrial Policy 1921–1943', *Studies* 32 (1943), 209–230, R.C. Geary, 'Irish Economic Development Since the Treaty', *Studies* 50.160 (1951), 398–418, pp. 403–407

12   National Economic and Social Council (NESC), *The Developmental Welfare State* (Dublin: Stationery Office, 2005), p. 36

13   M. Olson, *The Logic of Collective Action* (Cambridge: Harvard University Press, 1967)

14   T. Garvin, *Preventing the Future: Why Was Ireland so Poor for so Long?* (Dublin: Gill and Macmillan, 2004), p. 13. Also see M. Olson, 'Response to Lessons from Ireland', *Journal of Economic Perspectives* 12.1 (1998), 241–242

15   E. Ward, '"A big show-off to show what we could do": Ireland and the Hungarian Refugee Crisis of 1956', *Irish Studies in International Affairs* 8 (1996), pp. 131–141.

16   National Archives, NAI, D.T, S11007 (10 December 1956), Fanning, *Racism and Social Change*, pp. 90–94

17   D. Keogh, *Jews in Twentieth Century Ireland* (Cork: Cork University Press, 1999), p. 117

18   *Ibid.*, p. 54

19   Garvin, *Preventing the Future*, pp. 12–15

20   D. Rottman and P. O'Connell, 'The Changing Social Structure', in B. Fanning and T. MacNamara (eds), *Ireland Develops: Administration and Social Policy 1953–2003* (Dublin: IPA, 2003)

21   R. Crotty, *Ireland in Crisis: A Study in Capitalist Colonial Underdevelopment* (Dingle: Brandon, 1986), p. 84

22   J.J. Lee, *Ireland 1912–1985: Politics and Society* (Cambridge: Cambridge University Press, 1989), p. 552

23   P. Kirby, 'Tom Garvin and the Causes of Irish Underdevelopment', *Administration*, 54.3 (2006), 55–67

24   But in support of the Olsonian model, compensatory packages (grants for threatened firms from 1962 to 1967) were part of the price paid for support or acquiescence of business and trade unions. See C. O'Grada and K. O'Rourke, 'Economic Growth since 1945', in N. Crafts and G. Toniolo (eds), *Economic Growth in Europe since 1945* (Cambridge: Cambridge University Press, 1996) p. 141

25   J. Fitzgerald, 'Ireland's Failure and Belated Convergence', ESRI Working Paper No 133 (Sept 2000), p. 3

26   *NESC Report No. 26: Prelude to Planning* (Dublin Stationery Office, 1976) p. 20,

cited in Fiztgerald, 'Ireland's Failure', p. 276

27 S. O'Rian, 'Social Partnership as a Mode of Governance', *The Economic and Social Review* 37 (Winter 2006), 311–318, p. 313

28 G. Boucher, 'Ireland's Lack of a Coherent Integration Policy', *Translocations: Migration and Social Change* 3.1 (2007), 5–28, p. 6

29 E. Gellner, *Culture, Identity and Politics* (Cambridge: Cambridge University Press, 1987), pp. 15–16

30 D. George Boyce and A. O'Day, '"Revisionism" and "Revisionist Controversy"', in D. George Boyce and A. O'Day (eds), *The Making of Modern Irish History: Revisionism and the Revisionist Controversy* (London: Routledge, 1996), pp. 3–4

31 Conor McCarthy suggests that much of what is termed revisionism in Irish historical and cultural debates can be traced to the influence of modernisation theory. C. McCarthy, *Modernisation: Crisis and Culture 1969–1992* (Dublin: Four Courts Press, 2000), p. 17

32 D. Corkery, *The Hidden Ireland: A Study of Gaelic Munster in the Eighteenth Century* (Dublin: Gill and Macmillan, 1970)

33 S. O'Faolain, *King of the Beggars: A Life of Daniel O'Connell, the Irish Liberator, in a Study of the Rise of Modern Irish Democracy* (Dublin: Poolbeg, 1980)

34 M. Tierney, 'Politics and Culture: Daniel O'Connell and the Gaelic Past', *Studies* 27.107 (1938), 353–381, p. 354

35 *Ibid.*, p. 357

36 *Ibid.*, p. 358

37 Lee, *Ireland 1912–1985*, p. 665

38 Government of Ireland, *Investment in Education* (Dublin: Stationery Office/OECD, 1965), p. 350

39 D. O'Sullivan, *Cultural Politics and Irish Education since the 1950s: Policies, Paradigms and Power* (Dublin: Institute of Public Administration, 2005), pp. 105–115

40 Cited in *ibid.*, p. 109

41 Garvin, *Preventing the Future*, pp. 215–216

42 *Investment in Education*, p. 350

43 For example, in *Second Programme for Economic Expansion* expenditure on education was described as 'an investment in the fuller use of the country's primary resource – its people – which can be expected to yield increasing returns in terms of economic progress'. Government of Ireland, *Second Programme for the Economic Expansion Part II* (Dublin: Government of Ireland, 1964), p. 193

44 U. Beck, *Risk Society: Towards a New Modernity* (London: Sage 1992)

45 A. Giddens, *The Third Way: The Renewal of Social Democracy* (Cambridge: Polity, 1998), pp. 99–118

46 NESC, *Developmental Welfare State*, p. xxiv

47 On the conceptual relationships between self-reflexivity, habitus and reflexive capabilities see M. Adams, 'Hybridizing Habitus and Reflexivity: Towards an Understanding of Contemporary Identity?' *Sociology* 40.3 (2006), 511–528

48 Address at launch of *Managing Migration*, www.taoiseach.gov.ie

49 W. Philbin, 'The Irish and the New Europe', *Studies* 51 (1962), 27–43, p. 31

50 G. Fitzgerald, 'Second Programme for Economic Expansion: Reflections', *Studies* 53.211 (1964), 233–252, p. 250

51 T.K. Whitaker, 'The Civil Service and Development', *Administration* 9.2 (1961), 83–87, p. 86
52 Lee, *Ireland 1912–1985*, p. 682
53 Garvin, *Preventing the Future*, p. 170
54 D. O'Sullivan, *Cultural Politics and Irish Education*, pp. 272–274
55 Government of Ireland, *Report of the Commission on Itinerancy* (Dublin: Stationery Office, 1963) p. 70
56 *Ibid.*, p. 106
57 *Ibid.*
58 *DWS*, p. 23
59 *DWS*, p. 139
60 Government of Ireland, *Investment in Education*
61 Rottman and O'Connell, 'Changing Social Structure', p. 53
62 'Favourable aspects of the Irish economy', *Irish Banking Review* (December 1958), p. 8
63 Quoted in J. McLaughlin, 'Changing Attitudes to "New Wave" Emigration', in A. Bielenberg (ed.), *The Irish Diaspora* (Harlow: Pearson, 2000), p. 332
64 *Ibid.*, pp. 324–328
65 Lee, *Ireland 1912–1985*, p. 665
66 NESC, *Managing Migration*, p. xxi
67 *Ibid.*, pp. 74–75
68 *Ibid.*, p. 93
69 *Ibid.*, p. xx
70 *Ibid.*, p. 155
71 *Ibid.*, p. 14
72 Address at Launch of *Managing Migration*. Available at: www.taoiseach.gov.ie
73 *DWS*, p. 198
74 *Ibid.*, p. 198
75 *Ibid.*, p. 77
76 'Ferries Row Could Sink the Social Partnership', *Irish Times*, 16 November 2005, p. 14; ICTU, 'Congress Defers Decision on New Talks – "Timing is not right"', press release, 25 October 2005 (Dublin: ICTU). Available at: www.ictu.ie
77 R. Erne, 'A Contentious Consensus', in T. Schulten, R. Bispinck and C. Schäfer (eds), *Minimum Wages in Europe* (Brussels: ETUI, 2006), pp. 65–83.
78 D. Begg, 'Displacement: Real or Imagined?' 6 October 2008. Available at: www. ictu.ie
79 NESC, *Managing Migration*, p. xvi
80 In the Taylor Nelson Sofres poll, a third of those surveyed had a firm opposition to immigration and immigrants. Roughly 20 percent had a very positive position; 53 percent believed that migrant labour was making it harder to for Irish people to get jobs; 63 percent believed that immigration was pushing down wages; but 59 percent and 52 percent considered that migrants were good for the economy and society respectively. *Irish Times*, 22 January 2006
81 M. Rhodes, 'Globalisation Labour Markets and Welfare States a Future of "Competitive Corporatism"?' EUI Working Papers, RSC 97/36 (Florence: European University Institute, 1997). Also see Roland Erne, *European Unions: Labour's Quest for*

Transnational Democracy (Ithaca, NY: Cornell University Press, 2008)

82 C. Joppke, 'Transformation of Immigration: Civic Integration and Antidiscrimination in the Netherlands, France, and Germany', *World Politics* 59 (January 2007), 243–273

83 C. Joppke, 'Why Liberal States Accept Unwanted Immigration', *World Politics* 50(1998), 226–293

84 Joppke, 'Transformation of Immigration', p. 247

85 *Ibid.*, p. 272. Also see C. Joppke, *Selecting by Origin: Ethnic Migration in the Liberal State* (Cambridge, MA: Harvard University Press, 2005)

86 E. Gellner, *Encounters with Nationalism* (Oxford: Blackwell, 1994)

87 Directorate-General for Justice, Freedom and Security, *Handbook on Integration for Policy Makers and Practitioners* (Brussels: EU Publications Office, 2007), p. 8

88 *Ibid.*, p. 8

89 The 2005 *Common Basic Principles for Immigrant Integration in the European Union* are as follows: (1) Integration is a dynamic, two-way process of mutual accommodation by all immigrants and residents of Member States. (2) Integration implies respect for the basic values of the European Union by every resident. (3) Employment is a key part of the integration process and is central to the participation of immigrants, to the contributions immigrants make to the host society, and to making such contributions visible. (4) Basic knowledge of the host society's language, history, and institutions is indispensable to integration, enabling immigrants to acquire this basic knowledge is essential to successful integration. (5) Efforts in education are essential in preparing immigrants, and particularly their descendants, to be more successful and more active participants in society. (6) Access for immigrants to institutions, as well as to public and private goods and services, on an equal basis to national citizens and in a non-discriminatory way is an indispensable foundation for better integration. (7) Frequent interaction between immigrants and citizens of the Member States is a fundamental prerequisite for integration. (8) The practice of diverse cultures and religions is guaranteed under the Charter of Fundamental Rights and must be safeguarded, unless practices conflict with other inviolable European rights or with national law. (9) The participation of immigrants in the democratic process and in the formulation of integration policies and measures, especially at the local and regional levels, is a key to effective integration. (10) Mainstreaming integration policies and measures in all relevant policy portfolios and levels of government and public services is an important consideration in public policy formation and implementation ... Developing clear goals, indicators and evaluation mechanisms are necessary to adjust policy, evaluate progress on integration and to make the exchange information more effective, so as to transfer good experience.

90 Joppke, 'Transformation of Immigration', pp. 247–248

91 *Ibid.*, p. 272

92 Lee, *Ireland 1912–1985*, p. 375

93 D. Kiberd, 'After Ireland?', *Irish Times*, 29 August 2009

3

Social cohesion

It would be unfortunate if a politically correct progressivism were to deny the reality of the challenge to social solidarity posed by diversity. It would be equally unfortunate if an ahistorical and ethnocentric conservatism were to deny that addressing that challenge is both feasible and desirable. (Robert Putnam)

The implicit subtexts within debates about integration are often anxieties about social cohesion. Social cohesion is a term used in the social sciences to denote the bonds or 'glue' that hold people together in society. The focus of this chapter is upon ideological, normative and empirical claims about social cohesion that have a bearing on Irish responses to immigration. Within such debates, the terms 'integration' and 'social cohesion' are by no means clearly fixed in meaning; to some extent at least, understandings of the former depend on perspectives on the latter. This chapter emphasises the need to distinguish between normative understandings of integration and social cohesion (evident, for example, in taken-for-granted assumptions within policy documents), ideological perspectives (evident in statements about how immigrants 'ought' to integrate) and empirical understandings (the use of actual evidence to support claims about what works or does not work to promote integration and social cohesion, however understood). In making such distinctions, it draws on Emile Durkheim's classic sociological account of social cohesion to examine some of the underlying presumptions that have come to be influential in the Irish case. Two in particular are emphasised here.

An influential governance security perspective worked to circumscribe state commitments to integration. The subtext here was the implicit definition of social cohesion in terms of the existing bounded community; it cannot be simply depicted as ideological proposition; its underlying normative presumptions are examined using Durkheim's concept of the 'social fact'. The second proposition considered here is Robert Putnam's assertion that immigration undermines social cohesion. Again, the vantage point is that of a bounded community. By definition, newcomers unsettle bounded communities. In recent years Putnam has become one of the most influential figures within social policy debates. Social capital as he understands it has not just come to be emphasised as a key resource in the promotion of social cohesion; as a short-hand for social glue it has come to actually define social cohesion.[1] A third vantage point – the big international debate offstage about the crisis of multi-culturalism – has clearly contributed to Irish debates about immigration and integration; how and to what extent are considered separately in Chapter 6.

Such large-scale immigration as experienced over such a short period of time in the Irish case inevitably brings about some degree of dislocation. At the same time, debates about the effects of immigration on social cohesion so far have been dwarfed by extensive angst throughout the twentieth century on the social costs of emigration and the unravelling of 'traditional' ways of life caused by urbanisation and secularisation. It is important to note that there has been to date no explicit 'national' conversation about the impact of immigration on Irish social cohesion. Arguably, this is because there has been to date no demonstrable crisis of cohesion perceived to have resulted from immigration of the kinds that occurred in Britain in 2001 and France in 2005.

Perhaps the closest Irish equivalent in the last decade occurred in Moyross, a deprived area in Limerick city, where a spate of killings by rival gangs resulted in a crisis being declared. The crisis in Moyross had been a long time coming. In 1992 the then Mayor of Limerick, Jim Kemmy, described to the Dáil how the area had 80 percent unemployment, some 100 houses had been vandalised and were now boarded up and how some residents were being intimidated by others. During the ensuing debate it was claimed that Limerick was one of the most heavily policed areas in Western Europe; Moyross itself was served by twenty-five Gardai.[2] By 2006 the area experienced a spate of 'gangland killings' which, controlling for population, was close to making Limerick 'the murder capital of Western Europe'. A government minister from Limerick, Willie O'Dea, called on Limerick Corporation to look carefully at its housing policy, pointing out that an unusual number of gang members lived cheek-by-jowl with one another, believing that living as such gave them better protection from attack. The result was that 'ordinary working people' were being squeezed out of their homes by 'gangsters bent on turning neighbourhoods like Moyross into their personal fiefdoms'.[3] Moyross and Southill resembled nothing so much as the predominately black city of Baltimore, as depicted in *The Wire*. By 2008 the government had agreed to demolish over 2,500 houses in Moyross and in Southill, another deprived area in the city. A hundred extra Gardai were to be brought in.[4] No immigrant population lived in Moyross; if there had been one, what had occurred might well have been depicted as a failure of integration. The point is that social cohesion problems attributed to immigration or ethnic conflict are likely to have a number of other causes.

When Irish citizens are excluded from the predominant norms, ways of life and opportunities of mainstream society this is generally referred to as social exclusion; their integration is referred to as social inclusion. Social inclusion is seen to contribute to social cohesion, social exclusion to undermine it. A core argument of this book is that much of what works to socially include citizens is likely to further the integration of migrants. This argument has been promoted in various EU Commission reports, but its full implications are generally side-stepped.[5] For example, the comprehensive inclusion of migrants within the remit of social inclusion policies would require the removal of welfare strati-fications and differential levels of entitlement that impede their access. As currently defined by the (Irish) Office for Social Inclusion, 'social exclusion' occurs when, as a result of inadequate incomes, people become excluded and marginalised from participating in activities considered the norm for other people in society.[6] In effect, what matters are how extensive one's resources and capabilities are, compared to others' in the same society. The case for a social inclusion approach to integration and social cohesion was addressed in Chapter 1.

'Migrants and members of ethnic minority groups' were first envisaged as a distinct target group within Irish social inclusion policy in 2002. The *Revised National Anti-Poverty Strategy* set an objective of ensuring that these were not more likely to experience poverty than majority group members.[7] This signalled (in theory) an integration remit for Irish anti-poverty and social inclusion policy. The first comprehensive Irish report on integration policy, *Migration Nation: Statement on Integration Strategy and Diversity Manage-ment* (2008), acknowledged a 'strong link between integration policy and wider state social inclusion measures, strategies and initiatives'.[89] With respect to migrants, these have been little more than paper policies. Why this has been the case cannot be explained solely by the expectation examined in the previous chapter that immigrants would to be integrated via the economy.

The most apparently influential normative perspective, certainly when it came to legislation and constitutional change, was that of the Department of Justice, Equality and Law Reform (hereafter Department of Justice). An Irish security mindset can be traced through decades of Department of Justice memoranda, notably in its well-documented xenophobic and anti-Semitic responses to Jewish refugees; it was reinforced a decade ago by a heuristic borrowing of United Kingdom Home Office responses to asylum seekers and race-to-the-bottom Fortress Europe norms of punitive responses to forced migrants.[10] A governance security perspective justified restrictions upon migrant rights and entitlements, with scant consideration about how the effects of these might subsequently impede integration. Specifically, it advocated the exclusion of non-citizen migrants from the welfare solidarities and support systems commonly referred to as social inclusion measures and normatively understood to promote social cohesion amongst citizens. Why security perspectives have been taken more seriously than a social inclusion approach to integration is one of the questions addressed by this chapter.

In an effort to illustrate the empirical intersections between integration and social cohesion in the Irish case, I commissioned an analysis of five 2007 and 2008 studies of the well-being of children, families and neighbourhoods (hereafter WBCFN data) to examine how immigrant respondents fared as compared to their Irish neighbours in deprived communities, including Limerick. In all, some 1,633 households were surveyed; of these, 9.4 percent were immigrant (non-Irish citizen) households, rising to 28 percent in one Dublin inner-city area, the Liberties. In essence, this research compared 'socially included' immigrants with relatively low levels of social capital but high levels of human capital with 'socially excluded' Irish neighbours who nevertheless had high levels of social capital. Interpretations of the challenge to social cohesion depend on whether this is defined in terms of social capital (trust and reciprocity) or social inclusion (socio-economic and human capital terms).

Social cohesion as social fact

Debates about social cohesion all too easily become exercises in nostalgic yearnings for a past that never quite was. Such yearnings have long formed part of the repertoire of responses to social modernisation, urbanisation, information technology, various aspects of globalisation and, of course, immigration. To some extent there is always a perceived crisis of social cohesion. In 1894, in *The Division of Labour in Society*, Emile Durkheim depicted the unravelling of what he referred to as traditional 'mechanistic' forms of social solidarity by more complex 'organic' interdependencies. A few years earlier, in 1891, the first major encyclical on Catholic social thought (in Ireland it came to be taught as sociology) outlined a somewhat similar critique of modernity. Durkheim's archetype (for that is all it is, a model) distinguished between traditional 'mechanistic' forms of social solidarity and more complex 'organic' interdependencies. Mechanistic solidarity was grounded in resemblance. Individual members of society resembled each other because they cherished the same values and held the same things sacred.[11] Society was coherent because people living in the same place led very similar lives. A third contemporaneous account of the impact of modernity on social cohesion, by Ferdinand Tönnies, similarly distinguished between *Gemeinschaft* and *Gesellschaft*.[12] In effect, Catholic social thought idealised mechanistic solidarity and *Gemeinschaft*; society had been coherent because individuals presumably led very similar lives; most were born, lived and died in sight of the same church steeple. Each of these simple models presented a theory of social change whereby modernity threatened an earlier form of social cohesion; like the modernisation narratives discussed in the previous chapter, they told influential stories about social change in which there were winners and losers, and sides to be taken.

To a considerable extent, twentieth-century Irish anxieties about social modernisation were framed by such Catholic social thought. Community development, aimed at fostering social cohesion (by safeguarding the reproduction of religiosity from one generation to the next), was promoted by a Catholic social action movement. A parallel Catholic sociology within the universities influenced the training of social workers and administrators; a focus on the decline of traditional community emerged as a dominant research concern.[13] The Irish sociology journal *Christus Rex* was founded in 1947, about the time when developmental arguments began to emerge.[14] The critique of social change it offered bore clear similarities with secular sociological accounts of modernisation, even if the core concepts of the latter – such as anomie, alienation and rationalisation – were eschewed. In a nutshell, the Catholic thesis was that a spiritual life sustained by individual faith and social habits could be damaged by removal from a society within which religious norms prevailed. Existing Irish society was seen to be economically and socially unsustainable. Materialism threatened to undermine communal solidarities and weaken individual spiritual resilience.

Yet, social and economic innovation was needed to ensure their survival. Alongside polemics, *Christus Rex* published some pioneering research on rural economic development.[15] In 1967 it published a landmark study of urban poverty and disadvantage; the research was undertaken in Limerick city.[16] Fr Liam Ryan's 'Social Dynamite: A Study of Early School Leavers' warrants discussion here as a pioneering Irish account of urban crisis. It followed an analysis by Ryan the previous year of unequal access to university education by social class.[17] 'Social Dynamite' emphasised the role of educational disadvantage in creating urban inequalities. Ryan argued that one-third of all school leavers were being condemned, the great majority through no fault of their own, to unskilled labour, unemployment or emigration.[18] A complex of social, psychological and economic factors meant that the introduction of free secondary education would not, of itself, solve their problems. These, he argued, demonstrated a need to take into account the 'total situation' of a child's life rather than focus on poverty defined solely in terms of income levels. Ryan's study described the experiences of families now housed in 'Parkland', a social housing estate in Limerick. They had been transplanted, through a process of slum clearance, from old, overcrowded Georgian or Victorian buildings or smaller houses in the back-lanes and alleyways:

> It was felt that if you gave each family a house with a little garden they would become clean and respectable. And so they were uprooted, from being ten families in one house, or ten children in one cellar, they moved into beautiful big three-bedroom houses. But they just could not cope with the new situation. They lost many of their roots. Their friends and neighbours of years and years were lost. They had no choice as to where they would go or when they

would go; they had no choice as to what street they would live in or as to who would occupy the house next-door or across the street. The policy was to scatter the better families around in the hope that they would set the standard of the locality. Today it is not the best family in the street but rather the worst or the rowdiest who sets the standard.[19]

Fr Ryan emphasised that such housing policy had in fact undermined social cohesion. He identified an underlying fear and hatred of officialdom amongst residents that remained 'curbed' because their lives were too dependent on the goodwill of people in authority: 'All government officials are enemies, the Gardai, rent-collectors, welfare officers – all who have "fine soft jobs".' The same attitude sometimes extended to teachers and priests. Ryan described the difficulties encountered by interviewees in their own frank language.[20] 'Social Dynamite' alluded to an urban crisis in social cohesion in the making, engineered by bad social policy and deepening of educational inequalities. An account of 'Social Dynamite' on the Limerick Regeneration Watch website described it as more insightful than the report written in response to the crisis in the city some 43 years later.[21]

Durkheim's sociological project was concerned with the social problem of apparently diminished social cohesion in the wake of modernity. He employed the concept of anomie to depict the ruptures in social solidarity resulting from the decline of established religious moral authority.[22] He argued that there could be no basis for social cohesion without recognition of some higher moral authority. In the past this meant God; in the last paragraph of *The Division of Labour* he argued that a replacement basis for social solidarity in modern society was only beginning to take shape.[23] The anomie that had resulted from the nineteenth-century division of labour was viewed as a temporary disorder. This is a crucial point; what appeared like a rupture in social cohesion from a given temporal perspective was better understood as a change from one kind of functional social cohesion to another. Even the notion of individualism was in fact a product of society. It did not result in the breakdown of society but in the assertion of new systems of rights and obligations as a new basis of social cohesion.[24] New forms of social relations produced new forms of social solidarity.

The apparent shift from ethno-religious to developmental 'rules of belonging' examined in the previous chapter can be viewed in such terms. These 'rules', as I described them, drawing on various canonical policy reports, were but surface representations of underlying social facts about the social status of certain human capital and cultural-capital attributes over other forms of habitus. The stilted language of economists and administrators masked a visceral reformation, an Irish ethic and spirit of capitalism. For advocates such as Sean Lemass, economic development offered a more viable basis for social cohesion than the old order that was being superseded. Emigration fractured communities and families. Generation on generation population decline, resulting from emigration, wasted human capital, but it also blighted lives. On the other side of the fence the quest of post-Second World War Irish Catholic sociology was to repair existing forms rather than advocate new forms of social cohesion. Durkheim's point was that new kinds of functional bonds came to replace old kinds of social glue.

Yet, as put by Ray Forrest and Ade Kearns, writing about subsequent generations of sociologists, 'predictions of cohesion in crisis typically rest on assumptions that the social cement of a previous era is crumbling and that we are being collectively as adrift in a world in which the previous rules of social interaction and social integration no longer apply'. Durkheim's point was that new forms of functional solidarity replace older forms. Forrest and Kearns' general point is that it is all too easy to underestimate the continuities of everyday life. They argue that, from the ground-up perspective of everyday experiences, most people still live within narrow *Gemeinschaft* worlds of neighbourhood, small-scale domesticity and kin, that at an individual level social relations are usually confined to a fairly narrow segment of society; in this context social cohesion is about getting by and getting on at the more mundane level of every life.[25] A helpful distinction can be drawn between society-level social facts and the distinct circumstances of specific communities.

Durkheim emphasised the need to study the 'recognised truths' of any given society as 'social facts', to explore what made them accepted and thus better understand the basis of social cohesion.[26] In *The Rules of Sociological Method* he emphatically argued that social life is constituted wholly of collective 'representations' or 'ideas'; the technical term he used was *Vorstellungen*. Collective representations, that is, shared cognitive perceptions between individuals, impacted on the material world insofar as they affected individual consciousness. Collective beliefs about the nature of the world were social facts.[27]

Such shared ideas were, he emphasised, social inheritances: 'the greater part of our social institutions were bequeathed to us by former generations. We ourselves took no part in their formation, and consequentially we cannot by introspection discover the causes which brought them about.'[28] Social facts were identifiable in ways of 'acting, thinking and feeling external to the individual, which are invested with a coercive power by virtue of which they exercise control over him'. Social facts, in Durkheim's account, included legal and moral regulations, religious faiths, financial systems and other social institutions characterised by established beliefs and practices that individuals variously internalised or, in concert with other individuals, dealt with.[29] Integration, from such a perspective, cannot avoid a reckoning with the social facts of a given society. In Durkheim's sociology, collective representations of reality were attributed a functional role of meeting the needs of a given society. As such, mythical, religious or scientific representations, all very different from one another, by necessity reflected and expressed social reality as commonly experienced by those who shared and believed them. Collective representations, true or false, provided a milieu for communication between human beings in society. Such a perspective suggests that predominant understandings of integration and social cohesion are in effect social facts that cannot be ignored; their power is suggested by the often-low status of empirical facts in debates about social cohesion.

Security and social cohesion

In retrospect it seems that responses to asylum seekers in the late 1990s were remarkably heated as compared to subsequent attitudes towards immigrants, even if the former were so far fewer in number. The 2006 Census recorded over 400,000 recent immigrants, but the arrival of 3,883 asylum seekers in 1997, following 1,179 in 1996, was portrayed as a crisis by some politicians and officials; in media accounts Ireland was being 'swamped', something no newspaper headlines proclaimed subsequently about immigration. By the end of the decade the total number of asylum seekers in Ireland was less than 10,000. Over time they constituted a smaller and smaller proportion of overall immigration. Ireland had ratified the UN Convention on the Rights of Refugees in 1956 and had periodically admitted groups of refugees: Hungarians in 1956, Chileans in 1973, Vietnamese in 1979 and Bosnians in 1991, an official total of some 2,333 persons.[30] Some of these did not stay in Ireland very long. The Hungarians went on hunger strike, demanding relocation to the United States or Canada – at the heart of this were administrative difficulties in meeting their needs; but the small Vietnamese and Bosnian communities grew over time through family reunification. Ireland only got around to putting its obligations to refugees on a legal footing in 1996, when the Refugee Act was passed with all-party support.

However, the rapid rise in the number of asylum seekers was used to justify non-implementation of much of the Act. Amendments to the Aliens Act (1935) introduced on 29 June 1997 (the last day in office of the outgoing government) increased the powers of immigration officers to determine whether 'aliens' should be allowed to enter the country. The revised Act was implemented in a heavy-handed manner; although the amendments expressly did not apply to persons entering the state from Northern Ireland or Great Britain, some 600 of these were refused entry into the country during the first two months. About twenty had applied for asylum but were not permitted to enter the country by officials.[31] The asylum issue was portrayed by politicians and by officials as an administrative crisis. In 1999 the vista of asylum seekers queuing overnight outside the Mount Street 'one stop shop' established to process their claims was scathingly criticised both by Michael McDowell, later Minister

of Justice, and by Liz McManus, then a Junior Minister. Her statement that
the government's asylum policy was a 'shambles' prompted new restrictions
on asylum seekers rather than reforms aimed at meeting their needs. A new
dispersal policy was introduced, aimed at sharing the burden of asylum
seekers. The political rhetoric that emerged in response to administrative difficulties depicted asylum seekers as 'bogus' refugees and as welfare scroungers.

Subsequent policy changes made the Department of Justice almost entirely
responsible for the welfare of asylum seekers. Existing welfare entitlements
were replaced by a system of 'direct provision' that limited support for asylum
seekers to basic accommodation, meals and cash allowances of £15 weekly
for adults and £7.50 for children. Direct provision was designed as a punitive
system, and was found in a number of studies to cause extreme poverty.
From 2000 to 2009 these low rates of payment remained frozen, whilst most
other benefits rose with inflation year on year. In this context asylum seekers
depended considerably upon NGOs, religious organisations and community
groups for help to integrate. In effect, social policy became an instrument of
border policy; the internal borders it created needed to be policed.

For the first few years of the twenty-first century Irish immigration
debates continued to be preoccupied with national security, with controlling, deterring and being able to expel unwanted guests of the nation. A
raft of legislation did much to criminalise and make dangerous the act of
seeking asylum. McDowell, as Minister for Justice, Equality and Law Reform,
sought to undermine and then remove the constitutional right of the Irish-
born children of immigrants to citizenship, interpreted by the High Court in
1987 as a right to remain in the state with their families. The 1987 ruling had
allowed for the regularisation of a significant number of asylum seekers and
other immigrants with Irish-born children. A 'policy decision' was made to
begin to refuse leave to remain to asylum seeker families, in the knowledge
that this would trigger a further test case in the Supreme Court.[32] In April
2002 the 1987 ruling was overturned in the High Court (*Lobe* v. *Minister of
Justice*). On 23 January 2003 the Supreme Court upheld this ruling, in essence
holding that the Irish-citizen child of non-citizens could be deported with
its parents unless the non-citizen parent agreed to be deported without their
child. This ruling was effectively superseded by the June 2004 Referendum
on Citizenship, which removed the existing birthright to citizenship from the
Irish-born children of non-citizens.

The Irish Nationality and Citizenship Act (2001) superseded the Aliens Act
(1935). Significantly, it systematically replaced the term 'alien' in Irish legislation with that of 'non-national'. The term was used by the Department of
Justice Equality and Law Reform in security debates; in reports about crime,
human trafficking and illegal immigration, and by the Department of Enterprise and Employment to describe immigrant workers. By 2004 the 'national/

non-national' dualism had become the prevalent common-sense conceptual framework for debates about immigration.

The 2004 referendum undermined a definition of social membership set out in Article 45.1 of the 1937 Constitution which states: 'The State shall strive to promote the welfare of the whole people by securing or protecting as effectively as it may a social order in which justice and charity inform all the institutions of the national life.' Here, a concept of domicile entitlement, distinct from citizenship, was emphasised. It had been articulated in social welfare legislation that referred to 'every person in the state' rather than to citizens of the state. On top of this, the 2004 Social Welfare (Miscellaneous Provisions) Act restricted considerably the entitlements of 'non-nationals' to benefits such as children's allowances. These political and policy responses to immigration deepened constitutional and legal distinctions between citizens and non-citizens. In essence, the referendum outcome marked the end of a phase of Irish immigration policy, but not of a mindset preoccupied with deepening distinctions between Irish citizens and immigrants and with little or no focus on integration or social cohesion.

The quest for impermeable borders by one influential part of Irish government coexisted, as noted in Chapter 2, with an influential market case for porous ones. Between them, securocrats and economists shaped Irish immigration policy debates in way that stymied a focus on integration. Simply put, the security perspective defined social cohesion in terms of the existing bounded citizenry; measures aimed at controlling migrants, such as direct provision, were part of a repertoire of external and internal border controls aimed at protecting citizens from migrants. This deliberately impeded the integration of 'aliens' and 'non-nationals'. As observed by the Joseph Rowntree Foundation with respect to the British case, predominant security perspectives within government cognitively undermined social policy, community-based and civic leadership approaches to integration; securocrat thinking about social cohesion worked against a focus on concrete measures to achieve actual cohesion at a community level.[33] Economists emphasised the benefits of immigrants to the economy; in effect they defined integration in terms of participation in the labour market; the reports within which their perspectives dominated also gave little thought to social cohesion. Taken together, their counsel was to restrict where possible access to the kinds of social infrastructure and services deemed necessary to support the social inclusion of existing Irish citizens.

It is important to emphasise that security perspectives are by no means restricted to government officials. In many European countries anti-immigrant populism has demonstrably affected the responses of mainstream political parties towards new immigrants.[34] Positions that were once the preserve of racist and national front parties have found expression within the political mainstream of a number of European countries. In December 2003 the Home Secretary, David Blunkett, noted in the *Observer* that the British National Party (BNP) rarely campaigns these days as overtly racist: 'instead they focus on a sense of injustice borne out by poverty and insecurity; a sense that asylum seekers, immigrants, everyone who looks different, is getting an easier time of it than hard-working, white families'. Blunkett argued that failure to tackle immigration head on would open the doors wide to the extreme right.[35] Tony Blair similarly argued that New Labour could not ignore the electorate's genuine anxieties about asylum and so needed to be demonstrably tough on the issue. In a similar vein Anthony Giddens has argued – wearing his hat as architect of New Labour's 'Third Way' – that the Left could only defeat the Right by adopting policies that are 'tough on immigration (and) tough on the causes of hostility to immigrants'.[36] In 2003 New Labour put forward proposals to charging 'failed' asylum seekers for NHS treatment and to take their children into care if they refused deportation. Blunkett justified these harsh measures as an act of 'political courage' aimed at thwarting the extreme right and as an exercise in political realism.

The Irish context is somewhat different, for all that Irish civil servants borrowed ideas such as direct provision from across the water. Irish political parties have eschewed overt anti-immigrant populism, yet the Irish governance of immigration and integration effectively appropriated much of what was advocated by Blunkett. McDowell cast himself in an equivalent role to Blunkett in advocating the Referendum on Citizenship; he made repeated claims that asylum seekers were exploiting Irish health services. But this was so much smoke and mirrors. The manner in which Irish security perspectives prevailed in the governance of immigration suggests that a security perspective on social cohesion functioned as social fact.

Governance is something of a catch-all term that conveys implicit and explicit activities broader than the range of those traditionally associated with 'government'.[37] According to one definition, governance refers to the activities of policy communities and networks that cut across the domains of state, market and civil society, whether below, at or beyond the level of the nation-state.[38] In the face of globalisation, authority, responsibility and decision-making capacities are presumed to be diffuse. Whilst the system of sovereign states has persisted, it has done so alongside plural structures of power and authority that are, at best, weak or obscure mechanisms of accountability. As explained by David Held:

> The contemporary nature and scope of the sovereign authority of the nation-states can be mapped by looking at a number of 'internal' and 'external' disjunctures between on one hand, the formal domain of political authority they claim for themselves and, on the other, the actual practices and structures of the state and economic system at the national, regional and global levels. The powers

of political parties, bureaucratic organisations, corporations and networks of corporatist influence are among a variety of forces which put pressure on a range of decisions that can be made by the nation-state.[39]

Governance cannot be understood without taking questions about power into account. Responses to immigration, in Ireland as elsewhere, can be explicit or implicit. These might involve legislation, regulation or the development of specific policies. These might also include efforts to manage public debate and expectations. Theories of power relevant to understandings of governance have been influentially categorised by Steven Lukes, who distinguished between one-dimensional, two-dimensional and three-dimensional understandings of power. The first of these typologies focuses upon behaviour, decision-making, observable issues and observable (overt) conflict. Understandings of the workings of power will focus on identifiable subjective interests and preferences relating to specific policy options. The second typology, which he describes as two-dimensional, offers a qualified critique of the behavioural approach he associates with the first. This emphasises 'non-decision making' as well as decision making, and 'observable covert conflict' as well as overt conflict. Lukes advocates what he terms a three-dimensional perspective to the study of power. This, he suggests, would focus additionally on potential issues as well as actual political issues and observable (covert or overt) and latent conflicts.[40] Luke's three-dimensional perspective seeks to account for the ways in which political institutions and political leaders might exercise considerable control over what people choose to care about.[41]

Governance, from this perspective, can be seen to include the political management of debates about asylum and immigration. In the Irish case this included the introduction of direct provision without any demonstrable politically articulated demands beforehand; the aggressive legal assault on the rights of Irish-born children of immigrants and their families as interpreted by the High Court; and the introduction of the Referendum on Citizenship, again as a top-down attempt to manage immigration. Such initiatives might be understood as exercises in pre-emptive political management, aimed at deflating potential anti-immigrant politics. However, at times what is advocated, and how it is advanced, might not be very distinguishable from the racialised politics advocated by extreme groups. Of concern here is how the social facts underpinning immigration governance (to add a fourth 'social fact' dimension to Lukes's tripartite emphasis on values, cultural norms and social structure) tend to work against the social inclusion of immigrants. A simple way of summarising the pertinent social fact is the proposition that nation-states are defensive bounded communities.

Social capital and social cohesion

In a 2006 article, 'E Pluribus Unum', Robert Putnam emphasised a negative correlation between ethnic diversity and trust in the United States. Reputably, Putman had held off publishing this research for some time out of concern about how it might be received in a context of mainstream populist responses to immigration. Putnam is a leading figure in social inclusion debates; in particular, his work emphasises the role of social capital in promoting social cohesion. Drawing on data from a study of American cities, Putnam reported extensive findings that increased levels of diversity seem to trigger anomie and social isolation: 'In colloquial language, people living in ethnically diverse settings appear to "hunker down".'[42] In the United States the strongest predictors of levels of trust (controlling for everything else) are individual-level variables: age (younger people are less trusting), ethnicity (black people and Hispanics are less trusting) and socio-economic class (the well-off and homeowners are more trusting). Next in importance, according to Putnam, are several contextual variables: poverty (less trust in high-crime areas) and ethnic diversity (less trust amongst inhabitants of ethnically heterogeneous neighbourhoods).[43] However, Putnam asserted that economic inequality 'does not appear to cause, amplify or obscure the apparent effect of ethnic diversity on social capital'.[44]

Putnam's research correlated levels of trust of neighbours by US Census tract levels of diversity, controlling for other variables such as age, socio-economic status and home ownership. From his findings, he asserts that inhabitants from diverse communities tend to withdraw from collective life, to distrust their neighbours, regardless of the colour of their skin, to withdraw even from close friends, to expect the worse from their community leaders, to volunteer less, vote less, have less faith that they can make a difference and to huddle unhappily in front of the television.[45] In effect, diversity is seen to detrimentally affect in-group and out-group solidarity. At the same time Putnam asserted that 'many Americans today remain uncomfortable with diversity'.[46] In setting the scene for his analysis Putnam presented an archetype of inner-city social diversity where cosmopolitanism, diversity, anomie and poverty co-exist:

> Diverse communities tend to be larger, more mobile, less egalitarian, more crime-ridden and so on. Moreover, individuals who live in ethnically diverse places are different from people who live in homogenous areas. They tend to be poorer, less educated, less likely to own their own home, less likely to speak English and so on.[47]

Against this, Robert Sampson, drawing on a study of language diversity and social disorder in Chicago, concluded that a negative relationship between social cohesion and diversity is likely to be most pronounced within the most homogenous communities. This was 'hardly a surprising finding', insofar as such areas had historically been most resistant to racial and ethnic change. These were far more likely to be more perturbed by even small amounts of diversity than were already cosmopolitan urban areas by large-scale immigration.[48]

Furthermore, the appearance of social homogeneity is by no means a guarantee of social cohesion. Consider the argument by M.P. Baumgartner (one dramatised by the novels of J.G. Ballard) that the civility, peace and quiet and apparent social harmony of suburban neighbourhoods may be the product of some of the very things often presumed to bring about conflict: fragmentation, isolation, atomisation and indifference among people.[49] Such critiques suggest a potential disjuncture between hidden experiences of anomie and dominant presumptions about the extent of social cohesion (as social fact).

Putnam's analysis of social cohesion leans towards a political critique of diversity. It emphasises the role of social capital in promoting social cohesion in terms of homogeneity of values. It is predicated on the notion of some dominant identity gold standard and static model of society against which any social change, by definition, disrupts.[50] Specifically, Putnam defined social cohesion in terms of the absence of latent social conflict or polarisation, whether as income/wealth disparities, racial/ethnic tensions or disparities in political participation. Social cohesion is also defined in terms of the presence of strong social bonds (social capital measured in terms of levels of trust and reciprocity).[51] Diversity, by implication, is bad for social cohesion. Putnam's findings might be taken to endorse policies that limit immigration in a climate of concern about the dangers of too much ethnic and cultural diversity across the early twenty-first-century West.[52] But this is never Putnam's intention. The closing pages of 'E Pluribus Unum' depart from the strict empirical style of the main body of the article; under the sub-heading 'Becoming comfortable with diversity', Putnam offers stories from his own life and from that of his daughter's half-Costa Rican family as illustrations of the hyphenated American identities that work to bridge across ethnic divides. He discusses how previous phases of 'hunkering down' had in time been overcome, in part of a series of ruminations that end by stating a 'hunch' that the current phase of hunkering down will, too, be superseded by new shared senses of belonging. The tightrope Putnam walks is summarised by the following extract from his closing paragraph:

> Scientific examination of immigration, diversity and social cohesion easily could be inflamed as the results of research become part of the contemporary political debate. But that debate needs to be informed by our best efforts to ascertain the facts. It would be unfortunate if a politically correct progressivism were to deny the reality of the challenge to social solidarity posed by diversity. It would be equally unfortunate if an ahistorical and ethnocentric conservativism were to deny that addressing that challenge is both feasible and desirable.[53]

A similar challenge can be identified in the Irish case. The impact of immigration on social cohesion cannot be understood by merely considering the social facts that influence Irish perspectives on immigration. It is not enough to commend one kind of normative response over another. It is also necessary to consider empirical evidence, insofar as this is possible.

Social cohesion: an Irish case study

The data used to examine intersections between social inclusion, integration, social capital and social cohesion in the Irish case were obtained from a combined analysis of five studies into the well-being of children, families and neighbourhoods undertaken in Ireland during 2007 and 2008. Each WBCFN study focused on a sample population within a relatively deprived neighbourhood where, by definition, the host Irish community was defined as socially excluded.[54] Putnam defined social cohesion in terms of trust and reciprocity scores. Yet elsewhere he offers more expansive definitions of social capital and proposes for it a wider role in promoting social inclusion and well-being, one that is addressed by a substantial research literature.[55] The focus on neighbourhood-level data here differs, of course from the large-scale datasets used by Putnam to measure trust and reciprocity, though what was being measured was essentially the same.[56] Yet it reflects the micro context within which social capital may or may not benefit social cohesion. Unlike Putnam's study, it considers relationships between social capital and social exclusion, both of which propose alternative ways of conceptualising social cohesion.

Social cohesion, trust and reciprocity

At face value, Putnam's thesis that social capital is undermined by diversity seems to be borne out in the Irish case. The most diverse WBCFN population area (the Liberties) was characterised by comparatively low trust and the lowest overall reciprocity scores. When comparisons are made at sample cluster level, the most diverse electoral area (Merchants Quay B in the Liberties) scored comparatively low trust and reciprocity scores. However, the lowest trust scores of all were found in the least diverse population area (Limerick). In fact, the three least diverse sample clusters (where Irish accounted for between 98 and 100 percent) returned comparatively low rates of trust, whilst a number of other clusters with similarly higher levels of diversity (in each, Irish comprised 93 percent) had hugely divergent trust scores. All this suggests that 'hunkering down', if that is what it is, happens for a different balance of reasons in different areas.

Trust scores were highest amongst the elderly and lowest amongst homeless respondents. The highest levels of reciprocity were identified amongst two-parent families and owner-occupiers. Reciprocity scores were lowest amongst non-EU respondents, who scored lower than even the homeless, the artefact here being that only non-familial supports were defined as reciprocity. Trust scores for the other categories of migrants, UK citizen and other EU citizen (hereafter EU) respondents were markedly lower than for Irish WBCFN respondents as a whole. Overall, migrant levels of trust were considerably lower than for Irish respondents, suggesting (albeit in the absence of longitudinal data) that the presence of migrants may have reduced overall levels of trust in the Irish case. For example, by accommodation type, trust scores were found to be lowest in the private rented sector where EU and non-EU migrants were predominantly concentrated; their trust scores were lower than amongst Irish-citizen private rented sector respondents. Yet (again in the absence of longitudinal data) there is nothing to suggest that the huge and rapid increase in social diversity has eroded trust amongst Irish citizens. Low trust scores amongst migrants have, in effect, reduced *average* trust scores for the population. In essence, the WBCFN data do not reveal a breakdown in trust due to immigration, but find low levels of trust amongst migrants who are somewhat isolated within the deprived neighbourhoods in which they live.

How might these low levels of trust be explained? Being a home owner, being part of a two-parent household and, above all, being elderly contributed positively to overall trust levels. Being a member of a vulnerable group and not being a home owner contributed detrimentally to trust scores. The most likely explanation of low trust scores amongst migrants is that many of these are singletons living disconnected lives in new-built private sector accommodation. Even though these possessed attributes (such as relatively high education levels) often found to positively correlate with psychological well-being, their low social-capital indicator scores dragged down their overall composite well-being scores. What these scores suggest is not so much a deterioration of Irish social cohesion but the marginality of well-to-do migrants within relatively deprived communities.

Reciprocity scores (which measured non-familial interactions – a stronger indication of social capital than trust) were found to be considerably lower for migrants than for Irish respondents. These were particularly low for non-EU migrants, lower than even amongst the homeless.

Migrants from EU countries (close to half of all immigrant respondents and mostly Poles and Lithuanians) were found to have comparatively poor social networks as compared to Irish respondents. Reciprocity scores were also considerably lower amongst these than for Irish-citizen respondents. By way of context, the 2006 census found that 64 percent of Polish migrants (the largest EU immigrant group by far) were male, 70 percent were in the 30–34 age group and under 40 percent of adults were married, with an undisclosed number of partners not resident in Ireland. Most, according to the 2006 census, were found to be living in Polish-only households, with non-family households dominating.

Comparative Eurobarometer data for 2004 on trust and reciprocity reveal that reciprocity scores were extremely low in Poland (0.093) and Lithuania (0.134) as compared to Ireland (0.321). Immigrants from both these countries collectively made up almost half of non-Irish citizen respondents in the Liberties. Comparatively lower but modest differences in reciprocity scores were found for Poland (2.510) and Lithuania (2.050) and Ireland (2.372). The inference here is that post-2004 EU Accession Country migrants arrived with lower levels of social capital than the Irish host population. On just one aspect of social capital – meetings with neighbours (a kind that immigrants could not bring with them) – Lithuanian scores were considerably higher than Irish scores. However, Poles and Lithuanians were far less likely in their countries of origin to be members of, or to participate in, voluntary organisations.[57]

Non-EU migrants, on the other hand, were found to have slightly better social networks than Irish respondents. However, their reciprocity scores were comparatively low (lower even than for homeless respondents), suggesting that many may have had support networks based on kinship (not counted in the measurement of reciprocity). Such findings suggest that some immigrants are more likely to reduce overall social capital scores than others. For example, a 2009 study of Fingal (the local authority area that includes Dublin 15) found that levels of community engagement by African immigrants far exceeded those of Polish immigrants.[58] Arguably, if there had been an African population in the Liberties, overall social capital scores would have been raised, and by Putnam's metric, social cohesion would have improved. This goes against a prevailing view exemplified by media accounts of white flight, and addressed in subsequent chapters, that African immigrants in particular undermine social cohesion.

Social cohesion and social exclusion

The WBCFN study included a number of indicators of social exclusion.[59] It also included several indicators of individual well-being; specific questions sought to measure depression, life satisfaction, hope and various social-capital indicators of trust, reciprocity and support network levels. A standard claim within the social-capital literature is that poor neighbourhoods are more likely to lack the necessary qualities of self-help, mutuality and trust that could assist in their regeneration.[60] In essence, the claim is that low social capital undermines social cohesion, defined as high levels of social exclusion. Yet the WBCFN findings were that Irish citizens living in deprived areas tended to have high social-capital scores but also high levels of social exclusion, defined in terms of low income and low levels of education. In some respects, immigrant respondents were clearly better off than Irish-citizen respondents in the communities in which they lived. For example, 25 percent of all WBCFN respondents had third-level qualifications, with levels amongst the most vulnerable WBCFN groups being exceedingly low (5 percent of Travellers, 0 percent of homeless and 5 percent of Barnardos clients). However, some 50 percent of UK migrants, 57 percent of other EU respondents and 64 percent of non-EU respondents had third-level qualifications.

Immigrant respondents were found to score comparatively high in human capital but comparatively low in social capital. Their low social-capital scores contributed to comparatively low overall well-being scores, the artefact here being that trust and reciprocity scores were used (alongside ones for hope and depression) as indices of well-being. Nevertheless, the findings suggested that comparatively poor well-being amongst adult immigrants was partly explicable by greater levels of isolation than amongst long-standing but poorer Irish residents in the same areas. The available evidence suggested that the lives of many such immigrants revolved around work. As suggested by Forrest and Kearns, residents of poor areas spend more time in their neighbourhoods than do wealthier people in the places where they live.[61] In essence, the kinds of isolation and anomie identified by Baumgartner in well-to-do anonymous suburbs may also apply to the new inner-city gated apartment complexes within which migrants became over-represented in the Irish case.[62] The WBCFN findings suggest that Irish and immigrant respondents within the same locality to some extent inhabited parallel worlds – ones determined by architecture, urban planning and gentrification rather than by cultural differences.[63]

Amongst Irish respondents generally, with the exception of the elderly, a strong correlation between high social-need scores and poor well-being scores was found. Social need was defined in terms of levels of income poverty (entitlement to a means-tested medical card), low education, the percentage of lone parent and elderly respondents and neighbourhood problem levels. By comparison, EU respondents scored low levels of social exclusion; none (0 percent) were found to have a low education and the percentage in receipt of medical cards was half that for Irish respondents. Their depression scores were comparatively low, marginally above single respondents overall. Their life satisfaction scores and hope scores were marginally below those for Irish respondents overall. However, their trust, reciprocity and support network scores were considerably lower than for Irish respondents. Similarly, non-EU migrants scored low on levels of social need and, again, had psychological need levels marginally lower than amongst Irish respondents overall. Trust scores were higher than for non-EU migrants but lower than for Irish respondents overall. Reciprocity scores for non-EU migrants were lower than for EU migrants but their support network scores were higher, suggesting that their social capital was to a considerable extent based on family and kinship.

In summary, then, adult immigrants were typically less socially excluded than were their Irish adult neighbours in deprived communities. Yet immigrant respondents exhibited poorer well-being than their more deprived Irish neighbours. The main barriers to immigrant adult well-being were social-capital deficits (trust and reciprocity formed part of the index of well-being). Adults were also typically under-employed, given their education levels.

Social capital has been presented by some commentators as something of a magic bullet: good for individual well-being and social cohesion; but it is hardly a social inclusion or integration panacea. High levels of social capital can translate into limited benefits for those experiencing social exclusion. Irish-citizen WBCFN respondents for the most part demonstrated high levels of social capital and high levels of social exclusion. Migrant respondents had comparatively low levels of social capital but high levels of human capital and income. Within the WBCFN, disadvantaged Irish communities' social inclusion proved inversely related to social-capital scores. Forrest and Kearns suggest that there may be considerable social capital in deprived areas but the assets obtainable through it seldom allow participants to rise above their poverty.[64] Likewise, Li (in the Canadian case) finds that the socio-economic status of immigrant communities is significant in determining the effectiveness of whatever social capital they possess.[65] In other words, social capital cannot replace other forms of capital needed to produce economic opportunities and outcomes. Immigrant respondents, on the other hand, were found to be comparatively strong on human-capital attributes, which translated into a degree of economic participation above that of their Irish neighbours. The benefits of social capital in the absence of human capital in fostering social inclusion appeared negligible.

Only if we simplistically measure social cohesion in terms of social-capital scores does Putnam's assertion hold. When the relationships between socio-economic status, social exclusion and social capital are taken into account what emerges is a more complex scenario than the 'hunkering down' portrayed by Putnam. The WBCFN findings suggest that overall scores, arguably, matter less than the relative positions of groups in distinct social settings. Marginal groups, including migrants, may lack social capital without necessarily reducing the social-capital status of other groups. The Irish findings suggest that whilst migrants are impoverished in social capital by Putnam's metric (trust and reciprocity), they possess considerable relative advantage in the kinds of cultural capital emphasised by Pierre Bourdieu (habitus). Indications of this can be identified from the higher child well-being scores and higher educational-aspiration scores than were found amongst Irish WBCFN respondents. These findings are considered in Chapter 7, which examines evidence of educational advantage and disadvantage amongst immigrant children.

Challenges

How we think about diversity, whether we celebrate it, accept it, fight it or flee from it only to some extent defines the politics of integration. Some of the biggest challenges to social cohesion have nothing to do with immigration. The example given of socially deprived areas in Limerick emphasised the damage of generations of social policy failure. The communities uprooted were of the kind depicted by Frank McCourt in *Angela's Ashes*. Research undertaken in the 1960s described the damage to social cohesion resulting from the way in which they were rehoused. This occurred at a time when Ireland was moving towards an optimistic future; education was rapidly expanding but it was already clear that socio-economically deprived groups were being left behind. The bland term 'social exclusion' hardly captures the consequences of the assertion within the National Anti-Poverty Strategy that no society can view without deep concern the prospect of a significant minority of people becoming removed from the incomes and lifestyles of the majority, that as a result of inadequate income and resources people may be excluded and marginalised from participating in activities which are considered norm for other people in society.[66] In 1967, in Limerick, according to 'Social Dynamite', such a prospect was already a reality, as it has subsequently proved to be in other socio-economically disadvantaged communities. Social exclusion as a threat to social cohesion preceded the arrival of immigrants. It is crucial not to lose sight of this when, as may inevitably be the case, some immigrants living in poor areas are identified as a threat to social cohesion. If this comes to pass it will be no less due to failed social policies than has been the case for long-standing socially excluded communities.

The cumulative argument of this chapter and the previous one is that two dominant perspectives on immigration have worked against a social-policy focus on integration. Securocrats justified restrictions upon migrant rights and entitlements, with scant consideration of how the human misery these caused for some might subsequently impede integration. Economists prioritised economic growth above social cohesion and presumed that a laissez-faire approach to integration was sustainable, never thinking that migrants were real people with real families, the crooked timber of humanity rather than disposable factors of production. Both mindsets worked against a focus on social cohesion.

Yet the analysis presented here suggests that it is not just a matter of listening less to some officials or economists. What is termed a security governance perspective is in fact a deeply ingrained understanding of social cohesion, a social fact which places immigrants outside of the dominant imagined community, even as these become inextricably embedded within Irish society. Governments are required to protect their sovereignty and borders. Insofar as these borders have been made ever more permeable, by, for example, cheap flights, the temptation to ramp up internal distinctions between how citizens and non-citizens are treated has intensified. The kinds of internal border maintenance promoted by what I term a governance security perspective have made it difficult to get immigrants onto the social policy agenda.

One of the features of immigration in the Irish case has been the arrival of well-educated newcomers in some deprived localities; the impact of immigration on socio-spatial disadvantage is considered in the next chapter; Chapter 7 examines its impact on educational disadvantage. The well-being research examined in this chapter suggests that immigrants can indeed be socially included whilst living in socially excluded communities. Such research illustrates the incoherence of many social-capital inspired discussions of social cohesion. In large-scale studies social capital is reduced to a handful of trust and reciprocity variables. Homogenous areas, Putnam suggests, have higher social-capital scores when social capital is reduced to such variables. When Putnam claims that diversity undermines social cohesion he is basically saying that diversity undermines social capital. Putnam tends to present social capital *as* social cohesion rather than as a means to achieve social cohesion. In other words, social capital is presented as an end in itself rather than a means to an end. Ultimately, the importance of social capital to overall social cohesion is less clear than the benefits of social capital to individuals. Social capital is an individual-level resource, though in recent years it has been increasingly presented as a societal one. In the Liberties case study long-standing Irish-citizen local residents scored high on social capital as compared to immigrants, but this did not seem to confer any social-inclusion dividend. Immigrants, on the other hand, had lower social-capital scores but were socially included by developmental rules of belonging. Human capital translated into 'social inclusion' in a way that social capital did not.

The opening proposition of this chapter was that understandings of integration are influenced by understandings of social cohesion. From a governance security perspective the Irish locals of the Liberties are integrated. Yet from the same perspective some of the Irish residents of Moyross are not. From a developmental perspective Irish residents in the Liberties are less integrated than are recent immigrants, who, at the time of the research, had high rates of economic participation. This bears thinking about.

Notes

1 The World Bank in fact defines social capital as the glue that holds together the institutions of society. Cited in C. Farrell, 'Thinking Critically about Social Capital', *Irish Journal of Sociology* 16.2 (2007), 27–49, p. 29

2 Dáil Éireann, *Adjournment Debate: Moyross (Limerick) Vandalism*, vol. 417, 11 March 1992

3 'One more Killing and Limerick Is the Murder Capital of Western Europe', *Irish Independent*, 24 September 2006

4 '2500 Houses To Be Knocked in Moyross, Southill', *Limerick Leader*, 14 January 2008

5 H. Entzinger and R. Biezeveld, *Benchmarking in Immigrant Integration, Report written for the European Commission, European Research Centre on Migration and Ethnic Relations* (Rotterdam: ERCOMER, 2003)

6 Office for Social Inclusion, www.socialinclusion.i/poverty.html

7 Government of Ireland, *Revised Anti-Poverty Strategy* (Dublin: Stationery Office, 2002), p. 17

8 Government of Ireland *Migration Nation; Statement on Integration Strategy and Diversity Management* (Dublin: Stationery Office, 2008), p. 9

9 National Economic and Social Council, *Managing Migration in Ireland: A Social and Economic Analysis* (Dublin: Stationery Office, 2005), p. xxi

10 See the chapter on 'Ireland and the Holocaust', in B. Fanning, *Racism and Social Change in the Republic of Ireland* (Manchester: Manchester University Press, 2002)

11 E. Durkheim, *The Division of Labour in Society* (London: Macmillan, 1984 [1894])

12 F. Tönnies, *Community and Civil Society*, ed. J. Harris (Cambridge: Cambridge University Press, 2001)

13 B. Fanning, *The Quest for Modern Ireland: the Battle of Ideas 1912–1986* (Dublin: Irish Academic Press, 2008), pp. 124–129

14 Within the civil service its key architects were T.K. Whitaker and Patrick Lynch. An early landmark was their participation as junior Finance officials in a debate on full employment at the Statistical and Social Inquiry Society (SSIS) in April 1945. T.K. Whitaker, *Interests* (Dublin: Institute of Public Administration, 1983), p. 82

15 Fanning, *Quest for Modern Ireland*, pp. 125–126

16 Rev. L. Ryan, 'Social Dynamite: A Study of Early School Leavers', *Christus Rex* 21.1 (1967), 7–44

17 Rev. L. Ryan, 'University Education and Social Class in Ireland', *Christus Rex* 22.2 (1966), 118–124

18 Quoted from the *Irish Times*, 12 September 1966

19 Ryan, 'Social Dynamite', p. 40

20 As put by one respondent: 'At present you must have four children to qualify for a house. But how can they have children? They live either with a relative for a while. Then they get thrown out and move into the City Home. He is put on one side, and she on another. Where are they supposed to have sex; is it in the street? These were young married people.'

21 'Essential Reading for "Regeneration" Communities', *Limerick Regeneration Watch*. Available at: www.limerickregeneration.org

22 E. Durkheim, *Suicide: A Study in Sociology* (New York: Free Press, 1951 [1897])

23 Durkheim, *Division of Labour*, p. 340

24 *Ibid.*, p. 338

25 See R. Forrest and A. Kearns, 'Social Cohesion, Social Capital and the Neighbourhood', *Urban Studies* 38 (2001), 2125–2143, pp. 2126–2127; also see M. Mann, 'Social Cohesion and Liberal Democracy', *American Sociological Review* 35 (1970), 423–439

26 S. Lukes, *Emile Durkheim: His Life and Work: A Critical Study* (London: Penguin, 1992), pp. 490–496
27 E. Durkheim, 'Preface to the Second Edition', *The Rules of Sociological Method*, trans. S.A. Solovay and J.H. Mueller (New York; Free Press, 1938) pp. xlv–xliii
28 *Ibid.*, p. xiv
29 *Ibid.*, p. 4
30 Fanning, *Racism and Social Change*, p. 97
31 P. Cullen, 'Refugees, Asylum and Race on the Borders', in E. Crowley and J. MacLaughlin (eds), *Under the Belly of the Celtic Tiger: Class, Race, Identity and Culture in the 'Global Ireland'* (Dublin: Irish Reporter Publications, 1997), p. 105
32 D. O'Connell, and C. Smith, 'Citizenship and the Irish Constitution', in U. Fraser and C. Harvey (eds), *Sanctuary in Ireland: Perspectives on Asylum Law and Policy* (Dublin: Institute of Public Administration, 2003) p. 265
33 P. Cheong, R. Edwards, H. Goulbourne and J. Solomos, 'Immigration, Social Cohesion and Social Capital: A Critical Review', *Critical Social Policy* 27.1 (2007), 24–49
34 T. Theiler, 'Societal Security', in M. Dunn and V. Mauer (eds), *The Routledge Handbook of Security Studies* (London: Routledge, 2009).
35 D. Blunkett, 'I Can't Back Down on Asylum', *Observer*, 14 December 2003
36 See M. O'Connell, *Right-Wing Ireland? The Rise of Populism in Ireland and Europe* (Dublin: Liffey Press, 2003), p. 56
37 R.A.W. Rhodes, 'The New Governance: Governing without Government', *Political Studies* 44 (1996), 652–67, pp. 662–663
38 D. Held, *Democracy and the Global Order: From the Modern State to Cosmopolitan Governance* (London: Polity, 1995), p. 139
39 *Ibid.*, p. 99
40 See S. Lukes, *Power: A Radical View* (London: Macmillan, 1974), chapter 7.
41 M.A. Crenson, *The Un-Politics of Air Pollution: A Study of Non-decisionmaking in the Cities* (Baltimore, MD: Johns Hopkins University Press, 1971), p. 23, cited in Lukes, *Power*, chapter 7.
42 R.D. Putnam, '*E pluribus Unum*: Diversity and Community in the Twenty-first century', *Scandinavian Political Studies* 30.2 (2006), 137–174, p. 149
43 *Ibid.*, p. 153
44 *Ibid.*, p. 157
45 *Ibid.*, p. 151
46 *Ibid.*, p. 158
47 *Ibid.*, p. 151
48 R. Sampson, 'Disparity and Diversity in the Contemporary City: Social (Dis)order Revisited', *British Journal of Sociology* 60.1 (2009), 1–31, pp. 25–26
49 See M. Baumgartner, *The Moral Order and the Suburbs* (Oxford: Oxford University Press, 1988), p. 134. Anomie within suburban and urban gated communities has been a sequence of novels by J.G. Ballard, e.g. *Concrete Island* (1974), *High Rise* (1975), *Millennium People* (2003)
50 Cheong et al., 'Immigration, Social Cohesion and Social Capital', p. 35
51 R.D. Putnam *Bowling Alone: The Collapse and Revival of American Community* (New York: Simon and Schuster, 2000)

52 Cheong *et al.*, 'Immigration, Social Cohesion and Social Capital', p. 27

53 Putnam, '*E Pluribus Unum*', p. 165

54 The component studies were undertaken by the same research consultancy on behalf of five client agencies working with socially excluded families and children: Barnardos, the Respond Housing Association, the Bray and Wicklow Partnerships and the Liberties (inner-city Dublin) Regeneration Area.

55 J. Helliwell, 'Social Capital, the Economy and Well-Being', in A. Sharpe and K. Banting (eds), *The Review of Economic Performance and Social Performance: The Longest Decade: Canada in the 1990s* (Ottawa: Centre for the Study of Living Standards and The Institute for Research on Public Policy, 2001)

56 Trust was measured by asking: 'how many people do you trust in your neighbour-hood?' The response options were: 'most', 'many', 'a few' and 'none'. Reciprocity was measured by asking whether respondents had done a favour for a neighbour in the past six months (or received one) and whether they believed that neighbours look out for each other.

57 Cited in M. Gesthuizen, T. van der Meer, T. Scheepers and P. Scheepers, 'Ethnic Diversity and Social Capital in Europe: Tests of Putnam's Thesis in European Countries', *Scandinavian Political Studies* 32.2 (2009), 121–142

58 'Only 16% of Polish respondents reported membership of groups or clubs, compared to 44% of African respondents', E. Ó'Brian, *Towards an Integrated community: A Survey of Minority Ethnic Communities in Fingal* (Dublin: Fingal Development Board and Fingal County Council, 2009), p. 18

59 Five indicators of social exclusion and social need were included in the WBCFN surveys: (i) proportion of population with a means-tested medical card (used as an income proxy); (ii) proportion of population with primary education only (a proxy for earning potential); (iii) proportion of lone parent families; (iv) proportion of households indicating financial difficulties; and (v) proportion of older households.

60 Forrest and Kearns, 'Social Cohesion', p. 213

61 *Ibid.*, p. 2133

62 Baumgartner, *The Moral Order*, p. 134

63 This was clear from photographs taken of the buildings and streets from which research clusters were selected.

64 R.D. Portes and P. Landolt, 'The Downside of Social Capital', *American Prospect* 26 (1996), 18–21, cited in Forrest and Kearns, 'Social Cohesion', p. 2141

65 P.S. Li, 'Social Capital and Economic Outcomes for Immigrants and Ethnic Minorities', *Journal of International Migration and Integration* 5.1 (2004), 171–190

66 Government of Ireland, *Revised National Anti-Poverty Strategy* (Dublin: Stationery Office, 2002)

4

Some numbers and percentages

Out of timber so crooked as that from which man is made nothing entirely straight can be built. (Immanuel Kant, 1784)

The 2006 Irish Census identified a population of 4,239,848 persons. Of the 'usually resident' population 610,000, or 14.7 percent of the total, were born outside the Republic of Ireland. Of these, approximately 10 percent were 'non-Irish nationals'. Just over 10 percent of children in Ireland in 2006 were born in other countries. Of a total of 117,600 of those under 19 years, 46,900 were born in England and Wales, 9,900 were born in the United States, 5,900 in Poland, 3,800 in Lithuania and 9,800 in other EU countries.[1] Some 10,000 children were born in African countries – some of these are likely to have Irish-born siblings; and 9,000 children living in Ireland were born in Asian countries. In 2006, children made up 18 percent of the non-Irish citizen population. Some 7.4 percent of identified children living in the Republic of Ireland do not have Irish citizenship.[2]

Census calculations of the size of the immigrant population (including numbers of children) have frequently been disputed and, in any case, quickly become out of date. For example, in 2006 the Polish embassy estimated that about 120,000 Polish migrants currently resided in the Republic of Ireland; census enumerators counted 63,276. The embassy's estimate was not unreasonable; some 90,320 PPS numbers (registration required to be able to work in Ireland) were issued to Poles between May 2004 and December 2005. A further 25,679 were issued between January and the end of April 2006. Prior to EU enlargement in May 2004, Poles were part of a population of 133,436 Eastern European migrant workers.[3] PPS statistics took no account of those who came to Ireland but subsequently left.

Estimates of the size of the Chinese resident population have been even more widely divergent. Census enumerators counted 11,161 in 2006, some 91 percent more than the 5,842 recorded in the 2002 Census.[4] Other estimates, also from 2006, using work permit and student visa data, put the Chinese population at about 60,000. A total of 15,933 student visas were issued to students from China in 2004 alone. Media estimates put the Chinese population as high as

130,000. A 2006 report by the National Consultative Committee on Racism and Interculturalism (NCCRI) suggested that there were between 60,000 and 100,000 Chinese in Ireland; it predicted that the 2006 Census would show the Chinese to be the second-largest immigrant community after the Poles.[5] This optimism proved unfounded. In 2008, citing no evidence, the Chinese ambassador claimed that about 80,000 Chinese lived in Ireland.[6]

Some 80 percent of Chinese respondents to the 2006 Census lived in rented flats and apartments. Anecdotal evidence suggests that many of these had multiple occupants who were not identified by enumerators.[7] Those Chinese counted in the 2006 Census were predominately young adults in their twenties; 54 percent were male and 46 percent were female; 71 percent were single; 43 percent were on student visas. Almost all of the recorded Chinese population (95 percent) lived in either towns or cities; 50 percent lived in Dublin. In terms of their education, 28 percent were educated to at least degree level; a further 59 percent had completed upper secondary education or non-degree third-level courses; the remaining 13 percent were poorly educated. Over half of those in employment worked in hotels or restaurants; 19 percent were chefs or cooks, a further 6 percent were waiters and waitresses. It may be the case that such census data does not adequately represent some of the invisibles. Some of the qualitative research considered in the next chapter describes the experiences of undocumented and exploited Chinese migrant workers, the kind of people who are unlikely to have spoken to census enumerators.

The census profiles of some immigrant communities are augmented in some cases by statistically reliable survey data. A number of such studies examined in this chapter indicate that immigrants encounter specific barriers to employment and occupational status that equate to their levels of education and human capital. Others quantify experiences of racism and discrimination. Others again address risks of social exclusion and socio-spatial segregation. Quantitative data has a clear role in identifying levels of and barriers to integration. The importance of adequate and appropriate data and some of the difficulties in developing such data have been highlighted by the United Kingdom Cabinet Office:

> But one of the reasons why policies and services have failed minority ethnic groups in the past is the lack of information available about them. Much information that is currently collected is not broken down by ethnic group. In addition, because people from minority ethnic communities make up a small proportion of the population, their representation in many surveys is so low as to make it difficult to use the results with confidence. The resulting lack of detailed local and robust data that covers the whole country means that it is often difficult to adequately diagnose the problems experienced by minority ethnic groups, better target policies or services at addressing their needs, and monitor the impact on them.[8]

All European countries have immigrant populations that face disproportionate levels of social exclusion. Research has shown that migrant and
indigenous ethnic minority populations in the European Union are disproportionately represented in forms of poor and insecure work and are disproportionately unemployed. Furthermore, such inequalities have persisted within
second and third generations of some migrant descended communities who
have been born, raised and educated in European member states. In Britain
a picture emerges of shifts in the fortunes of some communities over time,
of the ongoing marginalisation of others and of communities experiencing
different forms and levels of disadvantage.[9] Disparities between ethnic groups
have been found in income levels, rates of employment and self-employment,
types of employment, occupational status, educational attainment and levels
of home ownership. Particularly vulnerable cohorts were identified within
some communities on the basis of age and gender. The British experience
indicates that racism, discrimination and other barriers to integration are
experienced differently and with different consequences by different groups.

This can be translated, in the Irish case, into a hypothesis that Chinese,
Polish, Lithuanian or Nigerian immigrants will experience different opportunities for and barriers to integration. At the time of writing it would be impossible to construct a chapter that methodically assessed the challenges facing
each such group. Partly this is because doing so requires longitudinal data,
the results of successive censuses and surveys that allow us to gauge whether
the overall situations of respective groups are improving or deteriorating over
time and, no less importantly, to understand distinctions within groups on the
basis of gender and social class. Such data is not yet available. No less important is disaggregated data that reveals challenges to integration within specific
geographical communities.

Debates about immigration are often driven by anecdotal information.
Journalists have on occasion written about fears and risks of immigrant
ghettos; here the focus tends to be on black immigrants rather than, as has
recently been the British case, Muslims. In one important respect Muslims
living in Ireland are more integrated than many other immigrant groups;
almost one third (31 percent) are Irish citizens. Many are comparatively long-
term residents. The 1991 Census recorded 3,873 Muslims; the 2002 Census
put Ireland's Muslim population at 19,147; the 2006 Census identified 32,539,
which amounted to less than 1 percent of the population. Most Muslims in
Ireland are Sunni; about 2,000 are Shi'a. They were found to have arrived from
42 countries: 7,693 were citizens of African countries; of these 1,990 were
Nigerian. Of those originating from Asia 4,853 were Pakistani, 1,284 were
Malaysian, 304 were Indian and 4,076 were from other countries. About 10
percent (estimated at around 3,500) are asylum seekers or refugees.[10] Owner
occupiers were 21 percent, while 23 percent lived in social housing (local

authority and voluntary sector). Just over half (17,330) of Ireland's Muslim population were found to live in the Dublin area, with 6,519 in Dublin City, 4,176 in South Dublin, 1,922 in Dún Laoghaire-Rathdown and 4,713 in Fingal. Just under 11 percent of Muslims were found in 2006 to be unemployed; 21 percent were educated to degree level or higher; 8.5 percent were recorded under the 'employers or managers' socio-economic group and 17.4 percent as higher professionals. The two most prominent occupational groups were 'personal services and childcare' (2,522) and 'health and related occupations' (1,765). Eight Muslims were identified as employed in either the Garda Siochána or the army; of these, one was female. Of those aged over 15 years, just under 13 percent described themselves as engaged in one or more voluntary activity. This compared to 16 percent for the Irish population as a whole. Such statistics aside, very little social research has been undertaken on the lives of Muslims in Ireland.

Comprehensively disaggregated data can serve to explode myths, such as those about ghettos considered in this chapter, as well as provide an evidence base to address actual risks of social exclusion amongst immigrants, particularly those who settle in disadvantaged areas. But the use of such data remains patchy at best. Whilst the Central Statistics Office has considerably extended the availability of disaggregated data to policy makers since the 2006 Census, immigrants remain for all intents and purposes invisible in much of the quantitative research that informs social policy at national and local levels. This chapter includes some case studies aimed at illustrating the kinds of issues such data might routinely address.

Human capital, social lift and occupational penalties

Comparative OECD data for 2001 found that only one other developed country (Canada) had a higher proportion than Ireland of its foreign-born population with third-level educational qualifications. By comparative standards, the human-capital advantage of immigrants in Ireland has been exceptionally strong. In 2001 the percentage of those educated to third level was 1.8 times that of the native population.[11] This reflected a period during which highly skilled non-EU workers were proactively recruited by the Irish state, particularly into the health sector. Asylum seekers comprised a second major strand of immigration; these too were highly educated as compared to Irish citizens. For example, 41 percent of Nigerians (many of who had arrived mostly through the asylum process) were found to be educated to degree standard or higher.

An analysis of the spatial distribution of immigrant human capital in Dublin (using 2006 Census data) found that immigrants provide at least some degree of human-capital lift in all electoral areas, and a considerable lift in overall education levels in deprived areas.[12] In essence, each electoral area in the city saw its overall educational levels rise between the 2002 Census and the 2006 Census, due to the presence of immigrants. In Dublin according to the 2006 Census over half (52.3 percent) of non-Irish/UK-born persons living in Dublin had third-level qualifications, compared with 34.6 percent among natives. Less than 15 percent of non-Irish/UK-born migrants had low levels of education (primary or lower secondary level only), compared with 37 percent among natives. In one key respect the educational advantage of the non-Irish/UK-born was overstated: Ireland had attracted a predominantly young immigrant population with a large majority aged between 20 and 39 years, an age group in which education levels among natives was also quite high. But even comparing like for like, immigrants still retained an educational advantage over Irish citizens of similar age.

What economists call 'immigrant quality' – the labour market strengths and levels of human capital possessed by immigrants on arrival – emerges as a crucial variable in the literature on immigrant spatial segregation. Earnings alone offer an inadequate measurement of immigrant quality because many immigrants are likely to enter the labour markets of host countries at levels not commensurable with their skills. Research in the United States on earnings convergence suggests that, controlling for human capital and skills transferability, immigrant earnings are likely to rise significantly over time from a low base. Overall, a strong inverse relationship between entry earnings and earnings growth is likely.[13] Human capital, transferable education and skills emerge as strong predictors of immigrant socio-economic status that need to be taken into account when modelling the likely impact of immigration on spatial segregation. For instance, different post-1970 immigrant ethnic minorities in the United Kingdom have had quite different experiences of social mobility over time, with the comparatively well-educated/highly skilled African Asians doing better than the comparatively low-skilled/poorly educated Pakistani and Bangladeshi communities, the latter being spatially concentrated in deprived urban localities.[14]

In the case of Ireland's predominantly first-generation immigrant community, the education and human-capital levels these posses on arrival are likely to be an important predictor of immigrant life chances over time. However, there is a need for caution in presuming that immigrant quality or levels of human capital alone can overcome initial wage-penalty disadvantage. For example, in Canada immigrant poverty levels have been only slightly ameliorated by the rising education levels amongst successive cohorts; immigrant quality rose following the introduction, during the 1990s, of selection criteria that favoured those with third-level qualifications. In 2000 some 40 percent of immigrants (aged 25–54) experiencing persistent poverty had a university degree, up from 12.6 percent from 1993. Amongst the 1993 cohort of new immigrants some 20.5 percent experienced a spell of 'chronic' poverty during their first five years in Canada as compared with 16.2 percent for the 2000 cohort between 2000 and 2005. Explanatory factors for the small degree of decline, due to a rise in immigrant quality, include poor matching of specific qualifications amongst immigrants to actual skills gaps and economic downturn. The Canadian experience suggests that education levels alone can have a negligible effect on the likelihood of immigrants escaping poverty. Those with a third-level qualification were found to 1.02 times more likely to escape poverty than those with just high school qualifications in 1993, rising to 1.12 times more likely for the 2003 cohort of immigrants.[15]

Whilst immigrants in Canada are slightly more likely to have tertiary education than is the case in Ireland, their position is considerably less favourable compared to that of the host population. Over half of the Canadian active population aged between 24 and 65 have a post-secondary college or university degree, with some 500,000 new undergraduates enrolling annually. Canadian data for 2005 reveals that 79 percent of secondary school leavers go on to tertiary education.[16] In Ireland the percentage of school leavers transferring to third-level education exceeded 50 percent for the first time 2005. In the Irish case, and in Dublin, immigrants have a comparative educational advantage over the overall host population. This also holds for 20–39 age group, within which the most highly educated Irish and most immigrants are to be found.[17]

Yet such human capital advantages have not translated into labour market advantage for many immigrants. Some reasons for this were suggested by an analysis of 2004 Quarterly National Household Survey data and of a 2005 Survey of Migrant Experiences of Racism and Discrimination in Ireland undertaken by the Economic and Social Research Institute (ESRI). This identified poor English-language fluency as a key factor in explaining lower immigrant earnings and employment status. It confirmed that in general, non-Irish nationals suffer an occupational penalty: 'holding age, sex and education constant they are less likely than Irish nationals to secure the more privileged jobs in the occupational structure'.[18] In the case of immigrants from the EU's new member states, it has been estimated that, on a like-for-like comparison with natives at similar skill levels, the immigrant wage penalty lies in the region of 10 to 18 percent overall and is particularly pronounced in the higher levels of the skills and earnings distribution, with almost no immigrant penalty at lower skills and earnings levels.[19]

Migrants from English-speaking countries were more likely than Irish nationals to be in professional, associate professional and technical occupations; this reflected the human capital of such migrants. In considering how human capital benefited migrants the ESRI study *Immigrants at Work: Ethnicity and Nationality in the Irish Labour Market* found that: 'Language of country of origin is important in occupational attainment: migrants from

English speaking countries show a more advantageous distribution of occupations for all migrant categories from non-English speaking countries.'[20]

Socio-spatial segregation and the myth of ghettos

A large body of research on post-Second World War immigration reveals that
immigrants and their descendants in the European Union have encountered
disproportionate levels of social exclusion. In Britain, for example, low income,
lack of access to local authority housing and racist discrimination contributed
to first-generation residential segregation on the basis of 'race'.[21] In Britain
and a number of European countries such segregation has continued, with
second and third generations of some immigrant communities encountering
disproportionate socio-spatial inequalities.[22] Overall, the literature suggests
that risks of poverty and disadvantage on the basis of race and ethnicity are
likely to combine with spatial forms of exclusion where minority ethnic groups
predominantly reside in deprived areas. This literature is for the most part
concerned with explaining a multi-generational scenario whereby present
inequalities are explained in terms of past racialised discrimination. Empirical
studies have given at best mixed support to such claims and have questioned
their explanatory power in accounting for migrant segregation.[23]

In any context new patterns of immigration become superimposed upon
pre-existing neighbourhood divisions.[24] Generally, levels of ethnic and 'racial'
segregation and socio-economic segregation are found in comparative studies
to be lower in European countries than in cities in the United States. Much of
this difference is accounted for by the experience of the black population in
the US, who underwent slavery and enforced segregation. When comparisons
are restricted to those who immigrated to European and American cities in
the last four decades, levels of segregation appear to even out.[25] The conclu-
sion, also drawn by leading researchers in the United Kingdom, is that social
inequality alone does not explain the nature and extent of ethnic segregation.[26]

The Irish case differs from those of the UK and other European countries
with histories of post-colonial immigration where prior cultural relationships as well as purely economic interdependencies pertain. However, when
it comes to recent immigration prompted by post-1990 global trends and
EU enlargement, the Irish experience is not unique. For example, Britain
has seen the establishment of post-EU enlargement communities in parts of
the country that had not previously been immigrant destinations.[27] The Irish
case is distinct in that the recent globalisation-era immigration it experienced
has not been superimposed on pre-existing patterns of ethnic segregation.
In essence, immigrants impacted on mono-cultural communities. Existing
patterns of socio-spatial segregation reflected class inequalities rather than

prior histories of ethnic segregation. An example of this considered in Chapter 2 is Moyross in Limerick. Crucial questions in the Irish case concern the future impact of immigrants on deprived Irish communities and the corresponding impact of living in deprived communities on immigrants who settle in them. The social lift hypothesis appears vindicated in the case of the Liberties area of south inner-city Dublin, as considered in the previous chapter.

Patterns of immigrant settlement in Dublin have been driven primarily by the availability of private rented accommodation. The contours of immigrant settlement considerably reflected the distribution of newly built apartments in the inner city (built to encourage social and economic regeneration) and the expansion of new suburban housing in areas like Blanchardstown and Swords to the north and north-west of the city. Immigrants renting the new inner-city apartments often lived in the midst of long-standing deprived communities. Data on some of those who moved into inner-city apartments was captured in the WBCFN study examined in the previous chapter. This revealed, for instance, that migrant respondents were better educated than Irish-born local residents. Those who rented in the expanding suburbs did not necessarily live in relatively deprived areas. That many immigrants have been unable to access social housing has worked to keep them out of some of the most relatively deprived urban areas. It may yet emerge that the classic associations between immigration, ethnic segregation and socio-spatial inequalities will emerge in Dublin, and perhaps the recent sharp economic downturn will make that outcome more likely. Yet the foundations laid during the economic boom have by no means made this inevitable.[28]

Nevertheless, alarmist media references to ghettos and white flight have emerged in Irish media. Many of these focused on Blanchardstown in Dublin 15. In November 2007 the *Sunday Tribune* dedicated several articles to 'the emerging phenomenon of 'white flight from certain areas in Ireland, racial segregation in schools, and clustering of ethnic minorities'.[29] Articles published under headlines like 'We are not making it easy for migrants to settle here and achieve their full potential' and 'The ghettos that are dividing the nation' drew on anecdotal information; in particular, perceptions of what was happening in schools (the focus of Chapter 6) both influenced and drove the debate.[30] The *Sunday Tribune* articles reflected claims expressed in other Western countries that immigrants are increasingly withdrawing into secluded communities and 'parallel societies' which 'hinder the integration of individual immigrants and contribute to societal tensions'. Anxieties about ghettoisation have featured in post 9/11 debates about multiculturalism and its discontents. Yet leading demographers conclude that levels of residential immigration segregation in Europe are moderate in comparison to the US and that 'the trends seem to be towards decreasing concentration, rather than towards consolidating ethnic enclaves'.[31]

In a speech on the July 2005 London bombings, Trevor Phillips, chairman of the Commission for Racial Equality, coined the catchphrase 'sleepwalking to segregation' that came to be frequently invoked within subsequent debates by politicians and academics.[32] Phillips maintained some ethnic minorities were becoming more and more segregated; that, for instance, the number of people of Pakistani heritage living in what were 'technically called ghetto communities' had trebled between 1991 and 2001. In support of these claims Phillips invoked index of dissimilarity calculations based on census data. In Phillips's summary:

> The figure tells us what percentage of any given group would have to move house to achieve an even spread across the district. Below 30 percent is regarded as low or random (for which read tolerable, even if we don't like it); 30–60 percent is moderate (for which read cause for concern); and above 60 percent is high (for which read that if a black person is seen in a white area, it's time to call the police; and if a black person is seen in a black area, he's lost.[33]

This overtly simplifies the findings and implications of research on ethnic segregation. Ceri Peach makes an important distinction between ethnic enclaves and ghettos. Ghettoisation required that (a) a high proportion of a group lives in a single area, *and* (b) the group accounts for most of the population of that area. The term was appropriate in the case of African Americans in Chicago, where two-thirds lived in tracts that were 80 percent or more black, not so with respect to Chicago's Irish Americans, where only 2.9 percent lived in 'so-called Irish ghettos' where these formed 34 percent of the population.[34] Ethnic residential segregation is by no means synonymous with social exclusion; enclaves are not necessarily cut off from wider society by poverty and disproportionate unemployment. However, the term 'ghetto' is often invoked to infer both social exclusion and cultural separatism. It presumes that ethnic segregation combines with socio-spatial segregation.

Specifically, an Index of Dissimilarity (IoD) compares the residential distribution of pairs of population groups in cities, showing the percentage of either group that would have to move so as to replicate the distribution of the other. Demographers have used the IoD to estimate levels of segregation between black and other groups in the UK, finding that while indices were low compared to black populations in the US, there were clear concentrations of Black Caribbeans in traditionally poor areas. The IoD is by no means a comprehensive tool for measuring segregation; rather, it measures spatial unevenness of one group compared to another. However, IoD scores can be used to test widespread perceptions that certain groups are significantly over-represented (or under-represented) in a given area. IoD is measured from 0 to 1 (the higher the number, the more segregation) but is also commonly expressed as a percentage, i.e. 1 to 100. Values below 39 are generally regarded as 'low', 40–49 as 'moderate', 50–59 as 'moderately high', 60–69 as 'high' and 70 or over as 'very high'.[35] D denotes the percentage of a population that would have to move their place of residence in order to replicate the distribution of the other group and is calculated using the following formula, typically comparing the white and black populations in a given area:

$$\frac{1}{2} \sum_{i=1}^{N} \left| \frac{b_i}{B} - \frac{w_i}{W} \right|$$

where b_i = the black population of the ith area, e.g. an electoral division
B = the total black population of the larger geographic entity for which the index of dissimilarity is being calculated
w_i = the white population of the ith area
W = the total white population of the larger geographic entity for which the index of dissimilarity is being calculated

In the United States the mean black/white IoD score for 207 cities was 87.8 percent in 1960 when policies of racial segregation were still enforced to a considerable extent. Equivalent scores for 1980 for the US northern metropolitan areas with the largest black populations found scores still in excess of 80 percent; Massey and Denton's 1993 book on these findings was not inappropriately titled *American Apartheid: Segregation and the Making of the Underclass*.[36] Nothing akin to such hyper-segregation (a term used to denote IoD scores over 70 percent) has been found in the UK, where white/ethnic minority segregation has declined over time. For example, the 2001 score for Pakistani in Bradford in 2001 was 51 percent; this had in fact declined from 54 percent a decade earlier. Aggregate IoD scores for 14 UK cities declined between 1991 and 2001 for Caribbean (43 percent to 37 percent), Indian (42 percent to 40 percent), Pakistani (56 percent to 51 percent) and Bangladeshi (69 percent to 61 percent).[37]

What, then, of the Irish case? On a county-by-county basis Irish census data reveals a pattern of broad immigrant diffusion, with 36 percent of immigrants residing in Dublin City and County, some 10.5 percent in Cork City and County (the largest and second-largest cities and surrounding areas), with the next highest percentages in other counties with cities (Galway 5.8 percent, Limerick 3.5 percent) and counties adjoining Dublin (Kildare 4.4 percent, Meath 3.4 percent). These figures are in broad keeping with the overall population distribution (Figure 1).

Nevertheless, there are two notable exceptions where relatively high concentrations of recent immigrants have settled in areas characterised by relatively high levels of socio-spatial deprivation. The first of these is the Dublin Inner City Partnership area (DICP), which covers most of Dublin's non-Irish nationals accounted for 30 percent of the p times the national average. The second is the Blanchard 15, where non-Irish nationals accounted for almost 22 twice the national average.[38]

By 2001 part of the north inner city came to be described as 'little Africa'. A number of asylum-seeker accommodation centres had been located in the area. African and other immigrant businesses became prominent on Parnell Street and Moore Street.[39] Within the DICP area a general pattern of immigrant clustering in comparatively disadvantaged electoral districts is discernible, particularly within the ten (of thirty-nine overall) DICP electoral districts classified as disadvantaged.[40] Each of the ten has more than three times the national average of non-Irish nationals, with five times as many in three EDs; in one of these, Mountjoy B in the north inner city, over 52 percent of the population are non-Irish citizens. Not only is Mountjoy B 'highly disadvantaged', it also contains the highest percentage of asylum seekers in the Dublin City area.[41] Data from the 2006 census Small Area Population Statistics (SAPS) find that just 2.17 percent of DICP population is black.

Analysis of SAPS data indicates that black immigrants are predominantly clustered in a small number of EDs. The black/white IoD score for the Dublin inner-city area turns out to be low as a whole (IoD = 32 percent).[42] While the segregation score is low for the DICP area as a whole, considerable clustering is evident in comparatively disadvantaged areas.[43] Anecdotal accounts tend to overstate the extent of black/white segregation. Africans comprised just four percent of the overall population of the ten most disadvantaged EDs.

The Blanchardstown Partnership Area comprises eight EDs: Abbotstown, Blakestown, Coolmine, Corduff, Delwood, Mulhuddart, Roselawn and Tyrrel-stown. Rapid population growth (25 percent) occurred between 2002 and 2006 (compared to 5.7 percent for Dublin as a whole); this was driven considerably by the settlement of immigrants in the area. In 2006 some 22 percent of all residents in the area, over twice the national average, were immigrants. Of these the largest groups were respectively Nigerians, Polish and Lithuanians. Overall, the black population of the Blanchardstown area was found to be 5.8 percent, almost six times the national average.

Roselawn, the most affluent ED in the Blanchardstown area, had at 4.2 percent the lowest percentage of non-Irish national residents.[44] Of all eight EDs, Abbotstown at 34.5 percent contained the highest proportion of non-Irish nationals. These were predominantly migrants from non-EU countries. Abbotstown was classified as 'marginally above average' on the relative index of deprivation scale. In 2006 Mulhuddart, the most disadvantaged ED, recorded unemployment levels at 19.4 percent, four times the then national average; 27.7 percent of its population were foreign nationals; this immigrant population was predominately African. Mulhuddart was found in the 2006 Census to contain almost thirteen times (12.69 percent) the national average of black people.[45] In 2006 some 42 percent of families in Mulhuddart were lone-parent families.[46]

In 2006 the black population of the Blanchardstown Partnership area, at 5.8

Figure 1 The spatial distribution of immigrants in Ireland (2006 Census)

County of usual residence	Total non-Irish Nationals	As % of total non-Irish national figure of 419,733 (%)
Leinster	**245,870**	**58.6**
Carlow	4,488	1.1
Dublin Co and City	150,933	36.0
Kildare	18,586	4.4
Kilkenny	6,071	1.4
Laoighis	5,111	1.2
Longford	3,511	0.8
Louth	9,035	2.2
Meath	14,476	3.4
Offaly	5,231	1.2
Westmeath	7,353	1.8
Wexford	10,283	2.4
Wicklow	10,792	2.6
Munster	**104,046**	**24.8**
Clare	10,837	2.6
Cork Co and City	44,224	10.5
Kerry	14,074	3.4
Limerick Co and City	14,581	3.5
Tipperary	11,381	2.7
Waterford Co and City	8,949	2.1
Connacht	**48,396**	**11.5**
Galway Co and City	24,137	5.8
Leitrim	2,983	0.7
Mayo	10,964	2.6
Roscommon	5,416	1.3
Sligo	4,896	1.2
Ulster (Part of)	**21,421**	**5.1**
Cavan	5,683	1.4
Donegal	10,572	2.5
Monaghan	5,166	1.2
TOTALS	**419,733**	**100**

percent almost six times the national average, was considerably higher than in the Dublin inner-city area. Yet the black/white IoD score proved very low (IoD = 18 percent). Again, however, black immigrants are unevenly distributed between across EDs. The highest percentage of black residents was recorded in Mulhuddart (12.69 percent), but the greatest number of black residents were found in Blakestown (the largest ED by far), which at 7.79 percent contained a proportionately smaller black population. Both case studies reveal low rates of segregation; by comparison to British IoD scores, Irish scores are low, but there exist grounds for concern about concentrations of marginalised black immigrants in relatively deprived areas.

Racism and discrimination

An ESRI study of immigrants in the labour market, drawing on 2004 (Quarterly National Household Survey) and 2005 (a dedicated Survey of Migrant Experiences of Racism and Discrimination in Ireland) data showed lower employment rates amongst both black and Asian respondents than amongst Irish nationals. The salient factor in the case of Asians was the finding that one third of respondents were students. Inability to speak English emerged as an important factor in explaining immigrant unemployment levels. However, profound racialised barriers to employment were also identified.

> We detect no difference between migrants from English speaking countries and Irish nationals in the risk of unemployment. The particularly high rate of unemployment amongst Black respondents that are participating in the labour market – nine times that of Irish nationals – may reflect difficulties encountered by those eligible to seek employment, having been granted refugee status or the right to remain in Ireland on other grounds.[47]

The 2006 Census identified a black or black African population of 53,318, of which Nigerians were the numerically largest group; the census recorded 16,677 Nigerian-born living in Ireland, of whom just 337 were Irish citizens.[48] A significant proportion of the overall black African population were former asylum seekers with Irish-born children.[49] In the case of Nigerians, females (8,929) outnumbered males (7,371). Overall, 61 per cent were aged 25–44 with more than 25 per cent under 4 years of age.[50] The 2006 Census reveals that 41 per cent of Nigerian-born migrants are educated to degree level or higher, as compared to just over 25 percent of Poles, 17 percent of Lithuanians and 28 percent of Chinese.[51] However, the apparent human-capital advantage is not reflected by the experiences of Nigerians in the labour market. The percentage of Nigerians aged between 15 and over in work in 2006 was the lowest of all the large immigrant groups, with male employment at just 50 percent and with 30 percent of females in paid employment. However, of those in employment some 15 percent fell within the 'employers and managers' and 'higher professional' groups, as compared to just 6 percent of Poles and 5 percent of Lithuanians. Nevertheless, Nigerians were clearly under-represented in the higher occupational groups when these were considered as a percentage both of those in employment and of the extremely large number who were unemployed.[52] Of the 16,300 Nigerian nationals recorded in the 2006 Census, some 12 percent were Muslim. The percentage of non-religious Nigerians (0.7 percent) identified by the census was lower than for any other nationality.[53]

A 2005 survey of non-EU migrants' experiences of racism and discrimination in Ireland conducted by ESRI found that black sub-Saharan Africans (hereafter Africans) were more likely than any other respondents (35 percent) to experience harassment on the street, on public transport and in public places. Findings were based on returned questionnaires from 345 work permit holders and from 430 asylum seekers. Amongst those with work permits, 32 percent of African respondents had experienced insults or other forms of harassment at work. Africans also reported higher levels of discrimination in access to work (34.5 percent) than other respondents.[54] The ESRI study was conducted on behalf of the European Union Monitoring Centre on Racism and Xenophobia. It concluded that 'even after controlling for other factors like education, age and length of stay' Black Africans experienced the most institutional racism as well as the most racism and discrimination in the work domain, in public places and in pubs and restaurants.[55] Some 47.7 percent of African respondents had third-level education; this was in keeping with the results of the 2006 Census. Of asylum-seeker respondents 44 percent had a third-level education. The ESRI findings were that highly educated respondents were significantly more likely to experience discrimination in two domains, employment and 'public arenas', than were other respondents.[56]

A 2009 survey undertaken by GALLUP on behalf of the Fundamental Rights Agency (FRA) found that 73 percent of sub-Saharan African respondents in Ireland believed that discrimination based on ethnic or immigrant origin was widespread in the country. Ireland was also found to be amongst the worst five amongst the 27 EU member states where people of African origin had experienced racist crime or victimisation such as theft, assault or harassment. All African interviewees in the Irish case lived in the Dublin metropolitan area. The FRA European Union Minorities and Discrimination Survey (EU-Midis) interviewed 23,500 respondents from selected ethnic minority and immigrant groups in all 27 EU member states. It is the first survey of its kind to have systematically interviewed minorities in all EU member states about their experiences of discriminatory treatment, awareness of rights and of where to complain about discrimination and being a victim of racially motivated crime.[57]

EU-Midis found that in different member states different immigrant groups perceive the highest levels of discrimination. For example, in Hungary the Roma perceive higher levels of discrimination than do other ethnic groups. In France 87 percent of sub-Saharan Africans (as distinct from North Africans) perceived that discrimination based on ethnic or immigrant origin was widespread in the country. In the Irish case the highest levels of perception of discrimination were found amongst sub-Saharan Africans; at 73 percent the level of such perceptions was lower than in the French case, but higher than in some other countries, such as Portugal, where 60 percent considered that discrimination based on ethnic or immigrant origin is widespread in the country.

Sub-Saharan Africans (hereafter Africans) in Ireland ranked second of the ten groups with the highest percentage (39 percent) of respondents who avoid certain places for fear of being assaulted, threatened or seriously harassed because of their immigrant or ethnic-minority background. Only the Roma in Poland (53 percent) were more likely to avoid certain places out of fear; Africans in Ireland were more likely to avoid certain places than those in other EU member states.

EU-Midis found that 76 percent of African respondents in Ireland did not know of any organisation offering support and advice to people who had been discriminated against. This strongly suggests that there is under-reporting of racist incidents in the Irish case. The 2005 ESRI study found that black Africans were more likely than other non-EU migrants to experience harassment by neighbours or on the street, but least likely to report such an incident to the police.[58] Estimates of racially motivated incidents recorded by the Gardai PULSE reporting system were 102 for 2002, 68 for 2003 and 67 for 2004.[59] Some 19.5 percent of respondents to the ESRI study described being badly treated by the Gardai on at least one occasion; this compared with 4 percent of Asian and 6.6 percent of other non-EU European respondents.[60]

In the same ESRI study 18.7 percent of Africans described being treated badly or receiving a poor service from healthcare services on at least one occasion; this compared to 9.2 percent of Asian respondents and 15 percent of non-EU European respondents. Of those who received bad treatment most (82.5 percent) did not make a complaint.[61] The ESRI study suggests high levels of under-reporting of racist incidents and discrimination in Ireland.

'Foreigners' and members of ethnic-minority groups are over-represented amongst crime victims, arrestees, pre-trial detainees, convicted offenders and prisoners in every Western country. The annual report of the Irish Prisons Service for 2002 showed that of the 9,716 persons committed to prison some 21 percent were non-Irish nationals; by 2002, when the census that year identified some 8 percent of the population as non-Irish nationals, these were already hugely over-represented within Irish prisons. Some 446 Africans were committed to prison in 2002, amounting to almost 4.6 percent of the overall prison population; compared to the other members of Irish society, again, these were hugely over-represented.[62] The 2002 Census identified an African population of 20,981. That year Africans in prison constituted some 2.1 percent of all persons in prison whilst the total number in prison as a percentage of the 2002 Irish population 3,858,495 was 0.0025 percent. Thus the percentage of Africans in prison was more than eight times higher than the overall percentage of the Irish population in prison. In his analysis, Ian O'Donnell states that it is not clear to what extent the 'sudden change in the make-up of committals to Irish prisons reflects targeting by the police, differential patterns of offending or sentencing or the shifting composition of the population.'[63] It can hardly be solely the latter, given the scale of the over-representation of Africans in Irish prisons.

A 2006 study of female genital mutilation (FGM) undertaken by the Health Service Executive estimated that 1,311 (19 percent) of Nigerian women living in Ireland had experienced FGM. The prevalence of FGM was estimated as extremely high amongst some African women (97.7% for Somalis and 90% for Sudanese) living in Ireland, though these were part of smaller communities. Overall, some 2,585 women, most from sub-Saharan African countries, were estimated to have experienced FGM. Most of these are likely to have arrived in Ireland as asylum seekers.[64]

Challenges

Integration occurs (or does not) in specific social and spatial settings. Experiences from other countries suggest that different immigrant and minority ethnic communities can have very different experiences of social exclusion and barriers to integration. Comprehensive disaggregated data is crucial if the complex effects of immigration on Irish society are to be understood. As applied to the entire population, disaggregation can identify risk factors of poverty and social exclusion, and hence barriers to integration, encountered by cohorts within particular immigrant communities. As applied to local area data, it can identify particular risks encountered by different immigrant communities living in specific social settings. The presumption is that such risks will be unevenly distributed between different immigrant groups and differently experienced *within* particular groups, for instance, on the basis of gender.

So who and where should 'we' worry about? Muslims in Ireland are highly educated and demonstrably more included in the labour market as compared to Muslims in France, the Netherlands or the United Kingdom. No strong indications of an immigrant penalty for Irish Muslims are discernable; over

20 percent are educated to at least degree standard but almost 24 percent are higher professionals, employers or managers. Some of the most excluded Muslims are likely to be Africans. Dublin's north inner city has a disproportionately large immigrant and black population, albeit low by international standards. Here the ingredients of the classic exclusionary cocktail often referred to as a ghetto – marginalised black immigrants over-represented in a socially deprived area – can be identified. That the numbers and percentages prove that no ghetto exists does not detract from the high risks of multi-generational exclusion such black immigrants face. Again, in Blanchardstown no ghetto exists. Yet Chapter 6 (on education and segregation) identifies serious challenges to the integration of black children in the Dublin 15 area. Given the range of barriers to employment encountered by black immigrants and the scale of their experiences of racism, the prospect of a rising generation of marginalised African Irish in Dublin 15 needs to be taken very seriously. Even the fact that Africans are likely to be better educated than their Irish-citizen neighbours in deprived areas can work against them. As recounted in 2005 by Darren Kelly:

> Interestingly, discussions with a prominent NGO group based in the Tallaght area working with non-Irish nationals pointed to the case whereby some of the difficulties for Africans living in the area have 'as much to do with class as race'. It was argued that some of the asylum seekers living in the area were middle class and were perceived as being 'snobby' by their working class neighbours, leading to malicious physical and mental bullying.[65]

Such an observation may sit uneasily in a chapter focused on the contributions of qualitative research. Numbers and percentages dealing with levels of human capital or employment levels only scratch the surface of the experiences of immigrants and host communities alike. While I was writing this book in 2009 two middle-class African families of my acquaintances were burnt out of their homes in north-west Dublin.[66] Such incidents suggest that integration cannot be presumed where socio-spatial data reveal a social lift in education, human capital or residential occupational profile resulting from the arrival of immigrants in an area.

Various ESRI studies have found that immigrants fare less well than Irish nationals in the Irish labour market in a number of ways, the exception being white immigrants from English-speaking countries. Immigrants with English-language capability deficits and black immigrants are apparently most at risk of experiencing the immigrant penalty. Explanations offered by the ESRI for such disparities include the absence of location-specific human capital, such as familiarity with local employment conditions and networks and transferability of qualifications and skills. Other key factors include higher levels of discrimination than are encountered by Irish nationals and poor English-language competence. The 2008 ESRI *Immigrants at Work* report did not highlight racism as an explanation for the hugely disproportionate levels of black unemployment identified in the Quarterly National Household Survey sample population that it examined. Instead, it suggested that the fact that many had once been asylum seekers was highlighted as an explanation for the hugely disproportionate labour-market exclusion they subsequently experienced.[67] The key underlying issue here is that asylum seekers are prevented by the state from working or undertaking employment training for up to several years. However, evidence that black immigrants experience high levels of racism by international comparisons suggests that racism as well as English-language capacity deficits, and barriers to support due to lesser rights (a key example being employment training), are contributing factors to the extremely disproportionate risks of unemployment experienced by black people in Ireland.

Immigrants at Work concluded firstly that its findings on immigrant experiences in the labour market confirmed the need for a planned and proactive public policy approach to integration as well as for systematic approaches to equality and integration by employers. Secondly, it emphasised the importance of ensuring that new migrants had access to training in English-language skills and made the case for 'state intervention' to ensure this. Thirdly, in response to disproportionate black unemployment, it argued for targeted active labour market programmes to assist refugees and others legally resident in Ireland (presumably including asylum seekers) to access employment on the same basis as Irish nationals.[68]

Notes

1 Central Statistics Office, *Census 2006 Non-Irish Nationals Living in Ireland* (Dublin: Stationery Office, 2008). Available at: www.cso.ie

2 Breakdown taken from C. Ní Laoire, N. Bushin, F. Carpena-Méndez and A. White, *Tell Me about Yourself: Migrant Children's Experiences of Moving to and Living in Ireland* (Cork: University College Cork, 2009), p. 20

3 See K. Kropiewiec and R. King O'Riain, *Polish Migrant Workers in Ireland* (Dublin: NCCRI, 2006), p. 21; on pre-EU Enlargement estimates, see B. Fanning, 'Denizens and Citizens', in M. Peillon and M. Corcoran (eds), *Place and Non-Place: The Reconfiguration of Ireland* (Dublin: Institute of Public Administration, 2004), p. 66

4 *Ibid.*

5 See, for example Y.Y. Wang and R. King-O'Riain (2006) *Chinese Students in Ireland* (Dublin: NCCRI, 2006), p. 18

6 'Building a Bridge to the East', *Metro Éireann*, 7 August 2008

7 A. Feldman, M. Gilmartin, S. Loyal and B. Migge, *Getting On: From Migration to Integration, Chinese, Indian, Lithuanian and Nigerian Migrants' Experiences in Ireland* (Dublin: Immigrant Council of Ireland, 2008), p. 126

8 Cabinet Office, *Minority Ethnic Issues in Social Exclusion and Neighbourhood*

Renewal (London: HMSO, 2000), p. 66.

 9 T. Modood, R. Berthood, J. Lakey, J. Nazroo, S. Patten, S. Virdee and S. Beishon, *Ethnic Minorities in Britain* (London: Policy Studies Institute, 1997).

10 G. O'Hanlon SJ, 'Asking the Right Questions: Christians, Muslims, Citizens of Ireland', *Jesuit Centre for Faith and Justice* (February 2007), www.cfj.ie

11 OECD, *International Migration Outlook* (Paris: OECD, 2007)

12 T. Fahey and B. Fanning, 'Immigration and Socio-Spatial Segregation in Dublin: 1996–2006', *Urban Studies* 47.8 (2010),1625–1642

13 H.O. Duleep and M.C. Rogers, *The Elusive Concept of Immigrant Quality: Evidence from 1970–1990* (Bonn: Forshunginstitut zur Zukunft der Arbeit/Institute for the Study of Labour, 2000)

14 T. Modood *et al.*, *Ethnic Minorities in Britain*

15 G. Picot, F. Hou and S. Columbe, 'Poverty Dynamics among Recent Immigrants to Canada', *International Migration Review* 42.2 (2008), 393–424, pp. 402–404

16 Statistics Canada (2007) *Youth in Transition Survey: Participation in Postsecondary Education*, www.statcan.ca/Daily/English?071120/d071120b.htm

17 Analysis and figures 2 and 3 from Fahey and Fanning, 'Immigration and Social Spatial Segregation', p. 1635

18 P. O'Connell and F. McGinnity, *Immigrants at Work: Ethnicity and Nationality in the Irish Labour Market* (Dublin: ESRI, 2008) p. ix

19 A.S. Barrett, S. McGuinness and M. O'Brien (2008), *The Immigrant Earnings Disadvantage across the Earnings and Skills Distributions: The Case of Immigrants from the EU's New Member States in Ireland*, Working Paper No. 236 (Dublin: Economic and Social Research Institute)

20 O'Connell and McGinnity, *Immigrants at Work*, p. 28

21 J. Rex, 'Urban Segregation and Inner City Policy in Great Britain', in C. Peach, V. Robinson and S. Smith (eds), *Segregation in Cities* (London: Croom Helm, 1981)

22 Cabinet Office, *Minority Ethnic Issues*

23 M. Samers, 'Immigration and the Global City Hypothesis: Towards an Alternative Research Agenda', *International Journal of Urban and Regional Research* 26.2 (2002), 398–402

24 R. Van Kempen, 'Divided Cities in the 21st Century: Challenging the Importance of Globalisation', *Journal of Housing Built Environment* 22 (2007), 13–31

25 S. Musterd, 'Social and Ethnic Segregation in Europe: Levels, Causes and Effects', *Journal of Urban Affairs*, 27.3 (2005), 332–348

26 C. Peach and N. Glazer, 'London and New York: Contrasts in British and American Models of Segregation', *International Journal of Political Geography* 5 (1999), 319–351

27 S. Drinkwater, J. Eade and M. Garapich, 'Poles Apart? EU Enlargement and the Labour Market Outcomes of Immigrants in the UK', Institute for the Study of Labor (IZA): Discussion Paper No. 2410

28 Fahey and Fanning, 'Immigration and Social Spatial Segregation', p. 1640

29 'We Are Not Making It Easy for Migrants To Settle Here and Achieve Their Full Potential', *Sunday Tribune*, 18 November 2007

30 'The Ghettos that Are Dividing the Nation', *Sunday Tribune*, 11 November 2007

31 K. Schönwälder, 'Introduction', in K. Schönwälder (ed.), *Residential Segrega-*

tion and the Integration of Immigrants: Britain, the Netherlands and Sweden. Discussion Paper Nr. SP IV 2007-602 (Berlin: Wissenschaftszentrum Berlin für Sozialforschung GmbH, Social Science Research Centre Berlin, www.wzb.eu), pp. 5–6

32 C. Peach, 'Does Britain Have Ghettos?' *Transactions of the Institute of British Geographers* 21 (1996), 216–235

33 *Ibid.*, p. 14

34 C. Peach, 'Sleepwalking into Ghettoisation? The British Debate over Segregation', in K. Schönwälder (ed.), *Residential Segregation and the Integration of Immigrants: Britain, the Netherlands and Sweden.* Discussion Paper Nr. SP IV 2007-602 (Berlin: Wissenschaftszentrum Berlin für Sozialforschung GmbH, Social Science Research Centre Berlin, www.wzb.eu), pp. 17–19

35 *Ibid.*, p. 23

36 D.S. Massey and N. Denton, *American Apartheid: Segregation and the Making of the Underclass* (Cambridge, MA: Harvard University Press, 1993), p. 86

37 C. Peach, 'Slippery Segregation: Discovering or Manufacturing Ghettos', University of Manchester Institute for Social Change working paper (2007), p. 13

38 C. Ryan, *Socio Economic Profile of Blanchardstown, Blanchardstown Area Partnership* (Dublin: Blancharstown Area Partnership, 2008). Available at: www.bap.ie

39 D. Kelly 'Dublin's Spatial Narrative – the Transition from Essentially Monocultural Place to Polycultural Spaces', *Irish Geography* 28.2 (2005), 209–224, p. 213

40 T. Haase, and K. Byrne, *Divided City: The Changing Face of Dublin's Inner City* (Dublin: DICP, 2007)

41 Kelly, 'Dublin's Spatial Narrative', p. 213

42 N. O'Boyle and B. Fanning, 'Immigration, Integration and the Risks of Social Exclusion: The Social Policy Case for Disaggregated Data in the Republic of Ireland', *Irish Geography* 42.2 (2009), 145–164, p. 151

43 T. Haase and J. Pratschke, *New Measures of Deprivation for the Republic of Ireland* (Dublin: Pobal, 2008). Available at: www.pobal.ie/live/dep/1003.html

44 Although Roselawn is the 'most affluent' electoral district in the Blanchardstown area, it is still only bordering on 'affluent', according to the Haase and Pratschke deprivation index.

45 Drawing from the 2006 Census of Population, Bailey and Brooke (see n. 46) indicate that 42 percent of families in Mulhuddart are lone-parent families (compared to a national average of 18 percent) and that approximately a fifth of this ED's working population were unemployed in 2006 (almost four times the national average as of January 2008).

46 N. Bailey and S. Brooke, *A Profile of the Needs of the Tyrrelstown Community* (Dublin: Burtenshaw-Kenny Associates, 2008), p. 54

47 O'Connell and McGinnity, *Immigrants at Work*, p. ix

48 Figure for number of citizens arrived at by subtracting number of Nigerian nationals (16,300) from number of Nigerian-born (16,667) living in the Republic of Ireland. See *Census 2006 Principal Demographic Results*, Table 20, p. 68 and Table 25, p. 73

49 B. Fanning and F. Mutwarasibo, 'Nationals/Non-nationals: Immigration, Citizen-

ship and Politics in the Republic of Ireland', *Ethnic and Racial Studies* 30.3 (2007), 439–460

50 *Census 2006 Principal Demographic Results*, Table 25, p. 73 and Table 26, p. 74

51 *Census 2006 Volume 10 – Education and Qualifications*, Table 33A, p. 109

52 *Census 2006 Volume 8 – Occupations*, Table 11A, p. 47

53 *Census 2006 Volume 13 – Religion*, Table 17, p. 109

54 F. McGinnity, P.J. O'Connell, E. Quinn and J. Williams, *Migrants' Experience of Racism and Discrimination in Ireland: Results of a Survey Conducted by the Economic and Social Research Institute for the European Union Monitoring Centre on Racism and Xenophobia* (Dublin: ESRI, 2006)

55 *Ibid.*, pp. iv–vi

56 *Ibid.*, p. vii

57 European Agency for Fundamental Rights, *European Union Minorities and Discrimination Survey* (Brussels: European Agency for Fundamental Rights, 2009). Available at: http://fra.europa.eu/eu-midis/

58 McGinnity et al., p. 40

59 Cited in *ibid.*, p. 41

60 *Ibid.*, p. 47

61 *Ibid.*, p. 49

62 I. O'Donnell, 'Imprisonment and Penal Policy in Ireland', *The Howard Journal* 43.1 (2004), 253–266, pp. 262–263

63 I. O'Donnell, 'Crime and Justice in the Republic of Ireland', *European Journal of Criminology* 2.1 (2005), 99–131, p. 119

64 Health Service Executive, *Ireland's National Plan of Action to Address Female Genital Mutilation* (Dublin: Health Service Executive, 2008), p. 22

65 Kelly, 'Dublin's Spatial Narrative', p. 214

66 In both cases their family homes were attacked using petrol bombs, the incidents were reported to the Gardai and both families felt it necessary to move out of the area.

67 O'Connell and McGinnity *Immigrants at Work*, p. xii

68 *Ibid.*

5

Some immigrant lives

People generally migrate to improve their circumstances on some dimension, either psychological, social, cultural, political, or economic, and sometimes all of the above. Migration is a principal mechanism by which human beings expand their choices, increase their opportunities, and enhance their capabilities. Migrants thus tend to be self-selected for drive, motivation, and ambition; and because migration inevitably entails costs, they are also selected for access to capital – financial, human, social, and cultural. Whether or not migrants are able to translate their intrinsic motivations and capital endowments into improved circumstances depends very much on the context of reception – the economic opportunities they encounter in the receiving society and the relative freedom they have to pursue them. (Douglas Massey and Magaly Sánchez)

So begins a 2009 United Nations research paper on how the exploitation of vulnerable migrants undermines their integration.[1] From Amartya Sen's capabilities perspective, freedom from exploitation depends on the options a person has in deciding what kind of life to lead, as well as the presence or absence of coercion. Much the same might be said about their capacity to integrate. The basic capabilities of any immigrant (or indeed anyone else) include rights and entitlements and the knowledge and ability to benefit from these, as well as human capital. The potential benefits of human capital to an individual may be undermined by language barriers or by other capability deficits. The real freedom people have to exploit their skills and abilities may be objectively constrained by other factors. The choices they make, their adaptive preferences in a given situation are formed by how chances of success or failure are internalised.[2] For some, the actual absence of rights, the perceived absence of rights they do in fact have (through inadequate knowledge and information), isolation brought about by not being able to communicate, or in other words, various kinds of disempowerment, can be understood in terms of capability deficits. Yet, such emphasis on individual capabilities and the rights and opportunities that facilitate these must be combined with a sense of the social context of immigrant lives.

The focus of this chapter is the role of capabilities, social capital and cultural capital as distinct layers of resources that might facilitate functional integration.

I have coined the term 'functional integration' to denote what migrant workers themselves might consider as viable lives in the host society as distinct from host-society integration goals. It draws on Sen's uses of the term 'functionings' to denote what a person can do with the resources and choices at their disposal.[3] Many migrants might envisage a temporary sojourn in Ireland that allows them to build better lives for families at home, only to encounter damaging levels of exploitation, risk and isolation. The first section is about intersections between migrant vulnerability and individual capabilities. Many of the experiences considered are those of migrants who have been trafficked into what the Migrant Rights Centre Ireland (MRCI) describes as bonded or indentured labour. In Ireland, as elsewhere, undocumented and status-insecure workers are amongst the easiest to exploit. Case studies compiled in various reports by the MRCI vividly illustrate how vulnerability, isolation, the lack of knowledge about rights and of information about the host society often lead to exploitation. In addition to such capability deficits many of the case studies depict exploitation by co-ethnics and complicity in such exploitation by Irish consumers, employers and the state.

The second part of the chapter considers the role of supportive social ties as a bulwark against vulnerability in the labour market. A case study of the experiences of the Brazilian community in Gort, County Galway is examined. This draws on research by Brian McGrath and Frank Murray on the positive and negative aspects of bonding social capital.[4] Robert Putnam has made an influential distinction between 'bonding' social capital, whereby membership of delimited groups or organisations confers advantages upon members, and 'bridging' social capital, which is outwardly focused and extends across social divides.[5] The focus here is on the benefits of social capital alongside individual capabilities in the functional integration of migrants.

But such functional integration hardly meets the needs of immigrants who are making long-term commitments to Irish society; nor does it meet the integration needs of the host society. The focus of the chapter's third section is on the attributes of some of the immigrants who have demonstrated considerable willingness to participate in Irish society. The case study draws on interviews with immigrant candidates who contested the 2009 local government elections. Many of these were also recent migrants; just one of the eighteen candidates interviewed had lived in Ireland for a decade. This research on immigrants in Irish politics considered the role of cultural capital in addition to individual capabilities and social capital as a third layer of resources that contributed to integration. As noted in Chapter 1, concepts such as capabilities and cultural capital overlap as accounts of non-material dispositional resources held by individuals. Cultural capital, as defined by Pierre Bourdieu, refers to knowledge, experiences and connections and ways of behaving that confer privilege and advantage upon individuals in particular social settings.[6]

Examples in the field of education might include familial knowledge of education systems (stronger amongst well-educated parents than amongst poorly educated ones), inherited positive attitudes towards education (stronger amongst their children than amongst children with poorly educated parents) or the non-material advantages conferred by access to elite schools and networks.[7] As considered here, cultural capital includes pre-migratory political socialisation as a non-material resource (political expertise) mobilised by some immigrants to further their integration.

Capabilities, vulnerabilities and dysfunctional integration

Kuldup Singh, an Indian Sikh, arrived in Ireland via England in 1976. For a few years he struggled to set up a viable business. In 1978 he travelled to London to purchase materials but was stopped by immigration officials who didn't believe he was legally resident in Ireland. Because he did not have his passport he was detained and deported from Britain to India. As a result, he lost his business. He returned to Dublin, started from scratch again, and subsequently obtained Irish citizenship. He became a founder member of the Sikh temple in Ballsbridge.

In his early years in Ireland he found Irish people to be helpful and he made lasting friendships. His business went well. When numbers of immigrants began to rise in recent years he noticed a shift in attitude; there appeared to be a general increase in negativity; comments were made to him such as 'go back to your own country'. Singh described his own experience as privileged, compared to many Indian migrants living in Ireland. Mostly these came to work in restaurants. Growing up, they had seen relatives home from the West for holidays. They brought back amounts of money that would be considered small in Ireland but seemed like an awful lot in India. So they came to Ireland expecting to do well. But when they arrived they got a big shock. They had no idea what accommodation would cost or how expensive it was to eat. On top of that, they were 'very prone to being taken advantage of'. Kuldap Singh described cases where it was agreed that a migrant would get £200 a month wages and £200 more sent back to his family: 'Before leaving home that seems like a reasonable arrangement. When they get to Ireland they quickly realise that they have been conned.' They were generally too scared to question anything about their situation. While not all employers exploited their workers, many did. Workers were told that if they complained they could be deported. Employers and recruitment agents played on the fears of migrant workers. Most such workers had paid something in the region of £1,200 to get to Ireland. The stock exploitation scenario described by Kuldap Singh, of vulnerable migrants with poor English and large debts and living in fear of deportation being forced to work extremely long hours ('anything from 10 to

14 hours' per day) has recurred again and again in cases highlighted by MRCI.[8]

In 2001 concerns about the widespread exploitation of 'third country' workers emerged in the Irish media. For example, there were reports of Filipino nurses being paid 30 percent less than their Irish equivalents and forced to live five or six to a room. Claims were made that some nurses who objected to working eighteen-hour shifts without any meal breaks were threatened with deportation.[9] In March 2001, Labour Affairs Minister Tom Kitt issued a statement that employment rights legislation applied to all 1.8 million people working in Ireland, whether they were Irish citizens or otherwise. On 8 May 2002 a Dáil debate on migrant workers referred to 'systematic exploitation over a wide range of sectors' and noted that the problem was particularly acute in the hotel and catering sectors, the meat industry and agri-related outdoor activities. It noted, again, that numerous cases of exploitation of foreign nursing staff had been highlighted. Complaints from immigrant workers included long hours, no overtime pay, having to work Sundays and at weekends for no extra pay and general insecurity with respect to conditions of employment. As explained to the Dáil by Deputy Flanagan:

> Many people are fearful of making a complaint lest they suffer deportation from the State. I know employees who have been told that if they bring a complaint to the authorities, they will be sent home immediately and will not have the opportunity to work any longer in the State.[10]

Some efforts by the state to address such exploitation followed. Additional labour inspectors were recruited. Migrants who sought redress through the Labour Relations Commission have tended to be successful; 80 percent of such claims were successful in 2002, rising to 85 percent in 2003.[11] Migrants generally had very strong grounds for the cases they took.

Yet, a lack of awareness of employment rights amongst vulnerable workers and of ability to meaningfully access such rights contributed to ongoing labour market exploitation. A 2002 Equality Authority study, *Migrant Workers and Their Experiences*, provided a snapshot of three sectors: agriculture, healthcare, and hotels, bars and general employment.[12] Gloria, a Filipino nurse, had responded to a newspaper advert placed on behalf of an Irish recruitment agency. In the course of a day she was interviewed by a Filipino agency, then by an Irish agency and then by a panel of three nursing directors as one of a batch of fifty nurses. Her first interview was at 6.00am, her second at 6.00pm. At stage two the Irish agency gave information about the expectations of the hospital and nursing responsibilities. She was shown pictures of the hospital. At stage three, she was told to bring warm clothes because it would be cold. Filipino interviewees reported paying recruitment fees of €1,000, the equivalent of one year of salary in the Philippines. They arrived in Ireland saddled with considerable debt. Whilst they encountered some of same dilemmas as the badly paid restaurant workers described by Kuldup Singh, they also demonstrated capabilities that enabled them to contest such exploitation.

Celia, a nurse, was recruited to work in the Dublin region. She received no pay from the nursing home during her induction period. Her contract stipulated that she would get paid once she had been registered as a professional and accredited nurse in Ireland. This did not happen. The nursing home refused to reimburse her. She experienced considerable stress. But she was able to seek help from the Irish Nurses Organisation (INO) and ended up working in a hospital. Roni had a better initial experience, but after registration in the hospital to which he was assigned his employers told him that he would continue as a 'student' for six months; after this time they would 'reimburse him' the amount of the accumulated back pay owing. He put up with this for a month and then, following complaints by another nurse, the hospital began to pay his proper wages.

Gloria, Roni and Celia fared comparatively well, compared to many of those described in the case studies below. They had capabilities that enabled them to contest their exploitation: they were able to speak English, they were able to acquire knowledge of their employment rights and access support in ensuring these were taken seriously. The subsequent experiences of other migrants vividly illustrate how, in the absence of such capabilities, even high levels of human capital may be of little benefit.

Anna had worked as a nurse before she came from Lithuania in 2004 to work on a mushroom farm. She shared a caravan on the farm where she worked exposed to chemicals in the mushroom tunnels with little regard for health and safety. She began to suffer from bad eyesight, breathlessness and coughing in the mornings. The women she shared the caravan with had similar health problems. Their caravan was used during the days as a canteen, toilet, smoking area and changing room for all the workers on the farm, even though each paid €45 every week rent for it. They had no means of heating their 'house' and sometimes no electricity or running water. The door of the caravan was broken and they couldn't lock it. They tied it tight with string to keep it closed. The steps up to the caravan were broken and there was a huge hole in the floor by the door. Anna was required to work long hours at low pay and never received overtime. Even though she had the right to work in Ireland without a visa she was considerably more vulnerable to exploitation than were the Filipino nurses. She was isolated, without friends from her own country and didn't speak English. She did not feel very comfortable around Irish people.[13]

Olena, a qualified horticulturalist who had worked as a landscape gardener and agronomist in for more than fifteen years paid a recruitment agency €1,750 for a work permit in the mushroom industry in Ireland. She had become unemployed after a long period of declining standards of living in

Russia. Before her departure she was assured that working conditions in Ireland would be good, that accommodation and protective clothing would be provided and that she would be expected to work no more than 8 hours per day. Needless to say, the reality proved different. She was required to work in the mushroom tunnels from 6.30am to 5.00pm but often finished as late as ten or eleven o'clock at night; for this she received €5.50 per hour and no holiday pay or time off in lieu. She was allowed only one day off per week. Her accommodation consisted of a bunk in a converted utility room in a two-bedroom house shared by six workers. Because of her professional expertise she had considerable concerns about health and safety, and rightly so; exposure to chemicals on mushroom farms has been known to result in skin abrasions and hair loss. She was aware that a lot of chemicals were used whilst the pickers were in the tunnels. Olena felt nauseous and the only protective clothing supplied was disposable gloves and a hair cap. Her employer promised that her work permit would be renewed but this did not happen. She became undocumented, unemployed and homeless after she left her job.[14]

In 2006 the MRCI report *Harvesting Justice: Mushroom Workers Call for Change* documented extensive abuse of migrant farm workers.[15] Typically, these were paid substantially less than the minimum wage and made to work up to 16 hours per day in the difficult conditions described by Anna and Olena. In another example, Sadka arrived in 2002 from Thailand, having left his wife and daughter at home, to work on a mushroom farm. His plan was to save enough to buy a house for his family in Thailand. He had borrowed in order to pay €6,250 to an agency but had since paid off this debt; it took him a year and a half to do so. He received a contract but was never paid as much as it stated; he received €5 per hour for a 70-hour working week with no overtime. His living and working conditions were much the same as described by Anna and Olena. He understood most of his rights but felt powerless to do anything to improve his circumstances because of the all-too-real fear that his work permit would not be renewed. Sadka explained how his employer manipulated work visa requirements to keep him in a position of vulnerability:

> I cannot take a holiday. The reason is that he waits until my permit expires before applying for a new one. He applies for a five month work permit. By the time the permit comes and I pay €100 for my Garda stamp in my passport and get my passport back my stamp is almost ready to expire. I cannot plan ahead to leave here to go and visit my wife and daughter. It is very difficult for me not to see them after so long. Sometimes I just want to leave here but I cannot.

In 2008 the MRCI published a report on Ireland's restaurant industry.[16] It was dedicated to the memory of Kubbath Miah, a Bangladeshi chef who had lived and worked in Ireland from 1998 until his death a decade later. He came in the hope of making a better life for his wife and three children. However, after three years of working under exploitative conditions in a Limerick restaurant he suffered a serious fall and injury, then lost his job and his legal status and became undocumented. He went on to work for a number of other restaurants, but because of his undocumented status remained separated from his family for several years. His mother died during this time and he was unable to return for her funeral. Years of tremendous stress, living in fear of deportation, coupled with long working hours and isolation from his family, took a major toll on his health. With help from the MRCI he eventually retrieved his legal status and he travelled home to be reunited with his family. He subsequently returned to his job with the hope of applying to bring his wife and children to Ireland. But soon after his return his health began to deteriorate and he died in June 2008.

Except for its tragic end, Kubbath Miah's life in Ireland was little different from those of many of the 115 interviewees in the MRCI *Exploitation in Ireland's Restaurant Industry* report. Of these, 53 percent were being paid less than the minimum wage. Almost half worked at least 9 hours per day, most got no overtime, over half did not receive a pay slip and most had not received a contract of employment. Of those interviewed, 22 percent reported that they had paid money to get their jobs to 'friends, agents or employers'; the fees ranged from €,1000 to the €30,000 charged to one chef from China. Respondents described verbal abuse, threats ('The boss is always shouting at us. He says he will cancel the work permit if he doesn't like what we are doing'), being afraid to complain and even threats ('If your son goes on holiday that he will have a problem returning to Ireland') being made to their families by telephone.[17] MRCI reported that 49 percent of respondents stated that they had suffered some kind of discrimination in the workplace; examples included non-EU workers being denied holiday pay given to those from EU countries, Irish workers being paid more than migrants, being allowed breaks denied to migrants and getting to work the best hours. Of those interviewed, 88 percent believed that the exploitation of restaurant workers in Ireland was widespread; 82 percent had not been in contact with a trade union.[18]

Stories of exploitation and extortion remain commonplace. Some migrants were required to raise fees so large compared to their subsequent earnings in Ireland that they effectively became indentured. They entered into such arrangements in the hope of providing for dependents in their countries of origin. Because they had borrowed from family and community at home, they felt they had no options other than to accept the situations they found themselves in; some respondents in this and other MRCI surveys talked about being intimidated by threats to themselves or their families if they did otherwise.

Jamal came from Bangladesh to work as a chef in County Wicklow in 2002, having paid €5,000 to his employer. He wanted to support his wife and family and help a younger brother to go to university. His employer had told him that he would earn around €300 a week in Ireland, but instead he just received €50 each week; he was never registered as an employee. He did not receive any contract of employment. He was made to work 72 hours per week.

Whenever he complained, his employer threatened that he would cancel his work permit. Jamal worked in the Wicklow restaurant for nearly five years. His weekly salary was increased each year by €25. In his five years in Wicklow he only got five weeks' holiday, without pay. After he left the job it took Jamal a long time to work up the courage to complain about his treatment. When he did, his employer phoned Jamal's family in Bangladesh and threatened that Jamal 'might have some big problems', should he return there. Jamal's family were very scared because the employer was wealthy and in a position to make life very difficult for them.[19]

In 2001 Li arrived in Wexford from the Fujian province in China to work as a chef. He had been promised £250 per week plus food and accommodation by a broker who charged 380,000 Yuan (€30,000). He borrowed the sum from relatives, friends and a money lender. When he arrived in Ireland he was paid just £150 per week in cash. His English was very poor; there were eight other employees in the same situation; they had all paid dearly for their 'work permits'. In their dealings with their Irish employer all were dependent on the Chinese agent who had brought them to Ireland. Li immediately tried to leave but the employer threatened to call the police and have him deported. He tried to communicate with the Irish woman who owned the restaurant but she was uninterested. He remained working there until January 2003, when he was sacked. But this had been engineered by the person who had brought him to Ireland; he was told that there was no longer a job for him, yet, as explained by Li: 'The truth is that in order to make another €30,000 the person who brought me to Ireland is the one who organised my dismissal, so that he could arrange for another person to replace me in the restaurant.'

Much of this kind of exploitation is enabled by manipulation of the lesser employment rights of migrants who are absolutely dependent on visas. People like Li or Jamal have the same employment rights as anybody else working in Ireland but they cannot meaningfully access such rights; their exploitation is, in effect, state sanctioned. Yet even secure residency status may offer inadequate protection against exploitation and coercion. The ongoing exploitation of migrant workers from EU countries has also been documented. Edita came to Ireland with her daughter from Lithuania; she began working in the kitchen of a restaurant in Blanchardstown in 2007. She was desperate to find work and her English was not very good. She was told she might have to work more than 39 hours per week; in fact she was required to work between 12 and 14 hours per day for up to six days a week. The roster posted with her work hours invariably did not match the number of hours on her payslips. She was paid €8 per hour for each of the 39 documented hours; for overtime she received only €5 per hour; she was also only paid for one week of her two weeks' annual leave. She felt she was 'treated like a dog' by her boss and supervisors. Irish workers, in her view, were treated better; they got better (more convenient) hours and, unlike the Lithuanians, were not bullied by their employer. After one year she could take no more and left her job.[20]

Some of the most grievously exploited migrants in Ireland are women trafficked into prostitution. Sex trafficking is characterised by considerable pre-migratory and post-migratory coercion. The dynamics of exploitation and deception are somewhat similar to those encountered by the most exploited vulnerable migrants in other sectors. As put in a 2009 report by the Immigrant Council of Ireland, *Globalisation, Sex Trafficking and Prostitution: The Experiences of Migrant Women in Ireland*:

> The stories of migrant women are of earning money to support their families, including their children and parents, who remain in their countries of origin. Their stories tell of the enormous expectations tied into the migration process – saving to build a house or set up a home, earning money to educate children in [*sic*] to pay hospital bills for sick parents. Most of them only intend to remain in prostitution for a short time to earn money.[21]

Similar dynamics of exploitation and capacity deficit are identifiable in the case studies citied in this report. These depict varying degrees of coercion, control and exploitation fostered by isolation from wider Irish society, coupled with, in some cases, threats of violence. Women's Health Project (WSE) staff described a case of a woman who decided to leave was gang raped and injured to the extent that a doctor who was also a buyer of sex was summoned to attend to her injuries. Despite her injuries, she was forced back into prostitution and a penalty of €20,000 was imposed for loss of earnings.[22] Another study, by Eilís Ward and Gillian Wylie, found that some women who had come to Ireland expecting to work in domestic service had in fact been trafficked to work in a brothel; in one case a women had her passport taken and was kept locked in a house where she was forced to have sex with men; another was required to work in prostitution to pay off her debt to traffickers but 'decided to remain working in that section' once she had done so.[23] Notwithstanding many examples of such coercion, Ward and Wylie highlight the role of individual agency in the choices made by many women.[24] They emphasise how many women made choices based on their own understandings of their options; most of their interviewees came from poor socio-economic backgrounds and, regardless of educational attainment, had few economic opportunities in their home country.[25] The Immigrant Council study emphasised a lack of alternatives perceived by many women working in prostitution; difficulties in pursuing education were discussed by a number of interviewees. Both studies concur that women perceived that they did not have other viable options in Ireland. In this, the apparently extreme exploitation of some sex workers has much in common with the much-documented exploitation of women working in domestic service.[26] In the international context, commonalities and intersections between these kinds of exploitation have been well documented in texts such as Barbara Ehrenreich's *Global Woman: Nannies, Maids and Sex Workers in the New Economy.*[27]

Few of the migrants whose stories were recounted above could be described as functionally integrated within Irish society. To varying degrees, exploitation and insecurity undermined their ability to manage their lives. Some were poorly educated but others had high levels of human capital. All experienced some or other kinds of capability deficits that limited their choices. Those dependent on the renewal of visas experienced knock-on barriers to those rights they had; those without the ability to communicate in English lacked the capacity for self-advocacy even when they had a secure right to work in Ireland. Poor language capabilities contributed to their vulnerability to exploitation. Very often such exploitation was exacerbated by a sense of isolation and atomisation, even when working for and amongst co-ethnics.

Social capital and functional integration

A 2004 newspaper article presented a bucolic account of Brazilian migrants in Gort, where some 600 had settled and now comprised 40 percent of the population of the town.[28] It described how local factory owner Sean Duffy had gone out to Brazil a few years earlier and recruited some skilled people. They got on well and others followed. Then a lot of the Brazilians brought their brothers and sisters and cousins and uncles and aunts to Ireland. 'An awful lot of the Brazilians who are in Gort are inter-related,' stated Duffy. 'All our signs in the factory are in both English and Portuguese. I go home to my wife speaking Portuguese at night,' he said with a laugh, 'you would pick it up.' Their arrival reversed generations of population decline in Gort and injected a new vibrancy into the social life of the town. They inaugurated an annual summer festival; once a year hundreds of Brazilians gathered in the town's square to celebrate the carnival season. As described by a local Irish observer: 'They all dressed in their costumes and danced from twelve in the morning till twelve at night. It's like Dirty Dancing here.' As put by Sean Duffy: 'The Brazilians are lovely people. We have Brazilian nights out. They don't drink very much but they would dance all night. We have translators in the factory as well to help people out but a lot of them have studied English and are quite fluent.' The article noted that Western Union had set up a branch in Gort because the Brazilians sent a substantial amount of money back home each week. The principal of the Convent of Mercy primary school said that there were more than thirty children from Brazil attending the school. The school had recruited two language-support teachers to help the newcomers with English. The children, she said, fitted in well. The Brazilians were 'lovely people and very polite and refined'.

Initially, Brazilians arrived to work in Duffy's meat factory. Over time the occupational distribution of the community diversified, with a number of Brazilians coming to work in the retail, catering, construction and transport sectors. Many of these remained on renewable one-year employment permits.[29]

In 2004 *Irish Times* journalist Ruadhán Mac Cormaic travelled to Vila Fabril, where many of the Brazilian migrants in Gort had come from and, as a strapline for his article put it, to witness an economic boom fuelled by the fruits of Irish toil.[30] Mac Cormaic describes being greeted by a local man in his mid-twenties who thrusts out an arm. 'Howaya. Are ye from Ireland?' he asks. 'I live in Clonee myself.' Then he introduces his friends, others like him who are home for the winter. There's a builder who lives in Naas, Co. Kildare, and a couple of meat factory workers who have been based in the West of Ireland for years. And then there's the shopkeeper, who has six nephews in Co. Clare. The young man points out nearby dwellings with an Irish connection; that woman's sister, husband, son-in-law and two nieces are living in Gort, 'a place so familiar to people here it might as well be a neighbouring townland'. Mac Cormaic describes the visible trappings of Irish money; extreme poverty and conspicuous wealth stand side by side. The older houses are uniformly ramshackle, mostly two-room shacks built with corrugated iron roofs held down by slabs of concrete. Their wooden doors are warped, and in places there are opaque sheets of metal where the windows should be. But among them, every fourth or fifth house is new and elaborately decorated. Some are adorned with steel gates, intercoms, satellite dishes and a new car in the garage. Vila Fabril is quiet, a local woman explains, because so many of its people are in Ireland.

Vila Fabril, a community of a few hundred homes, was built in the 1950s in the shadow of a nearby meat factory. This remained the largest employer in the area until the late 1990s, when the plant closed. The Irish connection dates from that time. One of its managers at the time was an Irishman who had been working in Brazil since the late 1970s. Through his contacts, the first twenty-five migrants arrived to work in similar factories in Ireland in 1998. Various meat factories' owners began to send representatives to Brazil to fish in the same pool of skilled workers. Among them was Sean Duffy Meat Exports in Gort, which recruited six Brazilians 1999. Gort subsequently became, in Mac Cormaic's analogy, to Vila Fabril what Springfield, Massachusetts was to the Blasket Islands.

Many of the migrants from Vila Fabril had clearly benefited from their sojourn in Gort and from the ongoing presence of family and relatives there. The Brazilians had apparently achieved what many of the unfortunates portrayed in MRCI case studies could only dream of. Mac Cormaic described how working in Ireland had worked out well for one family:

> Gomes has returned home for a few months to carry out some work on the house. The rest of his family – wife Marlene and sons Junior and Denisson – are in Gort, where they have lived for the past five years. He beams with pride in the new house, delighting in every detail of his family's five-year adventure. And well he might: as well as this home, they own two other houses, which are rented out, as well as 18 acres of land and three cars: an Opel Corsa and two Volkswagens – a Golf and a Beetle. Most of it has been funded by his wife's job as a cook and his casual work as a panel beater in Galway.

Mac Cormaic described how most Brazilians expected to spend a few years in Ireland, save as much as possible, then return home to a better life. However, it had become apparent that some now planned to settle in Ireland. Gomes described how one of his sons was engaged to an Irish girl and wanted to stay in the West of Ireland. Another of his sons now never spoke of returning to Brazil; both spoke good English and had what were regarded as good jobs. But not everyone who went to Ireland had such good fortune. One woman described how her family had sold their shed to pay for her husband's plane ticket. In December 2005 he was killed, along with his nephew, by the fumes from a home heater left on overnight in their rented house in Gort.

The study of Brazilians in Gort (hereafter the Gort study) undertaken by Brian McGrath and Frank Murray between 2004 and 2007 highlights the role of social capital in functional integration,[31] and revealed some of the underlying complexities of the Vila Favil/Gort intersection depicted by Mac Cormaic. McGrath and Murray had anticipated that close-knit family and community networks would emerge as key bonding social capital resources for migrants, especially in coping with the initial stressful phase of settlement. One of the apparent differences between the Brazilians and the mostly vulnerable migrants described earlier in this chapter was that the latter had often become disconnected from any discernable community support; they were often trafficked in ways designed to ensure their exploitation; unlike many of the Brazilians, they often had nobody to turn to for advice and support. McGrath and Murray examined the functional advantages and disadvantages of such ties.

Their Gort study concluded that those without good-quality social ties are vulnerable to being exploited by opportunists. One of the biggest problems facing migrants was found to be difficulties in obtaining accurate information about rights, entitlements and opportunities in the host society; the absence of reliable such information fostered certain 'exploitative' practices. It seemed to be an accepted practice for fellow Brazilians and even relatives to charge new arrivals for almost any type of help. This might include basic accommodation, such as sleeping on a sofa, help in interpreting forms, applying for

PPS numbers, paying to translate with medical professions or even for making phone calls to the Electricity Supply Board.

It was found that copies of work permits were being sold for as much as €1,000. Some of those who purchased such documents – later arrivals than the meat factory workers who were specifically recruited – were threatened with violence when they found it difficult to repay this amount. As numerous MRCI cases demonstrate, the practice of 'selling' jobs is hardly uncommon; research amongst Brazilian migrants (cited by McGrath and Murray) in the United States has found that the practice is not uncommon, and attributes such practices to intense competition for employment.[32] No such competition existed during the boom years in Ireland. One of the Gort study interviewees described how another Brazilian woman proposed to charge her €400 for acquiring a cleaning job. As she put it: 'I had no language and they knew the lay of the land a little bit so I had to go through them to get work.' Another described paying €500 for a job that lasted only four months; he was paid €350 a week. In effect, the broker took just under 20 percent of his earnings for that period.

Whilst some Brazilians, particularly the first wave to arrive in Gort, benefited from close social ties, some others who followed in their footsteps did not. Those with families and friends in the town found it easier to access jobs and accommodation. Others outside such networks found it more diffi-cult to break in. As put by one Gort study interviewee:

> They're all related, they're all friends, family and so that makes life difficult, more difficult for me or anybody who is not from that area because of course they help each other first. They keep the jobs in the family or, so it's kind of extra difficult if you're not, if you're from Brazil but if you're from a different part of Brazil from the vast majority here.

A further major challenge for many was an inability to speak English; this made it difficult for many to interact with anyone other than fellow migrants. By way of illustration, McGrath and Murray cite the following interview:

> I remember at the beginning, the language was so difficult that I would wait in the house the whole day for somebody to come home to go with me to the super-market to buy something simple like even rice. I was just terrified, no English … Well, if I had to do it all over again, I wouldn't do it, I wouldn't repeat it. No, to arrive here without the language and it was just very difficult. Very difficult. No I wouldn't have the courage to do it again.

The Gort study found that most Brazilian migrants learnt English on a 'need to know' basis, which effectively meant learning barely enough vocabulary to get by at work but not enough to enable them to find work independently. Like many of the others described earlier in this chapter, most worked long hours. Several interviewees described being simply too busy or too tired after work to attend formal language classes. Through satellite dishes most tuned into television stations from their home country. This contributed to what McGrath and Murray described as 'weak ties' with the wider Irish society. English fluency, they emphasised, was a crucial ingredient of bridging social capital.

English-language fluency, they also emphasised, confers relative advantage over co-ethnics and other migrants who cannot speak English. The Gort study documented a number of cases where this led to exploitation, including one instance of exploitation within family networks: one woman's sister-in-law actively discouraged her from taking English-language lessons, presumably to keep her in a state of dependency.

The exploitation of some Brazilian migrants by co-ethnics was depicted as resulting from dependency relationships. Those who could not speak English were dependent on those who could; being totally dependent on others was a recipe for exploitation. Migrants who lacked the capabilities to interact independently within Irish society were more vulnerable to co-ethnic and, indeed, Irish opportunism than were those with such capabilities.

The Gort study emphasised the importance of 'trustworthy community leadership'. It gave a number of examples. A Brazilian Association was established in Gort. One of its leading members studied community development at National University of Ireland, Galway. He established an internet café in the town which functioned as a public space for many in the community. He was described as providing trustworthy advice on how to complete forms and identifying reliable contacts for information about various issues confronting migrants.

A second example given was the role of religious social capital. Gort's Brazilian community consisted of Pentecostals, Mormons and Catholics. The Pentecostal congregation, Assembléia de Deus, set up a church in the area and was responsible for the annual summer carnival; it catered for 'approximately 150 attendees on any given night'. The Brazilian Catholic community was ministered to by a Limerick-based priest who had worked for twenty years in Brazil; he said mass in Portuguese every Sunday in the local Catholic church. Both supplied spiritual, emotional and concrete support to their members. The positive role of religious social capital in Gort recalls that identified by Abel Ugba in his much-cited study of African Pentecostals in Ireland. Those interviewed by Ugba emphasised how church membership and activities helped to give them the confidence and skills to cope with the demands of living and working in Irish society; a bonding social capital that helped them to overcome barriers to participating in the wider society.[33] One of the Assembléia de Deus congregation gave an example of the kinds of concrete support also identified amongst African Pentecostals by Ugba:

> For example there is one family, the man has serious medical problems. He can't
> work at the moment, they have a wife and two children so the church helps pay

the rent, he has to go to hospital, one of the children has to go to hospital two or three times a week in Galway, they take the child, they pay the expenses and they buy shopping for them and people generally help out, look for work for the wife who can work. These kind of things ... Yeah and the church also helps of course spiritually but sometimes in other ways, yeah, sometimes you can feel a bit battered by life and it's good to talk to people and the Pastor is very helpful.

Interviewees emphasised the role of the Pentecostal pastor and the Catholic priest as sources of practical information and as a protection against co-ethnic exploitation. This included helpful announcements after church services and the facilitation of public meetings aimed at 'shaming without naming' those Brazilians who were seen to be taking advantage of their own people. At a fortnightly Catholic mass organised specifically for the Brazilians, the priest would often emphasise and reiterate certain parts to ensure that key messages were understood:

The type of information typically made available covered such items as: availability of English courses and enrolment dates; updates on migrant rights; laws on re-unification of families; work permit bureaucracy; breaches of the law (i.e. buying false driving licences, putting false tax and insurance data in windscreens, drinking and driving, getting involved in fights, etc); behavioural problems which were deemed harmful to integration within the wider community (e.g. Brazilians exploiting each other, playing music too loud, not returning shopping trolleys, riding bicycles on the pavement, dumping rubbish in the wrong places, etc).

Other examples given by McGrath and Massey emphasised the role of sport and commerce. The local football team 'naturally benefited from Brazilian talent and experience' and some Brazilian shops opened in the town, giving a focal point for community interactions.

In a 2009 article Ruadhán Mac Cormaic wrote again about the Brazilians, this time focusing on the decline of the Gort community in the face of economic recession. The 2009 summer samba festival, which had become a fixture in the town, had to be cancelled, ostensibly because so many Brazilians had had to return home (the International Organisation for Migration reported that Brazilians accounted for 40 percent of all applicants in Ireland for its voluntary repatriation scheme).[34] However, such elegies are premature. A Brazilian businesswoman I spoke to in October 2009 was adamant that their presence in Gort was a permanent one. As for her own situation, she said that her business, importing clothes from Brazil for sale in her boutique, was doing well despite the recession. She said that whilst some of her compatriots had gone back to Brazil, this number included some seasonal migrants who might return. On the October Saturday that I visited the town it seemed as if every second adult and child doing their shopping and enjoying the unusually fine Irish weather was Brazilian.[35]

Local political integration: capabilities, social capital and cultural capital

Functional integration – the ability to cope as migrant workers in the host
society – falls considerably short of most expectations of what is meant by
integration. This section considers the attributes of some immigrants who are
intent on high levels of civic and political participation in Irish society. A total
of eighteen immigrant candidates who contested the 2009 local government
elections were interviewed. Of these, ten were African and eight were from
Eastern Europe. In some respects these were not different from many of those
depicted in the various case studies above. They had not necessarily lived in
Ireland for longer; none had lived in Ireland more than a decade, several had
arrived after EU enlargement. Just one was an Irish citizen.

All eighteen emphasised an interest in promoting the needs of their
immediate local area, as distinct from the interests of co-ethnics, when
explaining their motivation for entering politics. Crucially, sixteen of the
eighteen had children living with them in Ireland; in this respect, Polish candidates were markedly atypical of the wider Polish population as found by the
2006 Census. Some repeatedly drew on the experiences of their children and
other family members to illustrate the changes they hoped to effect within their
neighbourhoods. The following explanation by one African respondent was
representative of what a number of candidates had to say: 'My motivation is
basically [...] my community has no facilities. When I came here my daughter
wasn't able to meet friends or even play with neighbours and stuff like that.'
Much like other local candidates, African and East European ones emphasised
the need to improve local facilities and amenities. One African respondent
described her motivation to enter local politics in the following terms:

> Yes I'm a migrant, but I'm also a woman. I'm also a mum who has got children
> who are in school like everybody else so participation would have been a very
> big issue. There are a lot of things that impede participation of people at different
> levels, like access to education and access to healthcare services. And then access
> to employment as well. But also issues such as the environment and issues such
> as transport are big, big issues.

Another African candidate stated that he became politically active because of
anti-social behaviour and vandalism in his area; it was affecting his business.
A number of respondents depicted themselves as community activists rather
than career politicians. As put by one: 'I prefer to work with small communities, just to be a voice for a few people.' As similarly expressed by another: 'To
be honest I am not that interested in politics – about [political] parties and
things like that. But to do something in the community here you need to have
some power.'

Seventeen of the eighteen candidates emphasised a desire to foster integration when explaining their political motivation. Both African and East

European candidates described wanting to become a 'voice' for the wider (i.e. Irish and migrant) communities they lived in. A number of respondents argued that integration must take root at the local level. As put by one respondent: 'I believe so much in grassroots […] we have to cultivate good neighbourliness. If you live in a place you need to be friends with your neighbours. They will get to know you […] Let us on the local level organise things and bring people together.'

Culturally specific reasons for entering local politics were also identifiable. Five of the ten African candidates cited experiences of racism, discrimination and lesser rights as motivations for entering local politics. One candidate described her decision to enter into politics as 'the only available path left to try.' As put by another: 'Coming to Ireland and experiencing racism and discrimination […] once you've experienced it you know how it feels, you know where it hurts.'

Amongst Polish respondents in particular, the need to address social isolation amongst immigrants emerged as a distinct motivating factor; five of the eight East European interviewees expressed such concerns. They envisaged civic and political participation as a response (or antidote) to alienation and isolation brought about by economic circumstances. As put by one Polish respondent:

> Most Polish people came here for work, for economic reasons, so they try to save as much as they can and don't go out. That's why integration here is a bit worse. That's why I would like to have meetings with Polish and Irish people so they will work together and maybe socialise more […] it doesn't need to cost money. Maybe we could clean a part of the town, plant flowers somewhere, then after we could meet and maybe have a barbeque or something. That's one thing because in Poland there are usually meeting places in every town with a canopy over it. I think if I get into the council I will try to create a place like that.

International studies of immigrant civic and political participation emphasise the role of both capabilities and social capital. US research suggests that social connectedness (what Putnam measures in his studies of social capital) is a strong predictor of political participation across different ethnic groups.[36] One study of Latino political participation in the United States found that English-language proficiency had 'an enormous effect upon Latino political participation', but that once English proficiency was taken into consideration, the Latino variable ceased to be significant. To a lesser extent the same was true in the case of English-speaking Asian Americans. Capabilities and social capital, these people suggested, mattered more than ethnic identity in determining political participation.[37]

Church membership as social capital has been identified as explaining why African Americans have greater participation rates than would be expected, given their socio-economic status. Not so in the case of Latinos in the United States (their high rate of affiliation with religious institutions notwithstanding).[38] The underlying explanation offered here relates to differences in political socialisation between Protestant African American churches and Latino Catholic congregations. As found by Sidney Verba:

> Latinos, a mostly Catholic group, in spite of recent defections to evangelical Protestant churches – are relatively unlikely to have the chance to develop civic skills in the context of church activity. African Americans, in contrast are affiliated with Protestant churches that are especially rich in opportunities for the development of civic skills.[39]

Religiosity emerged as a potential determinant of immigrant social capital in the Irish case. For example, the proportion of non-religious Nigerians (the largest African community) identified by the 2006 Census was just 0.7 percent.[40] All but one of the ten African candidates interviewed described themselves as religious. Of the eight Christians, three were Catholic and the remainder were from various Protestant denominations. Seven in total, including one Muslim, described themselves as actively practising their religion. Six described themselves as active Christian churchgoers. Of these, three were members of Pentecostal congregations, one being an ordained pastor. A further two described themselves as semi-regular churchgoers.

Many African respondents emphasised the role of their church as a 'social place' that gave them a sense of belonging. A number discussed how their religious beliefs influenced their participation in politics. For example, one said that although his entry into politics was not in any way religiously or spiritually motivated, his religious beliefs nevertheless informed his politics; religion acts as a moral guide when faced with difficult decisions. Overall, African respondents perceived their political and spiritual lives as intertwined. As put by one: 'I can't divide myself,' and by another: 'We are all political, we are all religious [...] I'm not a fanatic but my Christian values feed into everything I do.'

African respondents tended to emphasise their involvement in community life through their membership of religious congregations, voluntary organisations and other associations. Whilst they did not always describe such involvement as the motivational impetus to enter politics (see below), it is suggested that religious and other forms of social capital fostered an ethos of participation.[41]

Of the ten East European respondents, six described themselves as actively religious Catholics. One identified himself as Catholic but claimed that he does not go to church; one claimed that she is not religious and one did not answer this question. The sole identified non-Catholic (Russian Orthodox) did not attend church. Of the actively religious Catholics, one described being pleasantly surprised to discover that a town council meeting he attended 'started with a prayer'. When he asked about this, a local councillor explained

that Fine Gael is a Christian Democratic party. For some Polish resp
membership of the Catholic church was experienced as a form of u.
social capital that helped them to integrate into Irish society.

It emerged that all but one of the African respondents were educated
to degree level. The one exception had a management diploma. Two had
master's degrees and one was completing a master's degree. Of the ten African
respondents, two were graduates in English and literature, one in economics,
one in marketing, one in information technology, one in communications,
one in industrial chemistry and mineral processing, one was completing a
master's degree in international relations, and one held three master's degrees
in adult and community education, business administration and healthcare
management.

Comparisons between their pre-migratory and post-migratory occupational status (using Central Statistics Office socio-economic group categories) revealed that four retained their pre-migratory status, two had moved
to a higher socio-economic category and two had moved to lower categories.
Just one was unemployed and three were self-employed. African candidates
were somewhat atypical of the wider African migrant population as identified
in the 2006 Census and in 2008 ESRI research which identified extremely
disproportionate unemployment amongst black people: nine times that of
Irish nationals.[42]

By comparison, four of the eight East European candidates were educated to
degree level; one of these held a master's degree. All had completed secondary
education. Of the four non-graduates, one had dropped out of third-level
education and one was in the process of applying to study accountancy.
When the occupational status of East European respondents was compared
to their pre-migratory occupational status, two fared better in Ireland, four
remained within the same socio-economic category and two fared worse.
This fits with other research findings that East European migrants experience
a considerably greater degree of downward occupational mobility on coming
to Ireland.[43]

Seven of the ten African respondents had distinct pre-migratory political
expertise. One stated that two of his brothers were local councillors in Nigeria,
one had been a party secretary for the Social Democratic Party at the local
level in Nigeria, one had been a member of the National Republican Convention in Nigeria and one had been a member of the African National Congress
in South Africa. Three had been active in student politics, one of them coming
from 'a family of politicians', in which father, uncles and grandfather were
active in politics in Nigeria. One with no pre-migratory involvement in
politics stated that two of his siblings were councillors in Nigeria. Another
African candidate with no such family history depicted experiences of being
a leader at school as a form of pre-migratory political socialisation:

The first time I think I really had contact with politics was when I was in secondary school. I was elected the class prefect [...] From then I was really noticeable wherever I went. I was the class prefect until my final year and then I was elected the general prefect of the school. During that time too I happened to lead seven organisations in school. So people felt there was something I could do [...] And right within me I am revolutionary, you know, I have to stand on my own and then mobilise people, be critical if there is a need about what is happening.

A number of other African respondents depicted themselves as putative community leaders, making statements such as, 'I think that part of leadership is you shouldn't be afraid to take up responsibility', and, 'as a leader I feel I can engender change from within'.

Six of the ten East European respondents stated that they had no pre-migratory involvement in politics. Three of these stated that whilst they had not been involved in formal politics they had been active in social or voluntary organisations as an alternative to engagement with the formal political system; a strong degree of antipathy towards the political systems of their countries of origin was evident. Nevertheless, all but one of the East European candidates interviewed chose to become members of Irish political parties. The sole exception had unsuccessfully sought a nomination from a political party.

All of the African respondents stated that they were members of community organisations and voluntary groups. These include AkiDwa and the Africa Centre; with one exception, each of these organisations represented Africans from diverse religious and ethnic backgrounds. The exception was an Ebo support group. In each case they identified themselves as members of Irish community groups and networks as well as of immigrant groups (although almost half of the male respondents did not elaborate on the nature of their involvement in 'immigrant groups', suggesting predominantly informal ties with other immigrants). The four female African respondents stated that they were members of immigrant groups, such as AkiDwa, and that they were also members of Irish organisations, including community and voluntary organisations and intercultural networks. On this basis, African female respondents appeared to possess both more bridging *and* bonding social capital than males.

Compared to African respondents, the level of participation of East European respondents in both Irish and immigrant organisations and networks was low. Just three East European respondents were members of Irish organisations; of these, two were female. Of the ten Eastern European respondents, five (all Polish) stated that they were members of Polish organisations but were not members of Irish community organisations or groups other than a political party.

Challenges

Various statements by Irish politicians on integration have emphasised the need not to make the same mistakes made in other Western countries. Usually these refer to the presumed failure of multiculturalism in other countries. But such countries also had to reckon with the legacies of the kinds of exploitation and injustice now being written into Irish history. The presumption that today's vulnerable migrants are temporary guest workers has not been borne out in other Western countries. Any future crisis of integration in the Irish case, however defined, will find some of its antecedents in the kinds of immigrant experiences recounted in the first parts of this chapter.

The approach of this chapter has been to document a continuum of immigrant experiences of adapting to life in Ireland. It has illustrated how individual capabilities to some extent influence the ability of immigrants to function within Irish society; even those with high levels of human capital can find themselves extremely marginalised unless they possess other necessary capabilities. This suggests that any serious commitment to integration on behalf of the Irish state should heavily emphasise the individual empowerment of migrants, especially against exploitation; this includes forms of exploitation licensed by the state. A capabilities approach emphasises meaningful choices; current state practices do much to undermine the ability of some vulnerable migrants to escape exploitation. In redressing this, key capabilities include the ability to communicate in English and knowledge of and meaningful access to employment rights. Simply put, Irish society needs to invest in the capabilities of vulnerable migrants. As put by the MRCI in *Realising Integration*:

> A holistic approach to integration that focuses on social inclusion must incorporate economic rights and entitlements. Exclusion from information, invisibility within the system and the high degree of control, segregation and isolation within the economic sphere are all barriers to participation in the economy, but also to integration down the line.[44]

But even a capabilities perspective does not go sufficiently beyond the human-capital approach to integration that seems to predominate in the Irish case. Capabilities matter, but so too do supportive community ties. Immigrant communities and familial support networks are crucial aids to integration. Vulnerable migrants aspire to family reunification; in the case of low-income migrant workers and refugees this often seems to be resisted by the state. Familial and co-ethnic community ties as bonding social capital clearly improve the quality of immigrant lives. They do so in a context where the state pretty much leaves integration to the labour market. In effect, bonding social capital, such as provided by immigrant churches, must fill a vacuum created by state under-investment in supports for immigrants.

Yet, in the absence of certain individual-level capabilities, co-ethnic ties can work against integration. The kinds of exploitative dependency relationships with co-ethnics and even family members described in this chapter are easier to overcome where migrants can communicate effectively with the host society, where they have knowledge of and meaningful access to rights. The ability to participate is crucial; a core goal of any meaningful integration programme should be to foster the capabilities and supports that enable immigrants to engage with wider Irish society.

A willingness to participate is also crucial. All but one of the 2009 immigrant candidate interviewees had children living with them in Ireland; they typically identified strongly with their localities; their success or failure (of which more in Chapter 8) depended on bridging as well as bonding social capital. Both African and East European candidates possessed high levels of bonding social capital; they were typically members of co-ethnic organisations. African candidates were also typically members of Irish-led organisations; their abilities to network were to some extent the benefit of transferable cultural capital, which gave them valuable political experience. Yet the life stories of many African candidates included periods of state-sanctioned social exclusion; many were former asylum seekers. Their own personal experiences of racism, discrimination and lesser rights emerged as key issues in their decisions to contest the elections. Some insisted that the redress of such barriers was a precondition to integration. In effect, they warned that failure to address the social and economic marginalisation experienced by many Africans in Ireland would undermine future social cohesion.

Eastern European candidates typically invested less in social capital than did Africans; they benefited from Catholicism as a form of bridging social capital with the majority community; some found their way into Irish political parties (the only kind of Irish organisation all but one had joined) through parish community networks. Like African candidates, they identified issues in the local communities that affected Irish as well as immigrant residents. Yet East Europeans highlighted experiences of alienation and isolation of fellow migrants working long hours; high levels of participation in the economy, they emphasised, did not translate into integration. Here they could have been speaking for many of the vulnerable migrants described in the first part of the chapter, rather than about the immigrant lives of their compatriots.

Notes

1 D. Massey and M. Sánchez, *Restrictive Immigration Policies and Latino Immigrant Identity in the United States*, United Nations Development Programme Research Paper 2009/43

2 W. Barros and G. Manfli, 'Approaching Migrant Youth Marginalisation through the Capabilities Approach: Methodological Proposals', *Social Work and Society* 7.1, (2009), 7–24

3 A. Sen, 'Capability and Well-being', in M. Nussbaum and A. Sen (eds) *The Quality of Life* (Oxford: Clarendon Press, 1993), pp. 30–53

4 B. McGrath and F. Murray, 'Brazilian Migrants in Ireland, Emergent Themes from Research and Practice on the Significance of Social Networks and Social Capital', *Translocations: Migration and Social Change* 5.1 (2009), 1–20

5 R.D. Putnam, *Bowling Alone: The Collapse and Revival of American Community* (New York: Simon and Schuster, 2000)

6 P. Bourdieu, 'The Forms of Capital', in J.G. Richardson (ed.), *The Handbook of Theory and Research for the Sociology of Education* (New York: Greenwood, 1986) p. 249

7 P. Bourdieu and J.C. Passeron, *Reproduction in Education, Society and Culture* (London: Sage, 1977)

8 'Interview with Kuldup Singh. Migrating to Ireland: The experience of an Indian Sikh', *Migrant News*, July 2003

9 *The Examiner*, 4 June 2001

10 *Dáil Debates*, 8 May 2002

11 K. Allen, 'Neo-liberalism and Immigration', in B. Fanning (ed.), *Immigration and Social Change in the Republic of Ireland* (Manchester: Manchester University Press, 2007), p. 89

12 P. Conroy and A. Brennan, *Migrant Workers and Their Experiences* (Dublin: Equality Authority, 2003)

13 Mushroom Workers Support Group, *Harvesting Justice: Mushroom Workers Call for Change* (Dublin: Migrant Rights Centre Ireland, 2006)

14 Migrant Rights Centre Ireland, Realising Integration: Creating the Conditions for the Economic, Social, Political and Cultural Inclusion of Migrant Workers and their Families in Ireland (Dublin: MRCI, 2006), p. 53

15 Mushroom Workers Support Group, *Harvesting Justice*

16 Migrant Rights Centre Ireland, *Exploitation in Ireland's Restaurant Industry* (Dublin: MRCI, 2008)

17 *Ibid.*, p. 19

18 *Ibid.*, p. 5

19 *Ibid.*, p. 22

20 *Ibid.*, p. 22

21 Immigrant Council of Ireland, Globalisation, Sex Trafficking and Prostitution: The Experiences of Migrant Women in Ireland (Dublin: Immigrant Council of Ireland, 2009), p. 84

22 *Ibid.*, p. 95

23 E. Ward and G. Wylie, *The Nature and Extent of Trafficking of Women into Ireland for Sexual Exploitation 2000–2006* (Galway: Galway Social Science Research Centre), pp. 23–24

24 E. Ward and G. Wylie, 'Lap Dancing Clubs and Red Light Milieu: A Context for Sex Trafficking of Women into Ireland?' in G. Wylie and O. McRedomond (eds), *Human Trafficking in Europe: Character, Causes, Consequences* (Basingstoke: Palgrave, 2010), p. 166

25 Ibid.

26 Migrant Rights Centre Ireland, *Private Homes: A Public Concern* (Dublin: Migrant

Rights Centre Ireland, 2004), p. 120. For international comparisons see R. Cox, *The Servant Problem: Domestic Employment in the Global Economy* (I.B. Tauris: London, 2006)

27 B. Ehrenreich and A. Russell Hochschild (eds), *Global Woman: Nannies, Maids and Sex Workers in the New Economy* (London: Granta, 2003)

28 *Independent on Sunday*, 10 October 2004

29 C. Healy, 'Carnaval Do Galway: The Brazilian Community in Gort, 1999–2006', *Irish Migration Studies in Latin America* 4.3 (2006), 150–153

30 R. MacCormac, 'Faraway Fields Give Gort New a New Gloss', *Irish Times*, 11 April 2007

31 The research in Gort drew, firstly, on fieldwork experiences of one of the authors working with the Brazilian community as an outreach worker between 2004 and 2007, funded by the National University of Ireland, Galway Adult and Continuing Education Office; and secondly, on a research project undertaken between November 2007 and May 2008, involving qualitative interviews with 30 couples and seven single parents (64 adults in total); 21 children/young people; two focus groups with teenagers at a local school; six interviews with local Brazilian and non-Brazilian activist members of the community (teachers and church leaders). See McGrath and Murray, 'Brazilian Migrants in Ireland'.

32 Studies cited by McGrath and Murray include F. Goza, *Immigrant Social Networks: The Brazilian Case* (Ohio: Center for Family and Demographic Research, Bowling Green State University, 2006)

33 A. Ugba, 'African Pentecostals in Twenty-first Century Ireland: Identity and Integration', in B. Fanning (ed.), *Immigration and Social Change in the Republic of Ireland* (Manchester: Manchester University Press, 2007)

34 The scheme, funded in Dublin by the Department of Justice and the International Organisation for Migration, offers asylum seekers and undocumented migrants a flight to their country of origin and 'reintegration assistance' to the value of €600 for each person, or up to €1,200 per family. See www.iomdublin.org

35 One Brazilian shop owner explained that some people had returned to Brazil because of the recession, but that many had returned home for seasonal visits and some to attend third-level education in Brazil.

36 H.E. Leighley and A. Vedlitz, 'Race, Ethnicity and Political Participation: Competing Models and Contrasting Explanations', *The Journal of Politics* 61.4 (1999), 1092–1114, p. 1110

37 W. Tam Cho, 'Naturalisation, Socialization, Participation: Immigrants and Non-Voting', *The Journal of Politics* 61.4 (1999), 1140–1158, p. 1147

38 M. Jones-Correa and D.L. Leal, 'Political Participation: Does Religion Matter?' *Political Research Quarterly* (December 2001), 54.4, 751–770, p. 753

39 S. Verba, K. Lehman-Schlozman and H. Brady, *Voice and Equality, Civic Voluntarism in American Politics* (Cambridge, MA: Harvard University Press, 1995), p. 523

40 *Census 2006 Volume 13 – Religion*, Table 17, p. 109. Available at: www.cso.ie

41 N. O'Boyle, 'Integration and Political Participation: Immigrants and the 2009 Local Elections in Ireland', *Studies* 95.389 (2009), pp. 59–70

42 P. O'Connell and F. McGinnity, *Immigrants at Work: Ethnicity and Nationality in*

the Irish Labour Market (Dublin: ESRI, 2008), p. 29

43 A.M. *Barrett* and D. *Duffy*, 'Are Ireland's *Immigrants* Integrating into Its Labour Market?' IZA Discussion Paper No. 2838 (2007), p. 14

44 Migrant Rights Centre Ireland, *Realising Integration: Creating the Conditions for the Economic, Social, Political and Cultural Inclusion of Migrant Workers and Their Families in Ireland* (Dublin: MRCI, 2006), p. 67

6

Education and segregation

What varieties of men and women now prevail in this society and in this period? And what varieties are coming to prevail? In what ways are they selected and formed, liberated and oppressed, made sensitive and blunted? (C. Wright Mills)[1]

In a widely reported speech in April 2008, Archbishop Diarmuid Martin, patron of the Catholic schools which comprise well over 90 percent of Dublin's educational system, criticised Catholics who withdrew their children from schools with immigrant pupils: 'I hear of parents – even those who might fit into the social categorisation of "good Catholic parents" – making decisions with their feet or with their four-wheel-drives to opt out of diversity in schools.'[2] The year 2007 had witnessed rising numbers of non-Catholic immigrant children being unable to secure school places in oversubscribed Catholic schools. The overwhelming majority of primary schools in the Republic are faith based: 3,032 Catholic, 183 Church of Ireland, 14 Presbyterian, with two Muslim, one Jewish, one Jehovah's Witness and one run by the Religious Society of Friends (Quakers); by summer 2007 just 40 were multi-denominational 'Educate Together' schools. As such, the overwhelming majority of Irish primary schools could invoke an exemption from the Equality Act (2000), as did some Dublin Catholic schools in 2007, that allowed them to discriminate on the basis of religious affiliation where there was competition for school places.[3]

The statutory obligation to provide education for all children resulted in the establishment of two emergency Educate Together schools in Dublin 15 in September 2007. On Monday 3 September a meeting in Balbriggan organised by the Department of Education and Science (DES) was attended by upward of seventy people who had not found primary school places for their children. A journalist present observed, 'As they take their seats, one thing becomes startlingly clear: apart from the organisers, myself and five or six others, everyone else in the room is black.'[4] The immigrants in question were non-Catholics who happened to be black and who had moved into a predominately Catholic and predominantly white community. The first emergency primary school in Dublin 15, Schoil Choilm, admitted eighty-three junior infants in September 2007, 'the vast majority of whose parents come from Nigeria, Colombia, Romania, Poland and Moldova.'[5]

That the 'crisis' occurred in Dublin 15 (D15) was unsurprising. Overall population in the area had risen rapidly, from 71,673 in 2002 to 90,974 in 2006, a growth of 26 percent as compared to the overall increase in the Irish population of 8.2 percent between the 2002 to the 2006 census periods. Immigrants accounted for much of the population rise in D15; in 2006 some 73 percent of the population were classified as 'white Irish'. The percentage so categorised was considerably lower in some parts of D15: in three electoral districts, Abbotstown, The Ward and Mulhuddert, 'white Irish' comprised between 50 and 60 percent of the population. Poor planning, according to Archbishop Martin, had created a vacuum which was contributing to segregation: 'Ghetto schools, which we all wish to avoid, are not necessarily just the fruits of bad educational policies, but of a range of other policies which create ghettoes for which the school cannot be held to blame.'[6]

This chapter draws extensively on the findings of the two most substantial empirical studies to date of the experiences of schools, *Intercultural Education: Primary Challenges in Dublin 15* (hereafter *Dublin 15*),[7] a 2007 report funded by the Social Inclusion Unit and the Department of Education and Science (DES), and *Adapting to Diversity: Irish Schools and Newcomer Students*, by the Economic and Social Research Institute (2009). The 2006 Census found that 53,000 or 12.6 percent of resident non-citizens were aged between 0 and 14 years, as compared with some 20.6 percent of the total population.[8] Of these, the focus of *Dublin 15* and *Adapting to Diversity* was upon what were termed 'newcomer' children, recently arrived migrant children whose parents were not Irish citizens.[9] Some of the findings of these studies, considered here from a cultural capital perspective, are contextualised by comparison with the findings of WBCFN research undertaken in 2007 and 2008 in deprived communities.[10] This research interviewed 1,633 households, of which 9.4 percent were non-Irish citizen households. The findings allowed some comparison between the respective perceptions of teachers and parents of how immigrant children were faring in deprived localities.

The impetus for *Dublin 15* came from a meeting of twenty West Dublin school principals in spring 2006.[11] At the meeting, 'the frustration and anger were palpable and was primarily targeted at the perceived lack of appreciation by policy-makers and administrators of the scale of the challenge and the extent to which long established rules and routines applying to staffing and resource allocation were no longer working or appropriate.'[12] A further meeting of all twenty-five primary school principals in D15 was convened. This agreed to document the extent of diversity and its impact on schools in the area; one of the principals, Enda McGorman, volunteered to begin the study; the group successfully applied to the DES for his secondment; a steering committee was formed to work out the research design brief. The resultant 2006–7 report drew on data from all twenty-five of the primary schools in D12, the part of Dublin that in recent years has experienced the greatest overall increase in population and has come to have the highest concentration of immigrant pupils in the Republic of Ireland. At the time of research, seven of these schools were designated as disadvantaged.

Adapting to Diversity drew on a postal survey of the principals of all 733 second-level schools and a sample of 1,200 primary principals selected to be representative of all primary schools in terms of size, location and disadvantaged (Delivering Equality of Opportunity in Schools – DEIS) status; it also includes some case studies where the approach was broadly similar to that of *Dublin 15*; principals, teachers and pupils were interviewed.[13] Both studies examined similar issues, the nature and extent of segregation, the perceived effects of language difficulties, perceptions of the motivation and educational attainment of newcomers compared to Irish children.

Segregation and enrolment

Dublin 15 expressed strongly worded concerns about the segregation of immigrant pupils in the area. A summary report by the authors of *Adapting to Diversity* claimed that for Republic of Ireland as a whole there was 'no evidence of school segregation in relation to immigrant students relative to international comparisons'.[14] The basis of comparison were figures for OECD countries which identified that just under 30 percent of pupils with an immigrant background attended schools where they comprised more than half of the school population.[15] That these levels had built up over considerably more time than Ireland's brief mass immigration period was not considered. Whilst both reports differed somewhat in tone, their findings were broadly the same. Firstly, both suggested that school enrolment policies worked to block newcomers in circumstances where there was a strong demand for places. These seemed to shunt newcomers towards schools that were under-subscribed and accounted for the over-representation of newcomers in schools designated as disadvantaged. Secondly, there seemed to be a tendency for some Irish parents to withdraw their children from schools perceived as having a lot of newcomers. Whilst *Adapting to Diversity* resisted the term 'segregation', it warned that the enrolment practices illustrated by its case studies could lead to more widespread segregation.[16]

Adapting to Diversity (using 2007 enrolment data) found that about 90 percent of secondary schools had immigrant pupils, as compared with just 56 percent of primary schools; primary schools tended to have fewer pupils than secondary schools, so it was more likely that there could be schools with and without newcomers in the same locality. Almost half of newcomer primary school pupils were found to be in schools where they consisted of more than 20 percent of the intake. One in five of these were in primary schools with an immigrant student body of more than 40 percent.[17] There were no newcomer students in 44 percent of Irish primary schools.[18] East European nationals predominated in forty percent of those primary schools with newcomer pupils (56 percent of all primary schools); Africans predominated, that is made up more than half of all newcomers, in around 15 percent of primary schools with immigrant children.[19] The report estimated that there were around 45 schools out of the total of nearly 3,300 with more than 50 percent newcomers.[20]

Dublin 15 found some evidence of what Archbishop Martin called a withdrawal from diversity. A tracking exercise conducted across thirty-seven Junior Infant and Second Class groups between 2003 and 2007 found that 175 pupils, almost one fifth of the initial enrolment, had left. A slightly larger number of 192 pupils joined the thirty-seven classes in the same time period. Of the 175 that left, 82 (or 47 percent) were Irish and 93 (or 53 percent) were non-Irish. Of the 192 who joined in the same period 40 (or 21 percent) were Irish and 152 (or 79 percent) were non-Irish. These figures suggest that for D15 as a whole twice as many Irish leave as join, and twice as many immigrants enrol as leave.[21] The findings suggested a net loss of 400 Irish pupils from D15 schools. *Dublin 15* insisted that this 'evidence indicates quite a serious trend and significant trend of Irish moving out and immigrants moving in'.

What, then, explained the absence of any newcomers in almost half of Ireland's primary schools? Both *Adapting to Diversity* and *Dublin 15* made considerable use of case studies to consider the ways in which religious and other admission criteria disadvantaged newcomers. The enrolment dynamics that pushed migrants towards disadvantaged and under-subscribed schools were found to be similar in both reports.

Adapting to Diversity considered case studies of both primary and secondary schools. 'Adwick Street', a large secondary school, was one of the 10 percent with no newcomer pupils. It 'was oversubscribed and had to refuse a lot of applicants'. Selection criteria prioritised siblings of existing pupils and daughters of past pupils. Other criteria included length of time on the waiting list; this had allowed 'locals' attending a local feeder primary school get on to the waiting list before most newcomers had even arrived in Ireland.[22]

Similarly, the selection criteria for 'Huntington Road', a medium-sized urban secondary school for girls with less than 10 percent newcomers were such that the only way of getting a place in the first year without a sibling already enrolled as a pupil was through having attended a primary school feeder. However, places for other than first-year newcomers had sometimes become available.

In 'Benthan Street', an under-subscribed rural school, the percentage of newcomer pupils reflected the proportion of migrants in the local area.

But under-subscribed schools were likely to have disproportionately high numbers of newcomer pupils. One such example, 'Wulford Park', though not classified as disadvantaged, 'had experienced declining numbers of Irish students in recent years as students were "attracted" to schools further afield and now catered for newcomers in the local area'. Two other under-subscribed schools examined, 'Ashville Lane' and 'Brayton Square', were both classified as disadvantaged. Both accepted referrals from social services and the Education Welfare Board; the latter took in pupils who had been expelled from other schools.[23] 'Thomas Road', a small, inner-city disadvantaged school with more than 20 percent newcomer pupils always had vacancies; pupil numbers had dropped over a number of years: 'They take everyone who applies, at whatever time of year.'[24] 'Van Buren Street' drew its pupils from a predominantly social housing area. The school had recently become known locally as 'the school for newcomers', although newcomers comprised less than 10 percent of pupils. It accepted those who lived near but had been turned away by a larger school 'on the other side of the river'. In the year prior to the research it had experienced a logistical crisis when twenty-five new pupils of varying ages had unexpectedly enrolled the day before school started; it then took a year to get approval for extra accommodation from the Department of Education and Science.[25]

Two of the primary schools examined had no newcomer children. Neither 'Dobbins Road', a large urban primary school, nor 'Greendale Avenue', a small rural school, was designated as disadvantaged. The former was over-subscribed, with priority given to siblings of existing students and local parishioners. The school was in a middle-class area where expensive housing worked to reduce the likelihood of newcomer applicants. 'Greendale Avenue' accepted all applicants, but was in a rural area with few migrants.[26]

In 'Adams Street', a small rural school designated as disadvantaged, some 30 percent of pupils were newcomers. The school proactively sought to attract newcomers; it advertised in Polish and Russian and operated what the principal described as an inclusive Catholic ethos. 'Adams Street' had become known locally 'as the school for newcomers'. But this profile also reflected 'the withdrawal of some Irish students from the school by their parents' because, according to the principal, 'they felt that their education was being compromised by the presence of newcomer children in the classroom and the extra attention teachers had to give them because of language difficulties'; other local schools had but a few newcomers.[27]

'Durango Street', a large urban primary school, illustrated 'how admissions policies promoting equality can be contested by the local community'. More than 20 percent of the pupils were newcomers. The school's former admissions policy of prioritising older children had worked to favour these over some residents with long-term ties to the area. From this, the school moved towards the common practice amongst over-subscribed Catholic schools of prioritising siblings of existing pupils and those from the local Catholic parish. As put by one teacher:

> We examined our enrolment policy and as a result of the pressure from a lot of quarters the following year we took Catholics first. It didn't sit well with us to do that, but we had no choice because we're a Catholic school.

'Durango Street' subsequently reconsidered this admissions policy and changed the criteria so as to accept up to a certain proportion of non-Catholics.[28] In effect, it adopted the formula, promoted by Archbishop Martin in a number of West Dublin Catholic schools, of setting aside up to 30 percent of places for newcomer children.

English-language acquisition and academic standards

Unsurprisingly, English-language competency has emerged as a key issue in research into newcomers' experiences of education in Ireland and a key factor in their integration within school and society. Over 10 percent of newcomer children in the entire country who qualified for English Language Support (ELS) were found to live in D15. These 2,084 ELS pupils constituted 21 percent of all children in D15 primary schools.[29] In six of these schools more than 30 percent of pupils qualified for ELS – rising to 60 percent in one of these and 57 percent in another. A further nine schools contained between 20 and 30 percent of ELS-eligible pupils. Of the 2,084 ELS pupils in D15, some 574 were Nigerian nationals (28 percent in total), but overall around 40 percent were Africans. Another 40 percent were Europeans; of these, Polish children comprised the largest group, followed by Romanians, with other EU-10 countries comprising most of the rest.

One teacher vividly described the challenges she faced on moving to a D15 school. She had worked previously in a school with few ELS pupils. Now she had a class of twenty-seven where only four pupils 'had English'. She emphasised the pressures this put on those without and with language-acquisition needs:

> It is quite frightening. I'm in fourth class – sometimes you look around your class and see one group playing ABC bingo from Junior Infants, and another groups writing their novel … you look around and wonder how is this happening, how am I going to bring these children up to a level where they can enter First Year and not be struggling?[30]

Adapting to Diversity found that the majority of newcomer children in Ireland were from non-English speaking countries. Over half of both primary and secondary principals reported language difficulties amongst 'nearly all' or 'more than half' of their newcomer students. Interviews with principals indicated that language difficulties had 'marked consequences for the

academic progress and social integration of newcomer students.[31] In designing the research it was anticipated that there would be a relationship between the extent of perceived language difficulties amongst newcomers and perceived achievement differences between newcomers and native pupils. This indeed proved to be case. It was correctly anticipated that the extent of language difficulties would have a stronger influence on how principals perceived academic performance than would the concentration of newcomers in the school; in other words, that any deterioration of overall academic standards might be explicable by the absence of language supports rather than, as some Irish parents seemingly believed, by the presence of significant numbers of newcomer children in a school. In line with expectations, academic difficulties were more prevalent in schools with more language difficulties amongst newcomer pupils.[32]

Principals of schools designated as disadvantaged were more likely than those in non-DEIS schools to report newcomers as having 'above average' academic achievement.[33] These perceptions were found to be affected by perceived levels of English-language difficulty; the higher the proportion of newcomer students with language difficulties, the less likely they were perceived to be above average in motivation by their principal.[34] Principals in 49 percent of secondary schools where nearly all newcomers had language difficulties nevertheless perceived newcomers as being above average in educational aspiration; this rose to 60 percent in schools where only a small proportion had language difficulties.

When principals were asked their views on the motivation of newcomer students in doing homework, relative to Irish students, less than 10 percent in both primary and secondary schools rated newcomers as below average. Newcomers were rated as above average by 30 percent of primary school principals and over 50 percent of secondary principals. With respect to educational aspirations, less than 10 percent of primary level principals and 5 percent of secondary principals considered that newcomer children had lower than average aspirations. At primary level, 30 percent and at secondary level, 50 percent considered that newcomers had above average expectations.

Adapting to Diversity had hypothesised that newcomers would be perceived as higher-attaining relative to native pupils, but that language difficulties might inhibit attainment. Except in disadvantaged schools, the first part of this hypothesis proved not to be the case. National Assessment of Reading Progress results have indicated somewhat lower reading scores amongst immigrants than for equivalent Irish students in first and fifth classes of primary school.[35]

Institutional failures in providing-English language support to such children were highlighted in an earlier (2005–6) study of eleven schools. That research was conducted in an unidentified urban area with a history of socio-economic disadvantage that had experienced unprecedented socio-economic change, and where now approximately one fifth of the population were not Irish.[36] Only two of the twelve teachers surveyed were qualified as language support teachers; three-quarters had not attended any training; the reasons they gave included difficulties arranging in substitution to allow them attend and 'poor perceptions' of the usefulness of the training. The study found that some teachers were 'confused' about the differences between language support and support for students with special educational needs; it was common for language support to be coordinated by the special needs coordinator. In at least one school bilingual students were placed in 'remedial' classes rather than receiving specific English-language support. In one school assessment tools designed for use with primary-school-aged native speakers with learning difficulties were used to assess bilingual students' language levels. Overall 'common delays and difficulties' experienced in accessing resources were compounded by the inexperience of teachers on the ground.[37] *Dublin 15* also criticised the inadequacy of language support provision; many teachers, the report complained, had received only one day of ELS in-service training.[38]

Adapting to Diversity found that disadvantaged schools at both primary and secondary levels were almost twice as likely as others to have newcomer children.[39] The concentration of newcomers in disadvantaged schools was substantially more pronounced in urban areas. In effect, newcomer children with language difficulties were disproportionately concentrated alongside children with learning difficulties. The generally used indicator distinguishes where more than 10 percent of pupils in a school have literacy and numeracy problems, emotional/behavioural problems and absenteeism. Newcomers comprised on average 8.3 percent of pupils in schools where more than 10 percent of pupils had behavioural problems, a figure likely to be much higher in many particular cases because 44 percent of schools were found to have no newcomer pupils at all.

One way of contextualising this '10 percent' is with reference to a widely used index of child well-being, the Strengths and Difficulties Questionnaire (SDQ).[40] The SDQ measures problems with conduct, emotional symptoms, hyperactivity, peer problems and anti-social behaviour. With each of these, child well-being (as revealed in parental perceptions) is assessed according to whether the child has 'no difficulties', 'some difficulties' or 'serious difficulties'. Findings that 10 percent of Irish children overall experience severe difficulties are consistent with findings from the United Kingdom that used similar SDQ indicators of child well-being.[41] However, SDQ 'serious problem' scores tend to be considerably higher amongst disadvantaged children. For example, Irish WBCFN research using 2007 and 2008 data found disproportionately high 'serious problem' scores for children of medical-card holders (18 percent), lone parents (17 percent) and other groups at risk of poverty. In one Dublin inner-

city area (the Liberties) some 21 percent of children were found to experience serious difficulties; there were indications that in at least one deprived
inner-city tower block 30 percent of children experienced serious difficulties. To some extent, SDQ scores offer a proxy for cultural capital; children
with serious difficulties patently lack many of the attributes that translate into
educational advantage. In other words, what are measured (from a psychological perspective) are individual characteristics and capabilities understood
(from a sociological perspective) to impede education, well-being and long-
term life chance outcomes.[42]

Cultural capital, racism and social class

Adapting to Diversity implied that over-representation of newcomers within
such disadvantaged settings was an obstacle to integration but also, possibly,
a social-inclusion boon:

> This suggests that some schools are dealing with, not only a larger proportion of
> newcomer students, but also considerable literacy, numeracy, behavioural and
> attendance difficulties, and a high proportion of other disadvantaged groups like
> travellers, which could place a considerable burden on their resources. There is
> also a possibility that newcomer students may raise the standard and learning
> expectations in schools with a disadvantaged student intake.[43]

Adapting to Diversity described a 'reference group' effect whereby teachers
in disadvantaged schools made comparisons between newcomers whose
parents had higher educational levels and commitments to education and
Irish parents without such resources.[44] It corroborated previous smaller-scale
studies that suggested that immigrant children were perceived by teachers
to have positive dispositions towards 'schooling and education in general'
because immigrant parents were highly educated. As one of these put it:

> Positive accounts of migrant children's work, for example, were located in an
> assumption that such children generally came from middle-class backgrounds
> and as a result provided positive role models for Irish students, especially those
> in working-class schools.[45]

The inference was that parental human-capital advantage translated into
educational-cultural capital advantage within deprived schools; migrant
children were depicted by teachers as having a potentially positive impact on
some of the more 'deficient' working-class students. Teacher interviewees in an
earlier (2002) study of eight schools by Dympna Devine were found to idealise
migrant pupils as 'extremely well-behaved, courteous, polite and dedicated', as
having 'values regarding respect for authority' and as being 'very education-
orientated, very anxious for it', with 'quite a contrast between them and our
own kids'. In deprived areas immigrants were depicted as role models for Irish

children. Teachers, in Devine's analysis, perceived working-class students 'in deficit terms' and their presumptions about migrant children were framed in terms of a middle-class ideal.[46]

Similarly, both *Dublin 15* and *Adapting to Diversity* teachers highlighted the motivation of many newcomer children, 'who brought with them a desire to work hard, to learn and to succeed'. Some newcomers were perceived as a positive influence, 'particularly in disadvantaged areas', where it was felt that the arrival of such motivated and high achievers served as a 'good role model to Irish pupils.'[47] As put by a 'Durango Street' primary teacher cited in *Adapting to Diversity*:

> Some of them, their parents are pushing them really, really hard to work, they've got a really strong work ethic, they come to school to learn, they work very hard at everything they do, they present their work nicely, any homework that goes home is done properly … sometimes the home background can make a big difference.[48]

Such perceptions are hardly surprising, given the findings of the 2006 Census that immigrants are generally better educated than the host population, and particularly likely to be so in deprived localities. Several studies concur that many newcomers, particularly those in disadvantaged schools, seem to possess a relative cultural-capital advantage.[49] Why this might be the case can be illustrated using the aforementioned WRCFN data from deprived communities. Irish respondents were found to considerably more likely to be in receipt of a medical card (a proxy for low income) and far more likely to have a low level of education than immigrant adults. In essence, the comparison was one between the long-standing Irish inhabitants of deprived areas and relatively educated migrants. When asked about educational expectations for their children, migrant respondents scored considerably higher than did Irish citizens: 62 percent of Irish respondents expected that their children would go to third-level education, as compared to 71 percent of UK-born respondents, 94 percent of 'other EU' and 88 of non-EU respondents. Inevitably, socio-economic status affected these scores. Some 72 percent of those not entitled to a medical card had high educational expectations, as compared to 49 percent of those with medical cards. Overall, adult immigrants were markedly more optimistic about the future of their children than were Irish respondents. These differences were most dramatic when scores for migrants were compared to those overall for the Liberties, a deprived inner-city area, where these made up 28 percent of respondents. In one Liberties electoral area where Irish citizens made up just 55 percent of the population, some 90 percent of respondents expected that their children would access third-level education.

Well-being (SDQ) scores for immigrant children were extremely high as compared with the children of their Irish neighbours. The striking findings were that 100 percent of EU migrant-child respondents were found to be experiencing no difficulties at all. Again, no (0 percent) children of respondents in the 'Other EU' and 'Other' categories were found to experience serious difficulties, whilst 12 percent of EU migrants reported some difficulties. Amongst non-EU migrants, 88 percent were found to be experiencing no difficulties. Overall, these findings suggest that some immigrant children living in deprived areas exhibit dramatically higher levels of well-being than do indigenous children.

Somewhat similar findings emerged with respect to levels of parental conflicts with children as measured using the Parent Child Relationship Inventory and Conflict Tactics Scale. Compared to the WBCFN baseline of 11.3, the score for the Liberties was 30.7. By comparison, the children of EU migrants fared better, with parental conflict scores of 12.3, and non-EU immigrant children had a markedly higher score of 24.3. These findings are in keeping with the findings of research in other countries on the relationship between socio-economic status and child well-being. Study after study has found that poverty and insecurity take their toll on parental mental health and detrimentally affect relationships between parents and their children.[50] In the Irish case, amongst the most vulnerable WBCFN groups a strong correlation between poverty and poor psychological well-being was clearly identified. Internationally, poverty experienced in early childhood has been found to be a strong predictor of children's ability and achievement.[51]

Adapting to Diversity found that in 70 percent of disadvantaged schools newcomers were perceived as motivated above average.[52] Yet, along with *Dublin 15*, it emphasised considerable variations in terms of motivation for different immigrant groups; 'a sense that children from Eastern European, Middle Eastern and Asian backgrounds were more motivated than children from African backgrounds'.[53] As ever, *Dublin 15* described the concerns of teachers more bluntly:

> a very strong sense across all the groups (of interviewees) at the lack of social skills exhibited by some newcomer children, in particular 'some African children and particularly boys'. Again and again, teachers in Junior schools pointed to the fact that many African children in the early years did not have the social skills to take part in class-groups of 29 children. This perceived lack of social skills, the teachers indicated, leads to considerable disruption. While teachers were somewhat reticent about 'naming' such concerns for fear of stereotyping particular ethnic groups, there was a strong sense also that remaining silent on the issue would allow it to fester below the surface, where 'it would be likely to become a throbbing racist sore.'[54]

D15 teachers highlighted cultural conflicts with African children and families about discipline. Interviewees referred to 'some children exhibiting hugely disrespectful behaviour towards female members of staff' and, as one put it, 'a general lack of respect of Nigerian and African boys towards teachers'. A significant number of newcomer parents, Africans by implication, seemed to feel that the school was too soft on their children ('a parent came in and said – "don't be afraid to hit him … You say 'please and thank you' to the children, that is not the way'"). Such parents seemed to use corporal punishment. Teachers repeatedly described being afraid to report misbehaviour to parents for fear of the child being physically abused at home: 'Teachers refer to instances where children cry inconsolably when the teacher lets the child know that s/he will be seeking to talk to their parents. The children report that they will be beaten if they get into trouble, so that teachers face a dilemma as to whether or not they should report misbehaviour'. Teachers reported finding themselves in difficult situations. If they found out about instances where children had been beaten at home, they 'had no choice but to invoke child protection procedures; this brought about a breakdown in trust between home and school'.[55] Somewhat similarly, an *Adapting to Diversity* interviewee stated: 'There is a much higher number of behavioural problems with African newcomer boys in our school'.[56]

Such perceptions of cultural conflict obscured other factors that potentially affected the behaviour of children. As put by Nowlan in her study of English-language support teachers: 'Bilingual students' linguistic abilities are not valued as cultural capital'.[57] D15 teachers identified frustrations amongst some children who 'were bright and anxious to get on' but inhibited by their lack of English. They got frustrated because they could not interact: 'An awful lot of heads go down and their behaviour deteriorates', and they would become angry ('I just can't take this anymore. In Poland I was able to do everything'). Previously well-behaved children would enter 'an angry phase' or 'the silent phase'. *Dublin 15*, in common with Nowlan's research a year earlier, implied that the skills amongst teachers to address such issues were underdeveloped.[58]

Teachers felt they had to contend with a simplistic policy debate in which the needs of newcomer children were primarily viewed as ELS needs whilst the main problems, as perceived by many teachers, were behavioural problems. ELS did not address, as one put it, 'the basic social skills to be in school in the first place'.[59] Interviewees emphasised the importance of pre-school socialisation. Children who had attended playschools and crèches had already been taught the routines required for classrooms to function, turn-taking, queuing, toilet training. It seemed that many of children without the required social skills for school did not have such pre-school experiences. Junior Infant class teachers recounted having to play catch-up on such skills for much of the school year instead of getting on with education. *Dublin 15* stated that many newcomer children arrived without having been outside of the home, without much contact with 'the outside world', and therefore faced a considerable culture shock when they began school.[60] Respondents emphasised that ELS needed to be backed up by comprehensive special needs support. Special Needs Assistants (SNAs), where available, were found to achieve considerable improvements in pupil behaviour. *Dublin 15* recommended that an SNA should be appointed to each class with a high concentration of newcomers.[61]

Furthermore, *Adapting to Diversity* quoted the views of some newcomer children that second-level education standards were higher in their countries of origin ('in Poland it's very difficult, it's a lot of subjects, lots of study but here it's not bad'); some Nigerian students described Irish schools as less strict, commenting on the absence of corporal punishment.[62] The inference was that lower educational standards and poorer quality of discipline within schools might both have a negative impact on the motivation and behaviour of some students. *Dublin 15* inferred that many Irish teachers were uncomfortable about managing discipline, mindful not only of laws against corporal punishment but of the history of authoritarian punishment in Irish industrial schools.[63] For such reasons, some felt uneasy about demands from some parents of newcomers that they impose discipline. Whilst teachers seemed sensitive to a wide range of explanations for newcomer behavioural problems, a tendency to reduce these to a dominant cultural-conflict narrative was evident. This portrayed African children and families as deviant. The authors of *Dublin 15* suggested that some of the comments of teachers about African children were 'much too generalised', inferring some degree of stereotyping by teachers. The case for undertaking child well-being research in Dublin 15 is a strong one. Strikingly, none of the children of African respondents to the 2007 and 2008 WBCFN survey (1 percent of families surveyed) was found to have a 'serious difficulties' SDQ score; this research did not examine Dublin 15. However, it does suggest a need to question depictions of African children as disproportionately affected by behavioural problems.

To some extent at least, the perceived behavioural problems of newcomer children cannot be explained by cultural factors. Racism and other negative experiences of the school system need to be taken into account. *Adapting to Diversity* identified a tendency for non-white children to become socially isolated within schools. As put by a 'Brayton Square' teacher, 'The Eastern Europeans mix very well. The Africans tend to stay amongst themselves'; as put by a teacher from 'Ashville Lane', 'the Chinese in particular are a very close knit group that don't mingle with other students'; and as put by an Irish student interviewee about the 'boys in our class from Africa', 'they don't get on well with other people like from Ireland or from different countries, they don't get on with that many people'.[64] African pupils were more likely to report bullying than were Eastern European pupils.[65] As put by a teacher in the earlier study by Devine, 'I would say that the non-nationals who are not black mix easier with the kids, if they have any kind of English at all they are accepted easier than the African kids'.[66]

According to Bourdieu, cultural capital is manifested in the skills, norms, habits and dispositions that confirm social advantage upon individuals; it is unequally distributed and contributes to the intergenerational reproduction of inequalities.[67] Particularly in the case of education, cultural capital may be understood as a form of intellectual capital that affects the life chances of individuals even as it reproduces a specific social order and cultural hierarchies alongside material ones. Specifically, in the case of education, Bourdieu identifies a 'hidden curriculum' loaded in favour of certain social groups and against others on the basis of class.[68] Teachers emerge as key arbitrators; the values, norms and behaviour these respond to positively count as cultural-capital advantage; conversely (and simplifying somewhat), cultural-capital disadvantages are those dispositions that teachers tend to reject. In this sense, education is as much a battle for the hearts and minds of teachers as for those of pupils.

The academic literature on education and racism is fraught with questions side-stepped in this chapter and in most the research cited above. It is predicated on a recognition that racism is as insidious as it is destructive and that with the best will in the world it is almost impossible for white researchers not to internalise and reproduce some racist presumptions about the attributes and behaviour of black and minority ethnic children.[69] Paul Connolly recounts the kinds of dilemmas that had come to the fore within British academia by the 1980s:

> It was felt that because the majority of researchers were white and middle-class, this meant they had very little experience or understanding of racism. It was therefore not surprising, it was argued, that these researchers would tend to overlook the importance of racism in minority people's lives and simply reproduce the assumptions and values that were taken for granted because they underpinned their own privileged social position. Rather than critiquing the white, middle-class 'norm' and the exclusionary processes and practices that formed its foundation, it was argued that many researchers simply used this 'norm' unquestioningly as the yardstick to assess the lives and experiences of the minority ethnic population.[70]

How is it possible not to fall short, especially so in Ireland, where few teachers and academics come from the communities whose children are considered here? Such concerns about unwitting racism are particularly relevant to the Irish case because Irish policy makers, teachers and researchers are still at the beginning of their own steep learning curve. Useful lessons about the need to take racism seriously can be learnt from decades of research in the United Kingdom. Study after study has highlighted how teachers have responded differently to black students than to other 'ethnic minority' or white students. Examples of findings include the role of stereotypes in disproportionate exclusions (temporary expulsions as a disciplinary measure) of black students, findings that black students tended to receive more criticism and negative feedback than white students and findings that even well-intentioned teachers, committed to inclusive ideals, unconsciously respond differently to black pupils than, for example, to Asian pupils, favourably perceiving the latter as of 'high ability' and socially conformist while perceiving Afro-Caribbean male students as having 'low ability and potential discipline problems'.[71]

A recent (2009) analysis by Steve Strand of the persistence of 'ethnic gaps' in educational attainment in England emphasised the importance of socio-economic inequalities in explaining educational outcomes for different black and minority ethnic groups and, indeed, white pupils. Strand cites findings that 29 percent of black children in England are eligible for free school meals (a commonly used indicator of poverty), as compared to just 14 percent of white children.[72] *Dublin 15* noted that the numbers of households in receipt of private rent supplement (again an indicator of poverty) rose from 1,433 in 2002 to 2,822 in 2006, almost doubling in during a period when unemployment remained low for Ireland as a whole. Some 894 were 'foreign nationals' in 2002, rising to 1,910 in 2006. Of these 1,910, some 61 percent were African, 22 percent from Eastern Europe and 5 percent from EU Accession countries. As noted in Chapter 3, Africans have been found to experience extremely disproportionate rates of unemployment, even though they are comparatively highly educated as compared to others in Irish society. Disproportionate risks of poverty amongst Africans in Ireland suggest that some African children face barriers to educational attainment that are better explained by racism and socio-economic status than by culture.

Yet, black pupils in Ireland or elsewhere are by no means homogenous. Nor, it must be emphasised, are white Irish pupils. Strand's analysis of English data on educational attainment finds that black African parents, as distinct from Afro-Caribbean parents, have higher levels of educational qualifications and higher educational aspirations for their children than other minority ethnic groups, and that black African pupils reported the most positive attitudes towards school and the highest levels of motivation of all minority ethnic groups. Younger African secondary school pupils (at key stage 2) were found to be behind their white British peers but to have subsequently achieved similar levels of educational attainment. However, black Caribbean pupils were found not to close the gap with their white British peers. In the British case, African newcomers did better than pupils of (third-generation) Caribbean origin; like their Irish counterparts, their parents were comparatively well educated. Yet the group that consistently experience the lowest levels of educational attainment are white British 'working class' pupils.[73] A voluminous academic literature emphasises the role of cultural-capital disparities in the reproduction of educational disadvantage on the basis of both class and 'race'. Those without the requisite dispositions to master what sociologists call the hidden curriculum are disproportionately likely to be perceived as deviant. Those students who are psychologically or culturally ill equipped to negotiate dominant social and behavioural rules of belonging are more likely to be stigmatised than others. Some children, on the basis of socio-economic status and where they live, are more likely to have a cultural-capital advantage than others. Children learn much from their peers, including how to expand or limit their aspirations. Some secondary schools routinely send most of their pupils to third-level education, others send hardly any. Some children inter-nalise expectations of future academic success, others learn early that such futures are not for them. The parents most aware of educational inequalities are often those best equipped to avoid them on behalf of their children and better able to afford to live close to well-regarded schools. The necessary concern is that a system that so strongly reproduces socio-economic and cultural-capital inequalities might now disproportionately fail some immigrant communities.

A scenario can be envisaged whereby the effects of racism, cultural-capital deficits and poverty become compounded for some immigrants, producing new patterns of intergenerational exclusion alongside those already experi-enced by some white Irish. *Dublin 15* alluded to such risks; it depicted the history of socio-economic segregation within Irish education as 'a deep systematic fissure'. Institutionalised inequality, bad planning and increased segregation around schooling were each perceived as now contributing to social fragmentation in D15.[74]

Challenges

The 'social lift' wager implicit in Irish educational policy is that the human-capital advantage of many immigrants will transfer into a cultural-capital advantage amongst their children. In nearly every study of newcomers in Irish schools an immigrant human-capital advantage is implied. The 2006 Census found that over half (52.3 percent) of the non-Irish/UK-born living in Dublin (the parents of newcomer children), had third-level qualifications, as compared with 34.6 percent among natives. The 2006 Census found that 41 percent of Nigerians (Ireland's largest African community) had completed a degree or higher-level qualification and a further 17 percent had completed a non-degree third-level qualification, making them better educated than the host Irish population; an equivalent educational advantage has been identified amongst Africans in the United Kingdom. Furthermore, the implicit wager is that human-capital advantage can counter the immigration gap in earnings and the segregation factors that have resulted in disproportionate numbers of newcomer children enrolling in deprived schools. Both *Dublin 15* and *Adapting to Diversity* suggest grounds for optimism in the case of many white newcomers but not, as perceived by teachers, in that of many African children.

Dublin 15 refers to the disproportionate poverty encountered by many African families. Whilst African parents arc likely to be well educated, a disproportionate number are now also likely to have long post-migration histories of unemployment and social exclusion. Arguably, their current marginalisation is in large part due to the deliberate social exclusion many encountered as asylum seekers, alongside experiences of racist discrimination.[75]

The findings of *Dublin 15* highlight the risks to future social cohesion in under-investing in newcomer education and diverse communities, a message that is all too likely to fall on deaf ears in the midst of Ireland's financial crisis. Respondents emphasised the value of building up contacts between schools and the parents of newcomers as a practical means of addressing the kinds of communication difficulties teachers perceived as cultural conflict. What seemed to work best, according to D15 interviewees, were parenting classes organised by schools in conjunction with the Home School Community Liaison Scheme, although such provision, like various other kinds of support services, was under-resourced. Many teachers interviewed in the D15 study highlighted difficulties resulting from poorly resourced support services such as the Education Welfare Board (EWB), responsible for ensuring pupil attendance ('it's a joke', 'the EWB is simply not able to cope'), and the National Educational Psychological Service, responsible for assessing pupils for special needs support; even where pupil intake had tripled in D15, schools were not able get increased access to such support services.[76]

Dublin 15 emphasised that many factors that affected educational outcomes were outside the control of individual schools. D15 interviewees recounted how schools and Irish children welcomed newcomers but described 'patience fatigue' amongst teachers and children in response to the dislocations caused by large numbers of newcomer children, especially those who arrived 'cold' into classrooms in the middle of the school year, and by excessive turnover of class composition. The report documented an overall 'sense of fragmentation' that put considerable organisational pressures on schools and undermined cohesion within the classroom.

Dublin 15 argued that having to deal with such pressures without credible levels of government support affected the perceptions of both teachers and Irish parents. Amongst the former, 'positive motivation and an appetite for making inclusion happen ... [was] unlikely to be sustained'; the latter would increasingly seek to withdraw their children from such surroundings.[77] Again and again, it emphasised that bad planning or an absence of any planning and a credibility gap between aspirational rhetoric and the situation on the ground were responsible for a growing latent hostility towards immigrants in the area.

Several reports published by the Joseph Rowntree Foundation in the United Kingdom suggest lessons for the Irish case. These emphasise that successful integration depends considerably on local perceptions of the impact of immigrants upon local infrastructure and the perceived social cost in terms of access to schools, services and housing. The arrival of new immigrants in deprived neighbourhoods can serve to increase competition for scarce resources and fuel animosity amongst existing residents.[78] The reports emphasised the need for central government leadership in supporting local communities to meet the challenges of new immigration.[79] Each of these studies suggests that large-scale immigration imposes social costs upon some host communities more than on others, resulting in potential damage to social cohesion. Each counsels against complacency and emphasises the need to continually invest in the social fabric at a community level.[80] The lesson for Ireland is that concrete actions in specific communities matter more than do national-level integration or anti-racism rhetoric.

Dublin 15 placed considerable emphasis on what might be termed social cohesion factors. It was somewhat ambivalent about pursuing an intercultural curriculum whilst failing to build real opportunities for engagement between children from different cultural backgrounds. Cultural exchanges in the classroom, it suggested, may be superficial, a kind of 'voyeuristic gaze' at the 'other' that unintentionally reinforces cultural hierarchies. What seemed to work best, it argued, was what might be termed a social-capital approach. *Dublin 15* found that newcomer children were far less likely to be involved in clubs or youth activities outside the school, in comparison to Irish children ('The children also commented that in many of their clubs, there were few children from other countries'). There was evidence that some newcomer children were becoming involved in after-school activities and in local community and support groups; teachers saw this as evidence of positive integration and were keen to encourage this for 'their children'. As put by one teacher: 'There is huge potential for sport groups etc. building up links with newcomer children and helping their integration through getting to know other children but also helping their language development.' But teachers highlighted the general shortage of such activities, particularly in the newer developing areas where groups such as the scouts and sports groups 'were only in their infancy'. Interviewees considered that special initiatives were needed so as to develop youth clubs and activities in such areas, with a special brief to be given for the promotion of inclusion of ethnic minorities. Here, *Dublin 15* suggested, was an obvious area to build integration and social cohesion within communities.[81]

Notes

1 C.W. Mills, *The Sociological Imagination* (Harmondsworth: Penguin, 1959)
2 Archbishop Diarmuid Martin, 'The Role of Education in the New Ireland', address to the NUI Convocation Centenary Annual Public Lecture at St Patrick's College Maynooth, Co. Kildare, 10 April 2008
3 Section 7.3c of the Equal Status Act (2000) states that faith-based primary and

post-primary schools (the overwhelming majority) are permitted to discriminate against persons from outside their faith: 'Where the establishment is a school providing primary or post-primary education to students and the objective of the school is to provide education in an environment which promotes certain religious values, it admits persons of a particular religious denomination in preference to others or it refuses to admit as a student a person who is not of that denomination and in the case of a refusal, it is proved that the refusal is essential to maintain the ethos of the school.'

4 Rosita Boland, 'Faith before Fairness', *Irish Times*, 8 September 2007
5 *Ibid.*
6 *Ibid.*
7 E. McGorman and C. Sugrue, *Intercultural Education: Primary Challenges in Dublin 15* (Dublin: Department of Education and Science, 2007)
8 Economic and Social Research Institute, *Adapting to Diversity: Irish Schools and Newcomer Students* (Dublin: ESRI, 2009), p. 9
9 *Adapting to Diversity*, p. 41
10 B. Fanning, T. Hasse and N. O'Boyle, 'Well-being, Cultural Capital and Social Inclusion: Immigrants in the Republic of Ireland', *Journal of Immigration and Integration* (forthcoming)
11 E. Smith, M. Darmody, F. McGinnity and D. Byrne, *What Do We Know About Large Scale Immigration and Irish Schools?* ESRI Research Bulletin 2009/2/6 (Dublin: Economic and Social Research Institute, 2009), p. xiii
12 *Dublin 15*, p. 19
13 *Adapting to Diversity*, p. 36
14 E. Smith *et al.*, *What Do We Know?*
15 OECD, *Where Immigrant Students Succeed: A Comparative Review of Performance and Engagement in PISA 2003* (Paris, OECD, 2006)
16 *Adapting to Diversity*, p. 67
17 *Ibid.*
18 *Ibid.*, p. 47
19 *Ibid.*, p. 58
20 *Ibid.*, p. 67
21 The tracking exercise considered 37 out of 375 class groups across the D15 schools. There was 'no evidence that tracking different classes would yield different results'. *Dublin 15*, p. 60
22 *Adapting to Diversity*, p. 61
23 Quotation from head teacher of 'Brayton Square', *Adapting to Diversity*, p. 62
24 *Ibid.*, p. 67
25 *Ibid.*, p. 65
26 *Ibid.*, p. 65
27 *Ibid.*, p. 66
28 *Ibid.*, p. 66
29 In order to qualify for English Language Support (ELS) assistance from the Department of Education and Science, schools must submit a detailed application form indicating the English-language proficiency of children for whom they are looking for assistance. (The form is 'Language Proficiency of Non-national Pupils'). The

form grades English-language proficiency into three bands: grade 1, very poor comprehension of English and very limited spoken English; grade 2, understands sufficient English for basic communication; grade 3, has competent communication skills in English. Grades 1 and 2 are considered by DES as eligible for support. Until recently pupils born in Ireland (of non-citizen parents) who fell into grades 1 and 2 were refused support.

30 *Dublin 15*, p. 77
31 *Adapting to Diversity*, p. xv
32 *Ibid.*, p. 158
33 *Ibid.*, p. 151
34 *Ibid.*, p. 153
35 *Ibid.*, p. 33
36 E. Nowlan, 'Underneath the Band-Aid: Supporting Bilingual Students in Irish Schools', *Irish Educational Studies* 27.3 (2008), 253–266, p. 259
37 *Ibid.*, p. 261
38 *Dublin 15*, p. 78
39 *Adapting to Diversity*, p. 50
40 The SDQ has been used in more than 50 countries. It is available in over 40 languages. W. Woerner, B. Fleitlich-Bilyk, R. Martinussen, J. Fletcher, G. Cucchiaro, P. Dalgalarrodo, M. Lui and R. Tannock, 'The Strengths and Difficulties Questionnaire Overseas: Evaluations and Applications of the SDQ beyond Europe', *European Child Psychiatry* 13 (2004), suppl. 2, 1147–54, p. 1147. See Youth in Mind, *Information for Researchers and Professionals about the Strengths and Difficulties Questionnaire*, www.sdqinfo.com
41 G. Lindsay *et al.*, *Parenting Early Intervention Pathfinder Evaluation* (London: Department for Children, Schools and Families, 2008)
42 Fanning, Hasse and O'Boyle, 'Well-being, Cultural Capital and Social Inclusion'
43 *Adapting to Diversity*, p. 51
44 *Ibid.*, p. 175
45 From a study of eight primary and post-primary schools undertaken in 2002, D. Devine, 'Welcome to the Celtic Tiger? Teacher Responses to Immigration and Increasing Diversity in Irish Schools', *International Studies in Sociology of Education* 15 (2005) 49–70, p. 64
46 *Ibid.*, p. 64
47 *Dublin 15*, p. 15
48 *Adapting to Diversity*, p. 151
49 Devine, 'Welcome to the Celtic Tiger?'; Fanning, Hasse and O'Boyle, 'Well-being, Cultural Capital and Social Inclusion'
50 G.J. Duncan, 'Income and Child-Well-Being', the 2005 Geary Lecture (Dublin: Economic and Social Research Institute, 2005)
51 J. Shonkoff and D. Phillips (eds), *From Neurons to Neighbourhood: The Science of Early Childhood Development* (Washington, DC: National Academy Press, 2000)
52 *Adapting to Diversity*, p. 154
53 *Ibid.*, p. 64
54 *Dublin 15*, p. 67
55 *Ibid.*, p. 69
56 *Adapting to Diversity*, p. 67

57 Nowlan, 'Underneath the Band-Aid', p. 262
58 *Dublin 15*, p. 78
59 *Ibid.*, p. 67
60 *Ibid.*, p. 88
61 *Ibid.*, p. 68
62 *Adapting to Diversity*, p. 106
63 *Dublin 15*, p. 88
64 *Adapting to Diversity*, pp. 95–86
65 *Ibid.*, p. 184
66 Cited in Devine, 'Welcome to the Celtic Tiger?', p. 63
67 P. Bourdieu, 'The social space and the genesis of groups', *Theory and Society* 14.6 (1985), 723–744
68 P. Bourdieu *et al.*, *The Weight of the World: Social Suffering in Contemporary Society* (Cambridge: Polity Press, 1999), p. 186
69 See various contributions to P. Connolly and B. Troyna (eds), *Researching Racism in Education: Politics, Theory and Practice* (Buckingham: Open University Press, 1998)
70 P. Connolly, 'Introduction', in Connolly and Troyna (eds), *Researching Racism in Education*, p. 3
71 On disproportionate exclusions see M. Blair. 'The Myth of Neutrality', in Connolly and Troyna (eds), *Researching Racism in Education*, p. 17, on disproportionate criticisms see B. Tizzard, P. Blatchford, J. Burke, C. Sarquhan and I. Plewis, *Young Children and the Inner City* (Hove: Lawrence Erlbaum, 1988), on different perceptions of Asian and Afro-Caribbean children see M. Mac an Ghaill, *Young, Gifted and Black: Student–Teacher Relations in Schooling Black Youth* (Milton Keynes: Open University Press, 1988), p. 64
72 S. Strand, 'Do Some Schools Narrow the Gap? Differential School Effectiveness by Ethnicity, Gender, Poverty and Prior Attainment', paper presented to the International Congress for School Effectiveness and Improvement, Vancouver, Canada, 4–7 January 2009, p. 4
73 S. Strand, *Minority Ethnic Pupils in the Longitudinal Study of Young People in England*, DCSF-RR029, 2007 (Warwick: University of Warwick, Institute of Education/Department for Children, Schools and Families), pp. 4–6
74 *Dublin 15*, pp. 13–14
75 B. Fanning and A. Veale, 'Child Poverty as Public Policy: Direct Provision and Asylum Seeking Children in the Republic of Ireland', *Child Care in Practice* 10.3 (2004). 241–52
76 *Dublin 15*, p. 73
77 *Ibid.*, p. 76
78 D. Robinson and K. Reeve, *Experiences of New Immigration at Neighbourhood Level* (York: Joseph Rowntree Foundation, 2006), p. 16
79 M. Hickman, H. Crowley and N. Mai, *Immigration and Social Cohesion in the UK* (York: Joseph Rowntree Foundation, 2008). Available at: www.jrf.org.uk
80 R.D. Putnam, '*E Pluribus Unum:* Diversity and Community in the Twenty-first Century', *Scandinavian Political Studies* 30.2 (2006), 137–74
81 *Dublin 15*, p. 65

7

Integration as social inclusion

No society can view without deep concern the prospect of a significant minority of people becoming more removed from the incomes and lifestyles of the majority. (National Anti-Poverty Strategy, 1997)

The first major Irish immigration policy statement, *Integration: A Two Way Process* (2000) advocated the integration of refugees and immigrants into Irish society through employment promotion measures and through addressing specific barriers of discrimination, non-recognition of qualifications and lack of fluency in English.[1] The repertoire of barriers to labour market participation was well known by 2000. The same issues cropped up again and again as core issues in many subsequent research and policy reports and within case studies set out by various organisations working with vulnerable and socially excluded migrants. Back in 2000, a substantial percentage of immigrants were asylum seekers; some of these were allowed to work and were found to experience such problems along with what emerged as core problems for many subsequent migrants, namely lesser entitlements to employment training and other kinds of support identified as needed by Irish citizens with equivalent needs.

I recall a conversation with a Department of Justice, Equality and Law Reform (DJELR) official in 2000, a time when the Department was extremely busy with the initial dispersal of asylum seekers. The official described how she had spent most of that day trying to document a single case where an asylum seeker had supposedly registered on a state-funded Foras Áiseanna Saothair (FAS) employment training course, with the aim of putting a stop to it. I had recently participated in research on barriers to employment encountered by the 3,000 or so asylum seekers who had been granted the right to work on a once-off basis – a pragmatic and humane response to an administrative backlog at the time. As part of this initiative FAS piloted an Asylum Seekers Unit in Tallaght; our interviewees included some of those being helped by FAS. Most of our respondents, including those in Tallaght, felt that they needed retraining in order to access the kinds of employment that would make use of their pre-migratory skills and qualifications; they had been told that they were ineligible for state-funded training. Instead, FAS was required to treat these as 'job ready', even those with poor English; they were deemed to be in need of help in finding employment, rather than in need of employment training.[2] Many of our respondents, on the other hand, described being told in job interviews that they needed training. In essence, the security governance mindset to immigration policy described in Chapter 3 required FÁS to disregard the criteria that it used in assessing the needs of Irish citizen clients who were similarly trying to make the transition from welfare to work.

During the following decade new welfare stratifications emerged which deepened the gap between the entitlements of migrants and citizens to some welfare goods and services. One knock-on effect was that their needs proved difficult to address within mainstream social policy debates on social exclusion and inclusion. Report after report detailing with social inclusion and anti-poverty policy kept references to immigrants vague, whilst non-entitled groups such as asylum seekers tended not to be mentioned at all. The officials who wrote such reports were, in essence, avoiding corporate liability; they avoided acknowledging similarities between the needs of socially excluded migrants and socially excluded citizens. The *National Report for Ireland on Strategies for Social Protection and Social Inclusion 2008–2010* illustrates this social-policy shell game. It reiterated the social inclusion objectives set out in earlier social inclusion and social partnership documents, including in the 2007 National Development Plan. These included:

> (d) access for all to the resources, rights and services needed for participation in society, preventing and addressing exclusion, and fighting all forms of discrimination leading to exclusion; and
>
> (e) the active social inclusion of all, both by promoting participation in the labour market and by fighting poverty and social exclusion.[3]

The report contained some references to immigrants, including a specific policy objective of 'facilitating participation in employment, facilitating access to services at national and local level including education and training, income support, health and language training'.[4] Inevitably, the proposal to facilitate fell far short of the aspiration to 'access for all'. There was, so to speak, an unmentioned elephant in the room. Clearly, by all the criteria underpinning Irish social inclusion strategies, many migrants had high levels of need. However, they were also deemed ineligible for programmes aimed at addressing such need. They were effectively excluded from social inclusion policy norms. They were also excluded by omission from the rhetoric accompanying commitments to social inclusion goals. Since 2000, various welfare reforms had undermined the welfare rights of many vulnerable migrants. No reference was made to the 2004 legislation that introduced a two-year habitual residence condition for eligibility to many core benefits, including children's allowances. In this context, no commitments could be made to the inclusion of immigrants within the mainstream of social inclusion policy. Instead, readers were directed towards *Migration Nation*, the 2008 report of the Minister of State on Integration. In effect, the specific measures outlined in *Migration Nation* were off to one side, outside the remit of mainstream social inclusion policy and practice. *Migration Nation* emphasised a 'strong link between integration policy and wider state social inclusion measures, strategies and initiatives', but neither mentioned nor discussed any of these.[5]

At one level, immigrants are a potential target group that Irish social-policy makers have not yet learned to address. At a more insidious level, the increasing differences between the rights of citizens and migrants over time (welfare stratifications) required an institutionalised cognitive dissonance. A bracketed debate on integration, with a presumed aim of including migrants within the mainstream of Irish society, became cordoned off from dominant norms and thinking about how Irish people became integrated into Irish society. This has persisted even after migrants and ethnic minorities were designated as a target group within Irish social inclusion policy. The emphasis of this chapter is firstly, on the 'family resemblance' between integration goals and social inclusion goals within mainstream Irish social policy. Secondly, developing on the discussion of security governance perspectives in Chapter 3, the chapter examines the legal and cognitive barriers that foster the exclusion of migrants from mainstream thinking about social inclusion. Thirdly, drawing on the examples of the former asylum seekers who make up much of Ireland's disproportionately marginal black population and of vulnerable migrants excluded from welfare safety nets, the chapter argues that such state-sanctioned contradictory thinking works to sabotage integration and future social cohesion.

Integration as social inclusion

The case for social inclusion, defined in terms of capacity to participate fully in society, quoted at the beginning of this chapter, was influentially outlined in 1997 in the first *National Anti-Poverty Strategy*.[6] 'Migrants and members of ethnic minority groups' were first envisaged as a distinct target group within Irish social inclusion policy in 2002; the *Revised National Anti-Poverty Strategy* set an objective of ensuring that these are not more likely to experience poverty than majority group members.[7] This signalled (in theory) an integration remit for Irish anti-poverty and social inclusion policy. The still-prevailing 1997 policy definition of social exclusion emphasised that relative income poverty and the relative lack of other material, cultural and social resources precluded them from having a standard of living that is regarded as acceptable by Irish society generally.

There is a broad agreement, evident within the Irish and EU contexts, that the terms 'social inclusion' and 'social exclusion' encompass concerns about

'poverty, deprivation, low educational qualifications, labour market disadvantage, joblessness, poor health, poor housing or homelessness, illiteracy and
innumeracy, precariousness and incapacity to participate in society'.[8] The wider
EU social inclusion agenda that Irish anti-poverty policy reflected includes
normative understandings of the structural causes of poverty and deprivation,
of the role of social policy in promoting social cohesion and, crucially, efforts
to measure social inclusion. The dominant EU and Irish paradigm defines
social exclusion in terms of poverty, related phenomena such as unemployment, the spatial concentration of multiple disadvantages and discrimination.
Here the focus is on processes of exclusion and processes of inclusion, on
relational understandings of social capital, on access to the resources needed
to achieve security and also to the attainment of societal norms. A normative focus on social cohesion, defined in terms of 'shared values, feelings of
common identity, trust, a sense of belonging to the same community' can also
be identified.[9] Also implied is the importance of what Sen refers to as capabilities; in addition to emphasising skills and language competencies, a number of
European-wide studies of social exclusion and social diversity view rights as a
perquisite of social inclusion. As explained in one such study:

> We understand the problems of social exclusion and the possibilities for social
> inclusion in terms of the problems and possibilities of access to social rights. For
> our purposes the key social rights and packages of social goods are those relating
> to work, income and recognition. We refer to these rights and social goods as
> 'personal social capital'… and as 'forms' of inclusion.[10]

The 2005 EU Common Basic Principles of Integration (CBPs) place considerable emphasis on social-policy understandings of integration (integration-
as-social inclusion). The sixth CBP states that: 'Access for immigrants to
institutions, as well as to public and private goods and services, on an equal
basis to national citizens and in a non-discriminatory way is an indispensable
foundation for better integration.' It summarises the integration case against
welfare nepotism (discrimination in favour of co-ethnics or fellow citizens)
in the following terms:

> The adverse implications of such marginalisation continue to be seen across
> generations. Restrictions on the rights and privileges of non-nationals should
> be transparent and be made only after consideration of the integration conse-
> quences, particularly on the descendants of immigrants.[11]

Such rights are emphasised as a means to an end (the promotion of integration
and social inclusion) rather than as an end in themselves (as an entitlement of
citizenship). What an EU integration-as-social inclusion project might involve
is most clearly spelt out by the empirical indicators devised on behalf of the
European Commission. These established a baseline 'common language' for
conceptualising and measuring social inclusion.[12] The purpose was to define

core EU social values and place a normative pressure on member states to pursue social inclusion policies, to 'define social indicators conceptually, to apply them empirically, and to use them in politics'.[13] A key mechanism here has been the requirement that member states devise National Action Plans on Social Inclusion (NAPincl) The eleventh (and final) CBP proposed these as the basis of EU integration-as-social inclusion projects:

> Although it is a process rather than an outcome, integration can be measured and policies evaluated. Sets of integration indicators, goals, evaluation mechanisms and benchmarking can assist measuring and comparing progress, monitor trends and developments. The purpose of such evaluation is to learn from experience, a way to avoid possible failures of the past.

Ireland became an early adopter of social-inclusion policy discourse, plans and targets; in 1997 it became the first EU member state to adopt a national poverty-reduction target.[14] Although migrants were identified as a social-inclusion target group in 2002 they still remain excluded to a considerable extent from such institutionalised thinking about social inclusion. The contradiction between security-driven welfare stratifications and growing welfare ethnic nepotism (distinctions between social rights of 'nationals' and 'non-nationals'), on the one hand, and the embedded logic of the social inclusion case for meaningful access to welfare goods and services, on the other, has proved difficult to bridge. Chapter 3 argued that the dominance of economist and securocrat perspectives in immigration and integration policy debates contributed to a de-emphasis on the role of social policy in Irish integration debates. In essence, the problem is a cognitive one as a well as a legal one of lesser immigrant rights and entitlements. Societal knowledge and experience of why and how the social exclusion of citizens should to be addressed becomes ignored in debates about the integration of immigrants. In effect, immigrants become excluded from thinking about social inclusion.

Exclusion from social inclusion

During the peak years of immigration before and after EU enlargement in 2004 there was little or no political debate in Ireland on either cultural integration or the role of social policy in furthering integration. The main debates at that time (Ireland hosted a conference on integration as part of its 2004 EU presidency) emphasised the role of the labour market as the principal instrument of integration.[15] Policy development gathered pace in 2007, with the establishment of Cabinet post with responsibility for integration. The first comprehensive report on integration policy was published the following year. *Migration Nation: Statement on Integration Strategy and Diversity Management* sets out the following 'key principles' which were claimed to inform Irish state policy on integration:

- A partnership approach between the Government and nongovernmental organisations, as well as civil society bodies to deepen and enhance the opportunities for integration
- A strong link between integration policy and wider state social inclusion measures, strategies and initiatives
- A clear public policy focus that avoids the creation of parallel societies, communities and urban ghettoes, i.e. a mainstream approach to service delivery to migrants
- A commitment to effective local delivery mechanisms that align services to migrants with those for indigenous communities.[16]

Overall, the principles could be seen to endorse integration-as-social inclusion. A number of specific measures identified in *Migration Nation* had fallen by the wayside by the end of 2008. These included additional funding for migrants in schools (undermining linguistic integration goals) and plans for a Commission on Integration. The stated reason was the need to make cuts in public expenditure in response to the global financial crisis. But state-funded bodies with anti-discriminatory remits were subjected to hugely disproportionate cuts (the Equality Authority) or were shut down altogether (the National Consultative Committee on Racism and Interculturalism).[17] The Combat Poverty Agency (CPA), which had for many years advocated the expansion of social inclusion policy in Ireland, was abolished.[18] Arguably, Irish governance had purged itself of many of its institutional advocates of integration-as-social inclusion. Significantly, *Migration Nation* (unlike the earlier *Integration: A Two Way Process*) did not cite or paraphrase social inclusion documents. It made no specific commitments to integration-as-social inclusion.

The CPA had been an early advocate of the inclusion of vulnerable migrants in thinking about social inclusion. It funded a number of Irish Refugee Council studies, beginning with *Asylum Seekers and the Right to Work in Ireland* (2000), *Beyond the Pale: Asylum Seeking Children and Social Exclusion in Ireland* (2001) and *Food, Nutrition and Poverty amongst Asylum Seekers in North-West Ireland.*[19] In effect, such studies presumed that the needs of asylum seekers should be considered using the same standards that were applied to marginal Irish citizens. Insofar as direct provision removed asylum seekers from the mainstream welfare safety nets it was hardly surprising that these studies found that asylum seekers experienced very high levels of deprivation. In 1997, 13 percent of Irish children lived in households where income levels fell below the 40 percent poverty line.[20] The 2001 study found that asylum seeker children on 'direct provision' typically were living below the 20 percent poverty line.[21] It argued that the lesser entitlements of asylum seekers to welfare, combined with the lack on an entitlement to work, were the main causes of such extreme child poverty. The exclusions experienced by asylum seekers and their children within Irish society are largely the result of having lesser rights and entitlements than Irish citizens. The barriers to integration that they faced were largely ones that been put in place by the state; they were deemed, from the dominant security perspective, to be outside of Irish society, whilst living within Irish communities. Local organisations seeking to respond to vulnerable immigrants in the group have argued that such welfare stratifications have made them hard to help. For example, a 2006 study, *Building a Diverse Mayo*, described the frustrations of local social workers and community groups attempting to make a 'special case' for funding to enable asylum seeker children to attend a local play group; Community Welfare Officers were reluctant to provide financial support because responsibility for asylum seeker childcare lay with the DJELR.[22]

In 2000 the Irish government removed asylum seekers from the mainstream welfare system; in effect, they became the responsibility of the DJELR, an entity with hitherto no history in the provision of welfare goods and services and one charged with advocating their deliberate exclusion from Irish society. The direct provision rates introduced in 2000 were considerably lower than the entitlements of citizens. Direct provision rates remained frozen year after year from 2000 to 2010, a time during which benefit rates within the mainstream citizen welfare system rose year on year. This strength of resolve (to ensure that the material circumstances of asylum seekers did not improve) points to the strength of influence of the security governance perspective discussed in Chapter 3.

In effect, asylum seekers were required by the state to live parallel lives to those of other members of Irish society. In some domains they had the same rights and entitlements as Irish citizens; examples here include rights to healthcare, to primary and secondary education (up to 18 years of age) and the right to vote in local government elections. In other domains they clearly had lesser rights and entitlements; examples include the absence of a right to work and the lower rates of benefits that they received under 'direct provision'. In yet other domains asylum seekers were normatively treated by the state *as if* they had lesser rights than Irish citizens, when, under Irish law, this was not the case.

A key example here has been the treatment of unaccompanied minors. The Refugee Act (1996) specifically extends the provisions of the Child Care Act (1991) to refugees and asylum seekers. Under the Child Care Act the Health Service Executive is required to 'promote the welfare of children in its area who are not receiving adequate care and protection'. However, what has emerged is a distinctly two-tiered system of child protection.[23] A 2003 International Organisation on Migration (IOM) report concluded that unaccompanied minors in Ireland were not being afforded the same child-protection rights as Irish children.[24] The IOM report identified that the ratio of social workers to children was 1:50, when the acknowledged desirable ratio was 1:12.[25] It revealed that some 250 separated children had disappeared from the 'care' of the health boards in the Dublin areas since 2001. These accounted for close to 10 percent of the total number (2,717) of separated children who were placed in state care between 1999 and 2003; by 2007 some 441 children had gone missing out of total of 5,300 unaccompanied minors who had passed through state care. Of these, only 51 (12 percent) were eventually accounted for.[26]

In essence, migrant children in care received a lesser standard of protection than equivalent Irish children. Irish children in residential care are covered the National Standards for Children's Residential Centres Regulations.[27] The conceit that permitted lesser standards of protection for migrant children in residential care was the administrative designation of their accommodation as adult or homeless hostels under Part 11, Section 5 of the Child Care Act (1991). Such hostels were deemed to fall outside the remit of the Social Services Inspectorate, an anomaly that has persisted despite media exposés and acknowledgement of the problems by the Minister of Health.[28] In May 2009 a Seanad (Senate) debate on the Ryan Report on Institutional Abuse noted that residential facilities for unaccompanied minors were still 'exempt from inspection'.[29] As a result, children as young as 12 years continued to live in hostels run by caretakers with little training in dealing with vulnerable minors and without meaningful outside scrutiny of conditions and standards.[30] A 2009 report by the Ombudsman for Children found that more than 120 separated children were housed in hostels with no case staff after 5pm. It identified stark differences between standards in such hostels and conditions in registered residential centres for children. It gave examples of separated children being left to sleep on bare mattresses because bedding had not been provided.[31] Many, the author of the 2005 IOM study emphasised, were at risk of ending up in the sex trade or in forced labour.[32] Similar concerns have been articulated in all subsequent studies of unaccompanied minors.[33] As put by a 2009 Children's Rights Alliance report, these were that separated children remained 'hugely exposed to risks, including traffickers who may lure them into prostitution and illegal exploitative work'.[34] Others, according to such reports, vanish due to fears of deportation on becoming 'timed-out' at 18 years of age.

Safety nets and welfare stratifications

In May 2004, to coincide with the enlargement of the European Union, the Irish government decided to remove many benefit entitlements from new immigrants and their families for an initial two-year period. Under the Social Welfare (Miscellaneous Provisions) Act (2004) immigrants not habitually resident in Ireland for two years were deemed not entitled to Unemployment Assistance, Old Age (Non-Contributory) and Blind Pension, Widow(er)'s and

Orphan's (Non-Contributory) pensions, One Parent Family Payment, Carer's Allowance, Disability Allowance, Supplementary Welfare Allowance (other than one-off exceptional and urgent needs payments) and Children's Allowances. Unsurprisingly, the removal of welfare safety nets and the loss of entitlement to children's allowances placed immigrants at disproportionate risk of poverty.

Some of the issues were highlighted by a 2005 report, *Social Protection Denied: The Impact of the Habitual Residency Condition on Migrant Workers*, published by the Migrants Rights Centre Ireland (MRCI).[35] The report emphasised that the way in which habitual residency was interpreted made it difficult for migrant workers on work permits working in low-paid and insecure employment to demonstrate their entitlement. One of the difficult-to-meet criteria in the regulations was a need to demonstrate that Ireland was their 'centre of interest'. The MCRI study found that applicants on one-year work permits were deemed not to be eligible and that Community Welfare officers could no longer refer homeless migrant workers who were not considered habitually resident to emergency accommodation. The criteria worked against the more vulnerable. For example, having a long-term lease on a property or having a mortgage implied 'future intention' to remain in Ireland in a way that staying with friends did not. A history of permanent employment in Ireland counted more in an applicant's favour than did one of successive, unbroken, short-term contracts. Migrants whose families lived in their countries of origin attracted the presumption of not being habitually resident, whereas having a home, close family in Ireland, being a member of clubs or holding Irish bank accounts counted in an applicant's favour. MRCI case studies illustrate the ways in which such restrictions compounded experiences of workplace vulnerability.

José arrived in County Galway from Brazil in 2004. He worked with heavy machinery and seriously injured his fingers in June 2005. He was medically certified for twelve weeks. He had made insufficient social insurance contributions to qualify for a disability payment. He was denied social assistance payments under the habitual residence condition. Friends from his home country supported him. His employer pressured him to return to work; he did so after seven weeks, in spite of medical advice.[36]

Natasha arrived in County Cavan from Latvia in May 2003, prior to EU enlargement, to work in a mushroom factory on a renewable work permit. She worked six days a week for up to 16 hours per day. She became unemployed when the factory closed down and then found work with a pet food manufacturer in county Longford on a five-month contract. Her contract was not renewed. She sought unemployment assistance in February 2005. She was refused payment because she had returned to Latvia for a one-week visit to finalise her divorce; the Deciding Officer considered that her centre of interest was not in Ireland and so she was deemed not habitually resident. However, her adult son also lived in Longford; she asserted that both had made Ireland their home. She received support from Longford Partnership in getting a P45 issued to her. However, the document omitted her first six months in employment. There was no record that social insurance contributions had been made by her employer on her behalf, even though she had a work permit and had had income tax and PSRI contributions deducted from her pay. She approached the Community Welfare Officer for support. She was given a one-off payment to be used to return to Latvia.[37]

Ravi arrived in Ireland in October 2003 to work in an Indian restaurant. He paid his employer €10,000 for a 'work permit' (in essence, a charge he was required to pay to get his job in Ireland) that in fact cost his employer €500. He had been promised €1,000 in wages per month but never received anything like that amount; his pay was cut from €125 per week to €80 per week. In July 2004 his one-year work permit and the residency stamp on his passport expired. In effect, his employer had engineered his undocumented status. From September 2008 he was paid nothing at all. As an undocumented worker he was not entitled to social assistance or emergency accommodation. He had to rely on friends for accommodation and food. He successfully took his case to the Labour Relations Commission and was awarded some compensation from his employer.

Somewhat similarly, Anish had worked as a cook in an Indian takeaway since 2002; his wife and teenage son lived with him in Ireland. Wages were paid in cash and he received no contract of employment. When Anish lost his job in August 2004 his family became homeless. Friends took them in. He applied for Supplementary Welfare Allowance but was refused because his 'centre of interest' was not in Ireland because he was now without employment. Because he had no P45 the Community Welfare Officer referred his case to the DJELR. The DJELR asserted that he had no 'current status' in Ireland; in fact he had a valid visa and work permit. He won his case before the Labour Relations Commission for unfair dismissal but became (at the time of research in 2005) undocumented and remained reliant on his friends.[38]

The MRCI research detailed many examples where migrants were not deemed eligible for social assistance and Child Benefit. Those treated worst by their employers were particularly at risk of failing habitual residence tests, for example, in the aforementioned cases where employers did not register employees or give them contracts.[39] Child Benefit is crucially important to low-income families but tends to be denied to families who do not meet habitual residence criteria. The habitual residence condition also applied to Irish citizens; by May 2005 some 454 Irish citizen applicants had their applications for benefits rejected on habitual residence grounds, whilst some 4,624 such persons were deemed to be habitually resident.[40] John and Katrina arrived in County Cork from Germany with their child in October 2004 and applied for Child Benefit in January 2005. They were subsequently deemed eligible from May 2005. The stated reason why no payments were due from January was that John had not been in employment at the time; he was not deemed to have fulfilled habitual residence criteria until he obtained a full-time job in May.[41]

Various MRCI case studies depicted difficulties in supporting vulnerable migrants in their dealings with several statutory agencies and administrative processes. Any single case might involve dealing with the Departments of Enterprise Trade and Employment (work permits), Justice, Equality and Law Reform (visa issues), the Labour Relations Commission (workplace exploitation) and the Health Services Executive (emergency needs payments) while at the same time trying to make sense of and explain to clients why they had been refused social assistance or emergency accommodation by habitual residence rulings by the Department Social and Family Affairs. Add to this language difficulties, and unfamiliarity with Irish bureaucracy, tax codes and welfare systems amongst vulnerable migrants, people who typical find it difficult to ask for help in the first instance.[42] In effect, such restrictions have reinforced workplace exploitation.

Unsurprisingly, the Habitual Residence Condition (HRC) has met with criticism from organisations working to support vulnerable migrants. A 2006 submission to the Homeless Agency by the National Consultative Committee on Racism and Interculturalism (NCCRI) stated that there was increasing evidence that some vulnerable migrants were relying on charitable institutions for food and shelter:

> The HRC is leading to additional pressure on voluntary and community sector organisations, particularly those who supply hostel accommodation and free or cheap food. Already limited resources are stretched even further to assist vulnerable migrants who have found themselves in extremely difficult situations. Cases have been reported of people being forced to live on the street or living in overcrowded accommodation with friends. People have been found sleeping in cars in shopping centre car parks or in tents in public parks and even in the grounds of Dublin City Council's Municipal offices.[43]

The NCCRI submission was particularly critical of the removal of universal entitlement to Child Benefit under the HRC. This, it argued, would deepen the levels of poverty to which asylum seeker children and their families were exposed. Furthermore, it was 'contrary to the intent of the National Action Plan Against Poverty which', it asserted, 'includes specific commitments in relation to migrants and ethnic minorities'.[44] Yet a 2006 European Anti-Poverty Network (EAPN Ireland) conference on the National Action Plan concluded that there was 'no serious integration policy' for new minorities. This was 'passing on a message to wider society that migrant workers are outsiders' and leading to the alienation of immigrants and their families.[45] Crosscare (the Social Care Agency of the Dublin Archdiocese, which ran a number of 'food centres' used by immigrants) emphasised how the HRC hampered access by vulnerable migrants to homelessness services. Entitlement to these often depended on eligibility for social protection. As described by the policy officer of the Crosscare Migrant Project in October 2008:

> Previously if you went to a homeless shelter they'd ask you very few questions. Now they ask you lots of questions and if you don't give the right answers they'll turn you away.[46]

Unless applicants could confirm that they had lived in Ireland for two years they often could not be helped. Various media accounts of homeless migrants in 2008 recorded the stories of vulnerable homeless migrants and those who queued at the twenty-first century equivalent of soup kitchens for food. Mohammad slept rough in a disused car park and hid his homelessness from those he met at the mosque. Pavel from Lithuania described 'in limited English' becoming homeless after becoming unemployed. Dorotha moved to Ireland from Poland with her twin daughters in 2007; previously she worked as a fashion designer; in Ireland she got a job as a cleaner on a construction site. Although she had somewhere to live she couldn't afford to feed her children.[47] In April 2009 there was substantial media coverage of queues of up to 400 for food parcels at the Capuchin Day Centre (one of the Crosscare projects) in north inner-city Dublin.[48]

Inadequate provision and legacies of exclusion

From a 'bottom-up' perspective the integration debate appears very different from how it is depicted either within the security/economic perspectives that dominate Irish immigration policy or in the ideological posturing about the dangers of multiculturalism that tends to dominate media commentary. NGOs, religious and other voluntary organisations and local support groups have in various ways sought to address the needs of newcomers deemed not entitled to support from the state; here they attempt to fill an obvious vacuum. Like equivalent organisations working in other areas, such as disability, they are also at the cutting edge on the ground of responsiveness and policy innovation. Their advocacy on behalf of individual clients or their efforts to promote reform backed by research (often arising out of such advocacy) make a significant contribution to Irish integration expertise, albeit one that tends to be ignored by policy makers.

At its best, the voluntary sector is the bearer of broader definitions of social membership than those institutionalised by the state. The barriers that prevent state agencies from offering a service to non-citizens (or thinking about their needs) do not apply to voluntary organisations. Some voluntary organisations have had to develop services that mirror those provided by the state to which some migrants are not entitled; these include services crucial to integration, such as education and employment training. Much such work seeks to ameliorate the exclusionary consequences of non-entitlement to various forms of state provision.

For example, a number of voluntary organisations offer English-language classes to asylum seekers who are not entitled to state-funded programmes specifically restricted to persons with refugee status. Various specialist immigrant advocacy organisations have emerged. Examples include Integrating Ireland, the Refugee Information Service (the two were being amalgamated at the time of writing), the Immigrant Council of Ireland and the Migrant Rights Centre Ireland. Integrating Ireland developed from 2000 to coordinate and support a large 'network of community and voluntary groups working in mutual solidarity to promote and realise the human rights, equality and full integration in Irish society of asylum seekers, refugees and immigrants'. It has focused on providing training and capacity-building programmes, in addition to facilitating research and campaigning; its website hosts a significant body of research into the experiences of immigrants. The Immigrant Council of Ireland (ICI) has similarly supported organisations working on the ground with immigrants; it developed a training programme on migrant rights and entitlements which has been delivered to state agencies, voluntary organisations and community-based groups. In 2006 it became an Independent Law Centre.[49] Furthermore, a number of mainstream voluntary organisations also include a strong focus on migrants in their work, such as Crosscare and the Society of St Vincent de Paul. The somewhat different activism of immigrant-led organisations is considered in the next chapter.

The Vincentian Refugee Centre (VRC) was established by the Vincentian Community and the Society of St Vincent de Paul in 1998. It has developed a range of advocacy and support services in Dublin for 'asylum seekers, refugees and people with permission to reside in the State'. These came to include a housing service for refugees (partly in response to racism in the private rented sector), English-language and literacy training, support services for unaccompanied minors and support and advice in accessing social welfare, health and accommodation. The services provided in a number of cases were in areas where asylum seekers had no statutory entitlement. Similar services are provided by voluntary organisations in places such as Cork (NASC, The Irish Immigrant Support Centre), Galway (The One World Centre), Limerick (Doras) and in Ennis (The Clare Immigrant Support Centre).

A 2007 report marked ten years of service provision by the VRC.[50] This recorded dealing with 5,100 individual client cases on behalf of people from 85 different countries during the previous year; 629 of those were new clients of the Centre. Since almost its inception it had run a homework club for unaccompanied minors. In the year covered by the report, thirty-five children were enrolled for the club, aided by thirty volunteers from the Society of St Vincent de Paul in Trinity College; four had successfully passed the Leaving Certificate and gone on to undertake further studies. VRC workers spent considerable time listening to unaccompanied minors discussing their anxieties about their status. The report recorded that Adijat Okusanya, a 19-year-old, was deported back to Nigeria, despite having no family members there. The project support worker visited her in prison prior to her deportation. Her case had a huge psychological effect on other separated children who knew her at the Centre. Staff spent a lot of time reassuring the children, despite knowing that there was little they could do, should any of them receive a deportation order when they reach age 19.

The VRC sought to keep in contact with such 'aged-out minors', some of whom obtained refugee status. One young woman refugee was successful in her application for family reunification and her child joined her. As the child was unable to speak English, the VRC secured a place for him in a pre-school run by the Society of St Vincent de Paul. The child was able to attend school during the summer and learned sufficient English to begin primary school. This in turn meant that the mother could complete her Leaving Certificate; subsequently the project support worker got a place for her on a FAS course. Another aged-out minor was hospitalised and the project support worker visited her and spent much time with her.

The report described literacy as a problem for many clients; one lone parent from Africa was described as turning up 'daily' looking for help in reading letters she had received from various government departments. Parents of younger children expressed concern that they were falling behind in school because they could not read; in some cases this was because the parents' own literacy skills were poor. It described helping clients who were experiencing difficulties in paying utility bills and other aspects of independent living, many clients having previously become institutionalised within direct provision. Many clients needed considerable support in looking for employment. The Vocational Educational Committee helped clients to prepare CVs, to look for jobs in the newspapers and online, to prepare for interviews, and in some cases clients were accompanied to interviews. Some – those with refugee status – were able to access courses run by FAS, adult education centres and even the university. Clients of the VRC often experienced multiple welfare problems that needed to be addressed before they were in any position to participate in education and employment training. Some had been in the asylum system for years and, as a result, some had not been in employment or had access to education or training for years; they had lived in conditions of enforced dependency; depression was a problem for many.

Some clients were women fleeing abusive relationships. Greta, a single mother with two children, approached the centre having lost her part-time job. They had moved into a bedsit but Greta could not meet the rent. The centre helped Greta to apply for Supplementary Welfare Allowance (SWA), to which she was entitled. Her application was refused and the VRC assisted Greta in lodging an appeal. The appeals officer asked Greta to attend a meeting to discuss her circumstances; the VRC supplied an interpreter. A lengthy meeting ensued, 'on foot of which Greta was advised to seek further documentation in relation to some aspects of her case'. The VRC helped with this and after some considerable time Greta was deemed entitled to SWA. During this time, Greta was 'in dire financial circumstances'. At the request of the VRC the Society of St Vincent de Paul met with her landlord, who, when the situation was explained, agreed to be flexible in relation to rent arrears. Subsequently, Greta had to move from her bedsit to a women's refuge; again, the VRC helped. Eventually, it found a house for her family in Drogheda and assisted her in reapplying for benefits there.

Olga received help in accessing alternative accommodation for herself and her two daughters after she too became a victim of domestic violence. She got help with application forms for benefits, rental accommodation and a referral the Child and Family Services. This in turn led to legal advice about how to secure maintenance from her former partner and how to respond to his application for access to the children. Like Greta, Olga was refused rent allowance on the grounds that her rent exceeded the cap set by the Health Service Executive. Both women were helped to appeal this successfully.

Patricia approached the VRC shortly after securing refugee status. She had a physical disability and, as such, had specific accommodation needs. The VRC housing officer found a ground floor apartment close to public transport in Balbriggan Town Centre but the rent was significantly above the rent allowance cap for a single person. He approached Patricia's GP, requesting letters of support for her rent allowance application. The VRC wrote to the relevant community welfare officer in support of Patricia's application. She was awarded the rent allowance she needed and subsequently moved into her new home. The VRC maintained contact with the landlady to keep her informed of developments. It assisted Patricia in planning her regular rent payments and managing the utility bills in her name. VRC staff visited Patricia on several occasions in order to help her settle. They helped her to apply for Disability Allowance, which was awarded, and pursued SWA arrears. Once her accommodation needs had been addressed, Patricia began to focus on her education; she enrolled on a course in Drogheda Institute of Further Education.

Elizabeth, an African with refugee status, was heavily pregnant and living with her infant child when she received notice to quit from her landlord. At the time, demand for housing was extremely high and even after several weeks the VRC housing officer could not find anything for her. After a brief stay in an unsuitable apartment she became homeless. She was deemed by the Asylum Seekers Unit (ASU) to have made herself intentionally homeless and was refused emergency accommodation. She had to sleep rough in Dublin City Centre for two nights, during which she was assaulted. She presented to the VRC the morning after with extensive facial cuts and bruises. Eventually she obtained temporary accommodation. Her case study, as presented in the VRC report, ended pessimistically:

> Like many of our clients Elizabeth is trapped in a cycle of insecure housing which threatens her health, the welfare of her family, her ability to recover from the trauma she has experienced in her own country and her settlement in Ireland.

During the year covered by its report the VRC succeeded in securing accommodation for thirty-eight people from eleven different countries. Much of its time was spent negotiating with landlords; sometimes, after it had viewed potential accommodation, the landlord decided to rent to someone who was not dependent on rent supplement. Home visits gave clients an opportunity 'to welcome someone into their home and for someone to listen to them without having to queue'. Much of the outreach work focused on practical assistance, such as how to read meters and pay bills. Other work included enrolling clients for literacy classes and other courses and helping clients to find employment. The outreach worker also assisted a number of clients from EU-10 countries who came to the VRC seeking repatriation. All of them had been sleeping rough for several days before coming to the centre.

The VRC also organised men's and women's support groups. The former sought to address 'loneliness as a major factor in the lives of single [asylum seeker] men'; in conjunction with the HSE Refugee Psychology Service it organised a ten-week course to help asylum seeker men learn skills to deal with stressful situations. Again, the women's group sought to address experiences of isolation and stress. Members had typically been living in direct-provision hostels for two years; this detrimentally affected their psychological well-being. As put in the report:

> Many of these women are suffering from mental health problems and experience great loneliness and isolation far from family and friends, often not knowing if their families are alive or dead. We try to put on activities that have a positive and supportive focus for the women. They spend most of their free time alone in the hostels, unable to work with a lot of time to think which most say is one of the hardest aspects of being an asylum seeker. They have too much time with nothing to do but think and worry about the future and their family back home. These women have experienced so much trauma prior to coming to Ireland. In the VRC we provide a safe and welcoming environment for them.

Such case studies emphasise that many asylum seekers are indeed vulnerable; the wider literature on asylum seeker experiences emphasises damaging post-migratory legacies of disempowerment which impede integration once – perhaps several years after their arrival – they become eligible for social inclusion.

A pioneering study of the psychological health of asylum seekers, undertaken in 1999, emphasised how pre-migratory stress was compounded by postmigratory experiences within the asylum system. *Asylum in Ireland: A Public Health Perspective* was undertaken by the Congregation of the Holy Ghost (in conjunction with academic and Health Board medical researchers), who used its findings to develop the voluntary employment training and psychological support services provided by SPIRASI.[51] Coincidentally, I had come to know one of the asylum seekers interviewed as part of the study. Like many, he was African. He desperately wished to complete the third-level education he had begun in Nigeria. He had become acutely dispirited by not being allowed to work and by an overall sense of disempowerment. Soon after his participation in the research he was accosted by two Irish men and thrown through the plate-glass window of a shop. *Asylum in Ireland* reported that 95 percent of respondents found racism and discrimination to be a problem.

It proved all too easy to predict the long-term consequences of the enforced parallel lives asylum seekers were forced to live. In 1999 *Asylum in Ireland* stated that 'those who would eventually be granted status' would find themselves disadvantaged as 'atrophy of skills due to disuse is enhanced by prolonged unemployment'. As noted in Chapter 4, black people living in Ireland have been found to be nine times more likely than others not to be in employment. Many of them began their lives of social exclusion as deliberately excluded asylum seekers. Many were highly educated. The 2006 Census found that 41 percent of (the mostly former asylum seeker) Nigerians in Ireland had thirdlevel qualifications. The disproportionate levels of unemployment they and other black people experience seem partly due to racism and discrimination (found to be experienced by very high percentages of black people in Ireland in study after study). A second explanation of such levels of social exclusion seems to be atrophy of their capabilities or the barriers to their development experienced by some.

Various studies of the barriers to employment faced by African former asylum seekers list factors such as non-recognition of qualifications, the poverty trap of welfare dependency and the difficulties of having to overcome perhaps several years of forced unemployment and racism. The consensus amongst service providers who deal with unemployed migrants is that Africans generally experience the greatest difficulties in accessing employment.[52]

A persistent problem for a decade now has been access barriers to postsecond-level education, including mainstream state-funded adult education, comprehensive English-language training and employment training.[53] Except where they can access services provided by the voluntary sector, adult asylum seekers are, in effect, excluded from language and skills training. Comprehensive voluntary service provision, such as provided by SPIRASI, is only available to a very small percentage of asylum seekers during their years in limbo. Whilst a number of voluntary organisations provide some English-language training – generally a few hours per student per week – this falls considerably short of the 20-hours-per-week immersion programmes that have been found to work best. Such programmes have expanded considerably over the last decade through the Vocational Education Committees (VEC), responsible for adult education. However, access to these depends on residency status; further education colleges require that applicants be in possession of a 'Stamp 4' designation, confirming that they are entitled to work without a work permit.[54]

How deliberate exclusions from measures and supports (deemed necessary for the social inclusion of everyone else) have sabotaged integration is vividly illustrated in interviews with voluntary and statutory service providers conducted in 2008 and 2009 by Ann Kinsella. A service provider interviewed in her 'Welfare Rights and Risks of Poverty' study illustrated the capability deficits of some former asylum seekers who languished without such training for up to several years. These were, according to voluntary sector interviewees, 'not in on the system', they did not have the know-how to successfully gain employment; although they had lived in Ireland for several years they lacked job-seeking skills.[55] One voluntary service provider described receiving almost 100 applications ('loads of them were Nigerian') for a post working with asylum seekers. The organisation would have been delighted to be able to offer the post to a former client. Yet most former asylum seeker candidates could not be short-listed because their application letters and CVs were 'very badly written'. Some were, in effect, begging letters, reflecting host-country practices of pleading with those in authority; they clearly lacked the cultural capital that worked in the Irish case; others could not realise their human capital because of language capacity deficits. As put by one voluntary sector interviewer:

> We interviewed four refugees. None of them were prepared, there was one man ... you could see, he's here I think at this stage in Ireland possibly about eight years; he was actually thinking in French.

As with previous such studies, the lack of recognition of qualifications gained in African countries and the lack of English-language skills (in particular, difficult-to-understand pronunciation and accents) came up as two of the main barriers to employment encountered by Africans. Other issues identified included length of time out of the labour market, lack of experience and lack of social networks:

> Of course here I would say one of the big reasons is the length of time people are out of the job market, if they come here and they're in the asylum process

for a number of years, they're stale, … it's also lack of networks, they don't have the sort of networks that Irish people would have, you know that sort of thing you're down the pub 'oh I want to leave me job' and somebody says 'oh there's something coming up in our place that'd suit you', you know they don't have that. They don't have maybe the right level of English, where their English might be fluent or good conversation, it's very different from ours, I'm talking more about people from Nigeria who obviously speak English as a sort of second or business language but quite different from the way we would do it.

Another recent study undertaken by NASC in Cork also described difficulties experienced by Africans attempting to find employment after many years of enforced unemployment and exclusion from education and training. Many felt discriminated against because of their skin colour. Some recounted incidents that they felt proved that they were being discriminated against. African respondents described being told by employers that there were no vacancies in their areas, only to subsequently see new employees from other immigrant communities being regularly taken on. Some were able to identify prominent businesses which were 'known among the African community' not even to accept CVs from black applicants. One African man described being turned down for a job as a cleaner in favour of a Polish woman who had just arrived in Ireland a few weeks earlier; he had met all the necessary requirements, which he was told were minimum criteria for the job.[56] Another described how both he and the only other African trainee on a FAS course encountered great difficulties in obtaining a work placement; the other sixteen white trainees found placements in a relatively short period of time.[57]

Challenges

Welfare stratifications introduced since 2000 have bequeathed two specific damaging legacies. Firstly, the deliberate and persistent social exclusion of asylum seekers to at least some extent accounts for the exceedingly high unemployment rates experienced by black people living in Ireland. Insofar as many asylum seekers went on to achieve residency status, in particular pre-2004 Referendum cohorts with Irish-born children, it has became retrospectively clear that the security approach has worked to undermine integration. It could not have been any other way, given the contradictory imperatives of security and social inclusion perspectives. The consequent damage of the deliberate social exclusion of asylum seekers continues to be seen in the hugely disproportionate unemployment levels experienced by African former asylum seekers. Those who badly needed to develop English-language, educational or cultural-capital capabilities were impeded from doing so. Some of those with high levels of human capital faced years of enforced atrophy. Africans in particular have run a gauntlet of deliberate exclusion by the Irish state; the

2004 Referendum on Citizenship, which removed the constitutional birthright from children of immigrants was not too implicitly directed against Africans; add to this barriers to employment due to racism and the 'cultural barriers' experienced by African children in schools described in the last chapter. After a decade, Ireland appears close to replicating levels of racialised exclusion that other Western countries have spent decades trying to overcome.

The security case for direct provision and for deliberate exclusion from employment training and other capability-building supports was based on the premise that most of those affected would eventually be deported. The logic of the security perspective breaks down once migrants enter Irish society with even a faint chance of staying. It is better to anticipate from the outset that some will stay and plan for their social inclusion from the outset. Obligatory English-language and skills training that addresses the kinds of capacity deficits highlighted in the VRC case studies would yield dividends in terms of better health and well-being, future employment chances and avoiding the culture of dependency that direct provision excels in fostering. The challenge for the Irish state is to make good the deliberate damage to the capabilities of African and other former asylum seekers and, no less importantly, to avoid such harm to others in future.

Secondly, the HRC hits the most vulnerable migrants. In the current economic downturn, high rates of unemployment are inevitable and disproportionately high rates of immigrant unemployment are likely. The HRC presumes that unwanted migrants will repatriate. However, it seems that many see themselves as having no other choice than to live extremely marginal lives in Ireland. The HRC is currently interpreted so as to routinely disregard time spent by many migrants on temporary but sequential permits when assessing eligibility for support. In effect, this compounds the exploitation encountered by many such workers. Chapter 4 emphasised the capability deficits experienced by many such persons who did not have meaningful access to their rights under Irish employment law. If they are treated as non-persons in social-security decision making it is likely that the exploitation of some will be compounded. Many such migrant workers have capability deficits which need to be addressed. Or, by the various criteria that inform Irish social policy, they are socially excluded.

In 1999 the Macpherson Report in Britain influentially defined institutional racism as the 'collective failure of an organisation to provide an appropriate and professional service to people because of their colour, culture or ethnic origin. It can be seen in processes, attitudes and behaviour which amount to discrimination through unwitting prejudice, ignorance, thoughtlessness and racist stereotyping which disadvantage ethnic minority people.'[58] The consequences of institutional racism (or institutional barriers more generally) are understood to include unequal access to services and unequal outcomes on the basis of ethnicity. As explained by Macpherson, services configured towards the cultures, expectations and needs of majority groups and which wittingly or unwittingly neglect those of minority ethnic groups are likely to produce unequal outcomes for minority ethnic groups. In a context where racism and discrimination meet with disapproval, or indeed sanctions – Ireland's Equal Status Act (2000) prohibits discrimination on the basis of 'race', ethnicity and several other grounds – it would be unsurprising if such institutional barriers were regarded as anything other than organisational failure.

Yet such dysfunctional provision of public services is deliberately promoted in situations where differential entitlements pertain. However bad it is (in every sense of the word) to encounter discrimination in accessing a public service, it is, in practice, worse not to be entitled to such a service at all. Macpherson conducted his inquiry (on policing in London) in a context of racist discrimination against black citizens. Yet in various Western countries overt discrimination against new migrants has deepened through the deliberate removal of various rights and entitlements; in effect, these people encounter structural barriers that might legitimately be depicted in some cases as structural racism. The following definition of structural discrimination is proposed:

> Structural discrimination is the failure of an organisation to provide an appropriate and professional service to persons deemed not to be entitled. It can be seen in legislation, administrative practices and cognitive distinctions that foster and justify the deliberately differential treatment of non-citizens on the basis of administrative categories within which these are classified.

Migrant children in state care experience a patently 'two-tiered' system of institutionalised inequality, their legal rights to equal standards to child protection notwithstanding. Immigrant workers encounter what the MRCI describe as a 'three-tiered' welfare system. It described this new architecture of inequality in the following terms:

> A three-tier system of rights and entitlements to social assistance is emerging in Ireland; entitlements for Irish people, for EEA nationals and for non-EEA nationals. At a policy level, the diminishing of social rights and welfare entitlements is significant. For those affected by this trend, the results can mean poverty and deprivation. While the HRC may appear to be blind to race and nationality because all applicants for assistance must satisfy the condition, the reality is that migrant groups and ethnic minorities are disproportionately affected by the application of the HRC and are being pushed into poverty and deprivation.[59]

Recent debates about integration, including *Migration Nation*, emphasise the dangers of allowing the emergence of parallel societies; the post-9/11 normative preoccupation tends towards anxiety about potential Islamic migrant separatism. Within such debates there is a presumption that migrants pull away, retreat into separatist cultural or religious pillars and refuse to integrate. The hard reality experienced by Ireland's black and largely former asylum seeker population is one of deliberate initial exclusion compounded, by subsequent indifference to the barriers many of them encounter. Other first-generation immigrants will have stories of hardship and discrimination to pass on to their children, though the dangers are that some of these will experience at first hand the intergenerational transmission of social exclusion.

Notes

1 Government of Ireland, *Integration: A Two Way Process* (Dublin: Stationery Office, 2000) p. 29
2 B. Fanning, S. Loyal and C. Staunton, *Asylum Seekers and the Right to Work in Ireland* (Dublin: Irish Refugee Council, 2000) pp. 63–64
3 The 2007 National Development Plan (NDP) cited in Government of Ireland, *The National Report for Ireland on Strategies for Social Protection and Social Inclusion 2008–2010* (Dublin Stationery Office, 2008)
4 *Ibid.*, p. 24
5 Government of Ireland, *Migration Nation: Statement in Integration Strategy and Diversity Management* (Dublin: Stationery Office, 2008), p. 9
6 Government of Ireland (1997) *Sharing in Progress: The National Anti-Poverty Strategy* (Dublin: Official Publications), p. 4
7 Government of Ireland (2002) *Building an Inclusive Society: Revised National Anti-Poverty Strategy*, Dublin: Official Publications, p. 17
8 T. Atkinson, B. Cantillon, E. Marlier and B. Nolan, *Social Indicators: The EU and Social Inclusion* (Oxford: Oxford University Press, 2002), p. 3
9 H. Entzinger and B. Biezeveld, *Benchmarking in Immigrant Integration, Report written for the European Commission, European Research Centre on Migration and Ethnic Relations* (Rotterdam: ERCOMER, 2003)
10 M. Roche, *Comparative Social Inclusion Policies and Citizenship in Europe: Towards a New European Social Model*, Targeted Socio-Economic Research (TSER) SOE2-CT97-3059 (Brussels: European Commission, 2003)
11 Quote from full text of the sixth CBP (Common Basic Principle)
12 H.H. Noll, 'Towards a European System of Social Indicators: Theoretical Framework and System Architecture', *Social Indicators Research* 58.1–3 (2002), 47–87
13 F. Vandenbroucke, 'Foreword', in T. Atkinson, B. Cantillon, E. Marlier and B. Nolan, *Social Indicators: The EU and Social Inclusion* (Oxford: Oxford University Press, 2002), p. vii
14 The National Anti-Poverty Strategy (1997) was developed following the 1995 UN Social Summit in Copenhagen. Atkinson *et al.*, *Social Indicators*, p. 53
15 B. Fanning, 'Integration and Social Policy', in B. Fanning (ed.), *Immigration and Social Change in the Republic of Ireland* (Manchester: Manchester University Press, 2007), p. 252, B. Gray, 'Migrant Integration Policy: A Nationalist Fantasy of Management and Control', *Translocations* 1.1 (2006), 118–138, p. 134
16 Government of Ireland, *Migration Nation*, p. 9
17 Particularly the Equality Authority, which was stripped of more than half of its

funding (several times the level of cuts required of other public bodies).

18 Bodies shut down included Know Racism and the National Consultative Committee on Racism and Interculturalism (responsible for anti-racism policy) and the Combat Poverty Agency, which since the 1970s has played a key role in the development of social inclusion policy. Its functions were transferred to the civil service (Office for Social Inclusion).

19 Fanning, Loyal and Staunton, *Asylum Seekers*; B. Fanning, A. Veale and D. O'Connor, *Beyond the Pale: Asylum Seeking Children and Social Exclusion in Ireland* (Dublin: Irish Refugee Council, 2001); M. Manandhar, S. Share, O. Friel, O. Walsh and F. Hardy *Food, Nutrition and Poverty amongst Asylum Seekers in North-West Ireland*, Combat Poverty Agency Working Paper Series 06/01 (Dublin: Combat Poverty Agency, 2006)

20 B. Nolan, *Child Poverty in Ireland* (Dublin: Oak Tree Press, 2000), p. 13

21 Fanning, Veale and O'Connor, *Beyond the Pale*, p. 25

22 Mayo Intercultural Action, *Building a Diverse Mayo* (Mayo: Mayo Intercultural Action, 2006), p. 105

23 M. Corbett, 'Hidden Children: The Story of State Care for Separated Children', *Working Notes: Facts and Analysis of Social and Economic Issues: Issue 59* (Dublin: Jesuit Centre for Faith and Justice, 2009) p. 20

24 Pauline Conroy, *Trafficking in Unaccompanied Minors in Dublin* (Dublin: International Organisation of Migration, 2003)

25 *Ibid.*, p. 48

26 Corbett, 'Hidden Children', p. 22

27 The National Standards explicitly state that young people in residential care should have a room of their own and that centres must have age-appropriate play and recreational facilities. There is also a requirement that the Health Service Executive be satisfied, by undertaking a proper risk assessment, that centres are safe and secure places for young people to live in. Yet, the poor quality of provision for unaccompanied minors has been the subject of ongoing concern. See B. Fanning, 'Asylum-seeker Children in Ireland: Racism, Institutional Racism and Social Work', in D. Hayes and B. Humphries (eds), *Social Work, Immigration and Asylum: Debates, Dilemmas and Ethical Issues for Social Work and Social Care Practice* (London: Jessica Kingsley Press, 2004) and B. Fanning, *New Guests of the Irish Nation* (Dublin: Irish Academic Press, 2009), pp. 71–81

28 Coverage in early 2005 of the under-protection of migrant children in the care of the Health Services Executive (HSE). Mary Harney, the Minister of Health, indicated that hostels for unaccompanied minors would come under the remit of the Social Services Inspectorate but, according to the Irish Refugee Council, it was 'unclear how high a priority this is'. Irish Refugee Council, *Post-Afghan Hunger Strike Reflections on Ireland's Asylum System*, 24 May 2006. Available at: www. irishrefugeecouncil.ie/press06/afghan.htm

29 Parliamentary Debates, Seanad, vol. 195, p. 13, 27 May 2009

30 Children's Rights Alliance (2009) 'Note on Separated Children'. Available at: www. childrensrights.ie/files/respondingrecommendationsCommissionInquireChildAbus240609.pdf

31 Office of the Ombudsman for Children, *Separated Children Living in Ireland I*

(Dublin, 2009); 'Asylum Seeker Children Placed in Hostels with No Care at Night', *Irish Times*, 20 November 2009

32 Pauline Conroy, cited, *Irish Examiner*, 5 January 2005

33 Corbett, 'Hidden Children', p. 23

34 Children's Rights Alliance, 'Note on Separated Children', p. 2

35 Migrant Rights Centre Ireland, *Social Protection Denied: The Impact of the Habitual Residency Condition on Migrant Workers* (Dublin: MCRI, 2005)

36 *Ibid.*, p. 69

37 *Ibid.*, p. 71

38 *Ibid.*, p. 61

39 *Ibid.*, p. 50

40 *Ibid.*, pp. 47–48

41 *Ibid.*, p. 58

42 *Ibid.*, p. 55

43 National Consultative Committee on Racism and Interculturalism, *Submission to the Homeless Agency on the Homeless Agency Action Plan 2007–2010* (Dublin: August 2006), p. 9

44 *Ibid.*, p. 15

45 WAPN Ireland, *Report to NAPS Social Inclusion Forum, February 2006: Focus groups on issues for the new NAPS Inclusion.* Available at: www.eapn.ie

46 Jo O'Brien, Policy Officer, Crosscare Migrant Project, cited by Viktor Posudnevsky, *Metro Éireann*, 23 October 2008

47 'Hundreds of Migrants Join the Breadline as Boom Goes Bust', *Irish Independent*, 9 March 2009

48 'Busy Times for a Brother in Alms', *Irish Times*, 11 April 2009

49 See www.immigrantcouncil.ie

50 *Vincentian Centre Annual Report 2007*

51 M. Begley, K.C. Garavan, M. Condon, I. Kelly, K. Holland and A. Staines, *Asylum in Ireland: A Public Health Perspective* (Dublin: Department of Public Health Medicine and Epidemiology, 1999). SPIRASI is an NGO run by the Congregation of the Holy Spirit (Spiritans), also known as the Holy Ghost Fathers

52 P. Dunbar, *Evaluating the Barriers to Employment and Education in Cork* (Cork: NASC, 2008), p. 4

53 L. Coakley, *The Challenges and Obstacles Facing Refugees, Persons with Leave To Remain and Persons Granted Subsidiary Protection, as They Seek To Access Post-second Level Education in Ireland* (Dublin: Refugee Information Service, 2009), p. 4

54 Colleges of Further Education are post-second level colleges that provide training or education outside the third-level system. Most courses provided are designed to give students the skills necessary for progression in employment or further study. All courses are certified by national accreditation bodies (such as FETAC) and by internationally recognised examining bodies. See Coakley, *Challenges and Obstacles*, p. 14

55 A. Kinsella, 'Welfare Rights and the Risks of Poverty for Immigrants in Ireland: Stratification and Access Barriers', MPhil thesis (Dublin: University College Dublin, 2009)

56 Dunbar, *Evaluating the Barriers*, p. 52
57 *Ibid.*, p. 15
58 W. Macpherson, *The Stephen Lawrence Inquiry: Report of an Inquiry by Sir William Macpherson of Cluny* (London: HMSO, 1999), p. 22
59 Migrant Rights Centre Ireland, *Social Protection Denied*

8

Politics and citizenship

The key challenge facing both Government and Irish society in the period ahead is the need to integrate people of a different culture, ethnicity, language and religion so that they become part of our nation, part of the Irish family in the 21st century. (Fianna Fáil, 2009)

This chapter examines immigrant political participation and the role of citizenship in the political integration of immigrants. Firstly, it considers bottom-up efforts of immigrants to participate in electoral politics since 2004, when two former asylum seekers were elected as councillors in the local government elections; the chapter draws on interviews with almost half of all immigrant candidates who contested the 2009 local government elections. Secondly, the chapter examines the institutional responsiveness of Irish political parties to immigrants as voters, candidates and party members; it draws on interviews and written responses from each of the political parties in 2003, 2004, 2007 and 2009. Most immigrants are entitled to vote in Irish local government elections, where the franchise depends on residency rather than citizenship.[1]

If by integration we mean the full participation of immigrants within the mainstream of society, then this necessarily includes civic and political participation, citizenship and inclusion in decision making. This has more than a little relevance to the Irish case, where, since 2004, automatic citizenship is for the most part restricted to the children of existing citizens. In a context where very few immigrants are yet citizens, political decisions about their integration effectively occur without engagement with immigrants. Yet the right to vote in local government elections provides an impetus for Irish political parties to engage with immigrants. In the run-up to the 2009 local elections political parties responded to immigrants as if they were citizens. Such responsiveness contrasted with an absence of political engagement with immigrants in the 2007 general election, where only citizens could vote.

Citizenship does not ensure integration, but its absence clearly impedes integration. Non-citizens are not just excluded from political decision making, they also find themselves excluded from cognitive, normative, legal and constitutional solidarities between citizens.[2] The cognitive distinctions that flourished in 2004 pitted 'nationals' against 'non-nationals'. Many of the barriers to integration discussed in the previous chapters might be understood as expressions of welfare ethnic nepotism: a willingness by 'nationals' to remove rights to welfare goods and services from 'non-nationals'. Some chapters of this book have emphasised security governance pressures to selectively remove integration-fostering rights from non-citizens. Simply put, the default emphasis seems to be on protecting 'nationals' from 'non-nationals' rather than upon integration and social cohesion.

In advance of the 2009 local government elections, Irish political parties, to some extent at least, treated immigrants *as if* they were citizens because there were potential electoral benefits from doing so. In essence, these eschewed ethnic nepotism by defining Irish society as the local government electorate rather than in terms of a predominantly monocultural citizenry. This temporary political openness contrasts considerably with an ongoing security-governance approach to policing distinctions between 'nationals' and 'non-nationals' through restrictive approaches towards naturalisation.

The promise of positive politics

In a context where most immigrants are not Irish citizens it is no wonder that the possibilities of political integration allowed for by the Electoral Act (1992), whereby anyone over 18 years of age is entitled to vote in Irish local government elections and stand for election after 6 months of residency, has captured the imagination of the immigrant media. In 2009 *Metro Éireann* ran many articles about the forty or so immigrant candidates who contested the local government elections. A building sense of expectation found its laureate in Roddy Doyle, a regular contributor to the immigrant-run newspaper. One month before the June 2009 election *Metro Éireann* began its serialisation of 'Local', Doyle's tale about Chidimma Agu, a fictional Fianna Fáil candidate standing in Dublin 15. Doyle artfully inserted his Nigerian protagonist into Irish political tribalism:

– I am your Fianna Fáil candidate in the forthcoming elections.
– Fianna Fáil?
– Yes.
– But they are rogues, said the woman, and she clicked her fingers above her head.
She took a step closer to Chindimma.
– You are Igbo, aren't you?
– Yes, said Chindimma.
– For shame, said the woman.
– You should be in Fine Gael.
– Fine Gael is the party of the Igbo.
And she too slammed the door.

My God, said Chidimma, to herself. What am I doing? I am starting a tribal war in Mulhuddart.[3]

The front cover of the same issue of *Metro Éireann* carried four adverts for actual African candidates. Two of these were standing in Mulhuddart. The slogan on Ignatius Okafor's (independent) advert was 'Vote for community empowerment and balance of power', Adeola Ogunsina (Fine Gael) deployed the official party slogan of 'A fairer Ireland'. By some curious symmetry, no advert for the real Fianna Fáil candidate appeared. However, a speech by Idowu Olafimiham, 'a businessman with interests in retail security', was the subject of a full article on page 7. The occasion was the official launch of his campaign by the Fianna Fáil Minister of Finance, Brian Lenihan.[4] Another article on the same page reported criticism by Okafor of his Fine Gael rival Ogunsina, who allegedly had promised passports and status for immigrants within six months if Fine Gael came to power.[5] Whether Fine Gael was the party of the Igbo was unclear, but a tooth-and-nail political battle of the hearts and minds of Africans was being played out in *Metro Éireann* and in Dublin 15.

In the run-up to the 2009 elections the main political parties all sought to attract immigrant candidates. One independent African candidate suggested that the parties were 'merely shopping for immigrant faces'. He had been approached to stand by a number of political parties (as had a number of immigrant candidates) but he refused such overtures because of concerns about tokenism. This was not the view of many of those who joined political parties. In the weeks prior to the elections Fianna Fáil ministers campaigned on behalf of non-citizen immigrant candidates; even the Minister of Finance took time out, in the shadow of impending economic catastrophe, to address a public meeting in Mulhuddart on behalf of Idowu Olafimiham. In the early summer of 2009 Irish politicians tried on a new suit for size, one that appeared comfortably inclusive, a dress rehearsal for a possible future Ireland in which integration was an everyday, lived political reality. At least that is what it seemed like in the pages of *Metro Éireann* and in mainstream media accounts of the election – at least until the election took place.

The origins of this inclusiveness dated from 2003 when the Africa Solidarity Centre (ASC) commissioned a study of Irish political parties in advance of the 2004 local government elections. The plan was a simple one. Ask each of the parties a handful of questions aimed at encouraging internal debate, explain in advance that a report would be published just prior to the elections and make the case for positive engagement with immigrants, as distinct from anti-immigrant populism aimed at appealing to the majority community. Each of the parties was asked to identify policies or good practices they had adopted to encourage members of immigrant communities and ethnic-minority groups to become party members; policies or good practices had they adopted to oppose racism in Irish society; whether they had selected candidates from immigrant and ethnic-minority communities to stand in the 2004 local elections; and to identify what initiatives were proposed to canvass for support amongst immigrant and ethnic-minority communities.[6] An account of the experience of undertaking this research was published in *Immigration and Social Change in the Republic of Ireland*. It had become clear that the business of engaging positively with immigrants was uncharted territory for all six political parties:

> Overall, members of the research team were surprised by the lack of professionalism of the majority of parties in fielding queries and in articulating their policies. When it came to written replies to the research questions the two exceptions were Fianna Fáil and Sinn Fein. The responses of both of these were considerably more polished than those of the other parties contacted even if, in the case of the former there was little or no engagement with the specific research questions. What was surprising (in an era of political spin) was the extent to which the responses of the others were unguarded and dismissive. A written reply from the Labour Party merely directed the researchers to its website. Senior officials from a number of parties remarked in telephone conversations that they had never given the issue of immigrant participation in politics any thought. Some patently struggled to understand the questions being put to their organisations. It became clear that many of the political parties contacted did not take the ASC survey seriously. In a number of cases there was little sense that party officials understood that an unwillingness or inability to address social diversity was either an issue for internal concern or a potential source of external criticism.[7]

The first ASC report, *Positive Politics: Participation of Immigrants in the Electoral Politics*, was launched in December 2003. Fianna Fáil facilitated a photo call at the Taoiseach's office in Dail Eireann and the report, or at least one of its findings, that the Progressive Democrats had a clause in its constitution which prevented non-EU member state citizens from becoming members, received considerable media coverage. The Progressive Democrats very promptly agreed to amend its constitution.[8] A follow-up survey in February 2004 repeated the same questions. The aim was to gauge shifts in the responsiveness of political parties to immigrants as potential voters, members or candidates. Fianna Fáil replied that it aimed to create a society based on the principles of equality and dignity and that it welcomed support from all people regardless of race or religion. The party reported that it had begun to advertise in *Metro Éireann*, inviting people to become members. It also reported the inclusion of an anti-racism section in the local elections manual that was supplied to all its candidates. This included a definition of institutional racism as: 'Processes that consciously or unconsciously result in the systematic exclusion of ethnic minorities … visible in the inequitable outcomes for minority ethnic groups from the policies and practices of organisations and institutions throughout society.'[9] All the parties reported tentative engagement with the idea of immigrant political participation; leaflets were being translated and commitments to anti-racism emphasised.[10] Meanwhile, a number of immigrant candidates stood as independents in 2004; two former asylum seekers were elected as town councillors, Taiwo Matthews in Ennis and Rotimi Adebari in Portlaoise.

Three years later the research was repeated, this time in advance of the 2007 general election. The same four questions were asked. Although various political parties included in their manifestos a commitment to establish a cabinet post with responsibility for integration, their electoral engagement with immigrants was minimal, primarily because most were non-citizens not entitled to vote in general elections.

In the aftermath of the 2004 election the ASC, renamed as the Africa Centre, along with other African-led organisations, notably the women's organisation Akina Dada wa Africa (AkiDwa), placed considerable emphasis on the importance of immigrant civic participation. Both had memberships that included Africans of different nationalities and religious backgrounds (including Muslims). Several of the female African candidates who stood in the 2009 election were AkiDwa members. The Africa Centre's strategic plan for 2005–08 had emphasised the need to strengthen the capacity of African communities to participate in Irish society, to promote 'genuine representation of minority communities' and to promote civic integration amongst African communities.[11] After the 2004 election it undertook action research aimed at fostering civic and political participation. The resultant *Inclusive Citizenship in 21st Century Ireland: What Prospects for the African Community?* depicted African respondents from Dublin, Dundalk and Waterford, as strongly engaged in community activities (63 percent), very strongly interested in becoming politically active (98 percent), but found that actual political partic-ipation rates were much lower. Just 2 percent of those surveyed described themselves as members of political organisations and just 27 percent had voted in the 2004 local government elections. Respondents identified a range of specific barriers to civic participation, including racism, language barriers and a sense of insecurity.[12] *Inclusive Citizenship* emphasised how 'civil society provides the space for the marginalised to assert themselves and to contribute to the public sphere – activities that embody the "stuff" of citizenship, often in the absence of its formal acquisition'.[13] Such civic activism emerged in a context where (or even because) Africans have found it difficult to integrate within the economy.

In a striking example of African political activism, asylum seekers living in the Mosney reception centre sought in 2004 to set up a Fianna Fáil cumann (branch). This placed Fianna Fáil, the dominant party in the coalition govern-ment that had introduced direct provision, in a quandary. As described by a former Mosney resident who went on to stand as an independent candidate in 2009, one-sixth of the camp's adult population, over 100 asylum seekers, held a meeting with the local Fianna Fáil TDs (members of parliament). These responded that the application of the asylum seekers to join Fianna Fáil would need to be considered by the party at a 'national level'. Their request was turned down. As put by the candidate: 'We later got feedback that because we are not residents we were not allowed to form a cumman.'

The election of Councillor Adebari as Ireland's first black mayor in 2007 received media attention around the world. The then *Ceann Comhairle* (Speaker of the House) John O'Donoghue hosted a reception at Leinster House welcoming Adebari to 'the heart of Irish Democracy'. O'Donoghue hailed 'a significant moment in Ireland's development' and voiced his hope that the 2009 local government elections would bring greater cultural diversity at council level. He also anticipated that, further down the line, immigrants would be elected to parliament: 'I am sure that it is only a matter of time before we see some "New Irish" elected to the Houses of the Oireachtas.'[14] In 2008 Conor Lenihan, the Minister of State for Integration Policy, emphasised the role of political parties in promoting integration:

> Given the number of migrants who live in Ireland it is essential that every effort is made to ensure that as many as possible engage with the political system and participate to the maximum extent possible ... It is clear that all parties have embraced migrants as members. The challenge is to further encourage more migrants to become active in political life both at local and national level.[15]

In the run-up to the 2009 local government elections a number of local authorities, notably Dublin City Council, and NGOs, notably Integrating Ireland, led immigrant-voter registration campaigns. The Office of the Minister for Integration (OMI) funded some of this work. Dublin City Council's 'Migrant Voters Project' produced materials on voter registration and the practicalities of voting in more than twenty languages.[16] Their effectiveness appeared limited. In the run-up to the 2009 election immigrants remained under-represented on electoral registers. Yet sufficient numbers had registered for them to be politically significant; in Dublin, in particular, the immigrant vote was worth seeking.

The March 2009 electoral register identified 337,925 persons eligible to vote in the Greater Dublin area.[17] Of these, some 14,010 were from EU countries (other than the United Kingdom) and non-EU countries. The 2006 Census found that the non-Irish/UK-born population of Dublin (as distinct from the smaller Dublin City Council area) had risen more than fourfold between 1996 and 2006, growing from 29,500 to 158,000 (that is, from 2.8 percent of the city population to 13.3 percent). Yet, within the Dublin City Council area, non-Irish/UK-born accounted for just over 4 percent of the electorate in 2009. Immigrants formed a larger percentage of the population and potentially of the registered electorate in some areas such as the north inner city and Dublin 15, where a number of immigrant candidates emerged.

All of the political parties reported attempts to engage with immigrant communities in the months prior to the 2009 elections. These included efforts to select immigrant candidates, to recruit immigrant members and to attract immigrant voters. Initiatives by various political parties had much in common. Party literature was translated into various languages. Top-down engagement with immigrant communities tended to be led by a party official with a specific designated role – the Women and Equality Officer in the case of the Labour Party and the integration officers respectively appointed by Fianna Fáil and Fine Gael a year or so prior to the 2009 election, although Sinn Fein stated that it did not have the resources to designate such a person.

In their responses to both the 2007 and 2009 studies, the Labour Party and Sinn Fein placed considerable emphasis on equality principles. In other words, rather than direct campaigns towards particular immigrant communities, the emphasis was on articulating principles of equality and inclusion that were understood to appeal to immigrants and ethnic minorities in general and upon issues (such as asylum or immigrant legislation). The approach to immigrants amongst the other parties was arguably more pragmatic. A number of prominent immigrant community activists were invited to stand by more than one political party. Taking into consideration its comparatively small size, the Green Party proved most open to selecting immigrant candidates. It selected five candidates, as compared to the nine selected by Fianna Fail, seven by Fine Gael and four by the Labour Party; Sinn Fein selected none.

Both Fianna Fáil and Fine Gael recruited integration officers in, respectively, late 2007 and the beginning of 2008; both appointees were Polish immigrants with academic backgrounds in politics and international relations. Inevitably, perhaps, much of their work consisted in engagement with the Polish community. Both were active members of Forum Poloyna, the main Polish Diaspora Network in Ireland, and one was a founding member of Polish Toastmasters. Even though Fianna Fáil (the largest party in government) and Fine Gael (the largest opposition party) were locked into intense electoral competition, both their integration officers and their Polish candidates met as part of the same Forum Poloyna network. On 25 April 2009 Forum Poloyna held a conference on the election attended by Polish candidates and Irish representatives from several political parties. Also present were Dublin City Council officials and Poles engaged in voter registration campaigns.[18]

Although both integration officers held briefs for encouraging immigrant political participation it was clear than most of their outreach work was explicitly directed towards Polish immigrants. The Fine Gael post-holder was described on the party website as 'Polish Liaison Officer'. Fine Gael's official response to the 2009 survey stated that the liaison officer was presently working with the Polish community and that the role of the liaison officer has been to encourage Polish migrants to get involved in politics, register to vote and potentially to run in local elections. It also stated that all Fine Gael 'New Irish candidates' were doing similar work in their own areas, including attending church services and community meetings.

Fianna Fáil's response to the 2009 survey emphasised that its Integration Officer had developed strong contacts with various New Irish communities. It described many concrete examples of outreach to immigrants, but most of these referred to engagement with Poles. As with Fine Gael, the party website gave an explicit impression that Fianna Fáil was primarily interested in securing the support of Poles. In both cases interviews with party officials did not contradict a general perception that Poles enjoyed most-favoured status and that comparatively little effort had gone into reaching out to many other immigrant communities. In the case of Fianna Fáil, John O'Donoghue had invoked Rotimi Adebari as a symbol of new inclusive politics. However, his party excluded any focus on Africans from its online recruitment campaigns.

When it came to selecting immigrant candidates, a more complex picture emerged. Fine Gael appeared to favour Poles over Africans; Polish interviewees were practising Catholics and perceived the party as Catholic; one interviewee emphasised the ideological connections between it and the Civic Forum in Poland, both members of the same EU parliamentary grouping. Yet Fine Gael recruited four African candidates and just two Polish candidates. Grounds for a thesis of racialised politics were stronger in the case of Fianna Fáil, where a plethora of measures to engage with the Polish community were identified and where just two of the nine immigrant candidates selected were African. Yet, senior Fianna Fáil government ministers campaigned on behalf of their African candidates (in the midst of a breaking economic crisis) and the party advertised extensively in the African media.

When it came to actual success in attracting immigrant members, the impression given by both websites appears to differ from what actually happened on the ground. Both parties had attracted members from across a range of immigrant communities, although both found it difficult to quantify how many members had been recruited. Whilst most Fianna Fáil political integration initiatives were focused on the Polish community, the party estimated that the number of Africans who had joined the party probably exceeded the number of Poles.

In summary, the main political parties made considerable efforts to reach out to non-citizen immigrants in the run-up to the 2009 elections. Four of the five parties selected immigrant candidates and all made efforts to encourage immigrant-voter registration. Whilst the economic crisis had resulted in the introduction in June 2009 of new worker visa restrictions, none of the five parties, including those in government, seemed tempted by anti-immigrant populism. The year 2009 witnessed the positive politics that the Africa Centre had called for in 2004 (when a low level of engagement with immigrants coincided with the Referendum on Citizenship). Yet, from the perspective of the political parties, 2009 was very much an experiment. Perceptions of how well or poorly immigrant candidates performed would most likely influence future political engagement with immigrants. No less important are the conclusions that immigrants might draw from their bottom-up efforts at political inclusion.

Once the results of the 2009 election were announced, the optimistic mood in *Metro Éireann* dissipated. The front-page headline of the first post-election issue concerned the ongoing exploitation of vulnerable immigrant workers ('Slaves; Forced Labour is a Fact of Life in Ireland'). Analysis in *Metro Éireann* of immigrant candidates' perception of their experiences explored various reasons why candidates had failed to get elected. One article, headlined 'Migrant election failures "big blow" say candidates', quoted Patrick Maphoso, who had stood unsuccessfully as an independent candidate in north inner-city Dublin, saying the result was 'a big blow to the integration. Irish people are not ready to welcome immigrants by voting for them.' Maphoso stated: 'It will take another 10 to 15 years to have a voice in Ireland. I am vindicated now about racism in Ireland.'[19] During his election campaign Maphoso had experienced a racially motivated assault: 'One of them said to me, if I don't "want a bullet in my head" then I must leave. Why I kept asking. "Why me. Why pick on me?" He said black people made him sick. "All you f***ing foreigners make me sick."'[20] A number of other African candidates had reported racist incidents prior to the election. Several of those interviewed by Neil O'Boyle in 2009 described their experiences of racism as a motivation for standing for election. In January 2009 a website that featured stories on immigration with headings such as 'Non-nationals Steal Irish Jobs', and deportation as 'money well spent' came under investigation by the Gardaí for incitement to hatred. The Migration Watch website published the phone numbers and addresses of a number of immigrant candidates.[21] Several candidates made complaints to the Gardaí, the Office of the Minister of Integration, or their party leaderships. The site was shut down following various complaints.[22]

Media analyses of the failure of some African candidates to get elected suggested that racism amongst voters was a factor. For example, an editorial in the *Dundalk Leader* (under the headline 'Racism Rears Its Ugly Head') criticised anti-immigrant views expressed by some local people.[23] In his analysis of the Dundalk case, Kevin Howard quotes a Fine Gael supporter who did not vote for Benedicta Attoh, one of the two Fine Gael candidates in Dundalk South: 'As much as I hate Fianna Fáil [a vote for Attoh], that'd be going too far.'[24] In an interview with the *Irish Times* Attoh described being told by some Fine Gael party members that they would not vote for her ('I thought it was a joke, but it wasn't').[25]

For some, the intense competition between candidates within the same political party came as a shock. In *Metro Éireann* Catherine Reilly described how two African candidates in Letterkenny were trounced, mostly as a result of within-party competition:

'Most of my friends couldn't vote for me,' reveals Oladapo, of the information in those calls. 'I even helped register lots of foreigners – Indians, Filipinos – but they couldn't vote for me either.'

What Oladapo hadn't realised, and her Fianna Fáil colleagues not told her, was that the official boundaries of Letterkenny Town had not expanded to encompass many newer developments where she had extensively canvassed with her team of 16 (most were friends and not party members).

Homework not done, but the community activist wasn't alone in her misunderstanding. A fellow Nigerian – Fine Gael's Michael Abiola-Phillips, who was also running for Letterkenny Town Council – made the same error. In fact, Abiola-Phillips discovered that he couldn't even vote for himself.

Four Fianna Fáil candidates, all incumbents, were re-elected onto the council, but their colleague Oladapo – who's lived in Letterkenny for eight years and been a party member for seven – received just one transfer, on the second count, before being eliminated on 40 overall votes. Abiola-Philipps got 193.

Earlier this year, Fianna Fáil had selected Oladapo after Fine Gael declared countryman Abiola-Philipps, dividing the immigrant vote. But neither will be warming seats in Letterkenny's civic offices this time around.[26]

Yet in Dundalk the two African candidates who were not elected performed well. Attoh had run in Dundalk South on a joint ticket with Mark D'Arcy a sitting Fine Gael councillor and former chairman of Dundalk Council. The two campaigned jointly under the slogan: 'For Strong Effective Local Representation in Louth'. Once all the valid votes (11,505) had been collated and the quota (1,644) established, the ratio of D'Arcy's first preferences to Attoh's was slightly over 3:1 and D'Arcy was elected on the first count, with 1,918 votes to Attoh's 585 votes. Attoh received one quarter of the first preference Fine Gael vote. Whilst she stated in interviews that she had not received support from Fine Gael supporters, she nevertheless picked up a third of D'Arcy's surplus as well as transfers from across the political spectrum. These were insufficient to reach the quota, and she was eliminated following the eighth count. Whilst nearly two-thirds of those who gave D'Arcy their first preference voted across party lines to give their second preferences to non-Fine Gael candidates, Attoh nevertheless performed better than a number of white candidates.

A second immigrant candidate, George Enyoazu, ran in the Dundalk Central constituency on behalf of the Green Party. As in Dundalk South, a Sinn Fein candidate topped the poll. Enyoazu obtained 352 first preference votes, slightly over 7 percent of the total poll. Arguably this was a strong result for a Green Party candidate; the party performed very poorly in the 2009 election and most Green councillors across the country lost their seats. Moreover, Enyoazu picked up transfers from across the spectrum, in particular from independents, finally being eliminated after the ninth count.

Whilst just four immigrant candidates were elected in 2009, several other immigrant candidates performed well and it became apparent that a number of Irish candidates benefited from voter transfers from immigrant candidates in their party who were not elected. The former mayor of Portlaoise, Rotimi Adebari, retained his seat on the town council and gained one on the county council, while a Dutch immigrant, Jan Rotte, won a seat for the Labour Party in Lismore, Co. Waterford. In Co. Monaghan two immigrant candidates were elected, the Green Party's Kristina Jankaitiene, a Lithuanian standing in Carrickmacross, and Fianna Fáil's Russian-born candidate, Anna Rooney, in Clones. In Ruadhan Mac Cormaic's *Irish Times* analysis others performed well without clinching a seat. Among them were Fine Gael's Adeola Ogunsina in Mulhuddart (against competition from two other African candidates), Anna Michalska of Fianna Fáil in Kilkenny, the Green Party's Tendai Madondo in Tallaght (in spite of the swing against the Green Party) and Labour's Elena Secas in a part of Limerick City where the party had a poor track record of electoral success.[27]

Voting patterns for the three Nigerian candidates who competed against one another in Mulhuddart revealed how Irish political tribalism (traditionally low rates of transfer between Fianna Fáil and Fine Gael) combined with competition between African candidates to prevent an immigrant being elected in Dublin 15. Fine Gael's Adeola Ogunsina attracted 965 first preferences and was only eliminated on the ninth count. Fianna Fáil's Idowu Olafimihan attracted 611 first preferences and was eliminated on the sixth count. Just one third of Olafimihan's votes then transferred across to Ogunsina, the others being transferred to Irish candidates. The independent candidate Ignatius Okafor got 464 first preferences and was eliminated early in the count; his transfers scattered widely, rather than to the other African candidates.[28]

Roddy Doyle's serialised story about a fictional African candidate in Mulhuddart (Chidimma Agu) ended with her Irish election agent breaking the bad news to Chidimma:

– It's not looking good he said.
– Oh dear.
– Desperate, said Gerald. – But you're in with an outside chance if the other fella's transfers go to you.
– The other fellow?
– The African lad
– Chindi, Abebisi?
– Exactly.
– What about Paddy and Niamh's transfers? Chidimma asked. – Are they going to me?

– Not many, said Gerald. – Look. This time you're the black candidate. Next time, you'll be the candidate. Do you understand?
– Perfectly.

The lessons from 2009 for immigrant candidates and Irish political parties are hardly as simple as suggested by Doyle. Even where immigrant candidates did not get elected the parties that selected them benefited to some extent. If the aim of political engagement with immigrants was to attract immigrant voters, then this was to some extent successful. Some immigrant candidates were clearly poorly prepared for the election; some decided to stand only shortly before the election, many had not been able to build up the teams of canvassers they needed, many underestimated the degree of competition within parties that characterises Irish politics and many, it emerged, did not understand the importance of second and other transfer preferences under the Irish proportional representation system.[29] Many, nevertheless, did better than some Irish candidates in areas where immigrants comprised a very small percentage of the electorate. There is obvious potential for increased immigrant participation in future local government elections both as candidates and as voters; ongoing work on immigrant voter registration is crucial; research on the responsiveness of political parties to immigrants as potential members suggests that political parties need to improve their outreach to various immigrant communities.[30]

Yet their willingness to do so depends on a wider calculus about the extent to which immigrants can participate in general elections, the main event, as citizens. In their responses to the 2007 study a number of political parties suggested that the timing and scale of their future responses to immigrants would be shaped by pragmatic electoral considerations, namely the fact that most immigrants, as non-Irish citizens, were unable to vote in general elections. As put by one political party:

> It will obviously take time for such communities to become established members of society and of the party and it will most likely require a few election cycles before such members find themselves in a position to contest an election or propose themselves for election.[31]

Inevitably, the future approach of Irish political parties to immigrant communities is likely to be a 'pragmatic one'. Behind the rhetoric of inclusion and integration there may be little real commitment to political integration unless there are votes to be won, as put by one party official in 2007, a few election cycles from now, which would put the matter on the back burner until at least 2017. The underlying presumption was that there would be a critical mass of immigrant citizens by then and that this 'New Irish' citizen vote would be worth chasing. The on/off engagement of political parties with immigrant voters in local and general elections reveals a profound disjuncture between a genuine political willingness to include, on the one hand, and exclusionary approaches to immigration governance that work to impede the naturalisation of immigrants and their political integration within Irish democracy, on the other hand.

Helots and citizens, nationals and non-nationals

After Independence, under Article 3 of the 1922 Constitution a default entitlement to Irish citizenship was extended to any person born within the jurisdiction of the new state and to all those who were living there for not less than seven years.[32] In 1930, changes to Article 3 were mooted as part of a review of the (pre-Independence) Nationality and Status of Aliens Act 1914, undertaken by the Department of Justice. At stake within any redefinition of Irish nationality were the terms for admittance of non-citizens with reciprocal entitlements within the British Commonwealth, of which Ireland was then a member. In the behind-the-scenes debates of 1930, when the provisions of what later became the Aliens Act (1935) were thrashed out, the Department of External Affairs promoted the reciprocal rights of non-citizens so as to protect the equivalent rights of Irish citizens to domicile in Commonwealth countries. The Department's view in 1930 was that Irish law should grant automatic residency status to British and other Commonwealth subjects living in Saorstát Éireann. It proposed a wording that would grant 'all and every of the franchises, rights and privileges conferred by law on citizens of Saorstát Éireann' to them. It also argued that the children of persons resident in the state for seven years should be regarded as 'natural born citizens'.[33]

In keeping with the 1922 Constitution, the 1937 Constitution set out a constitutional right of citizenship for all people who were citizens of Saorstát Éireann at the time it came into operation. It also provided that, apart from the specific right of those who already had citizenship, the right for citizenship would be set out in legislation. In 1998, following the Belfast Agreement (also called the Good Friday Agreement) and a constitutional referendum, a new Article 2 was inserted into the Irish Constitution affirming the entitlement of anyone born within the 'island of Ireland' to Irish citizenship. The implication of Article 2 was that the Oireachtas (parliament) no longer had the power to decide whether or not citizenship could be withheld from any person born in the island of Ireland. In summary, those born on the island of Ireland (north and south), any child of an Irish citizen and any child of a person entitled to become an Irish citizen had an automatic right to Irish citizenship.[34]

The 2004 Citizenship Referendum and subsequent constitutional amendments to Article 2 led to restrictions being imposed on the constitutionally protected right to citizenship by birth. In 1989, the Supreme Court had ruled in the Fajujonu case[35] that Irish-citizen children had the right to the 'company, care and parentage' of their parents within a family unit. Subject to the exigencies of the common good, this right could be exercised within the state, with parents asserting a choice of residence on behalf of their children. Following on from the Fajujonu judgment, non-national parents were routinely granted the right to remain in Ireland on the basis of the children's right to the 'company, care and parentage' of their parents. This practice was to change in early 2003. In January 2003, the Supreme Court ruled in the L. and O. cases[36] that the automatic right of residence granted to the parents of Irish-born children, regardless of the legal status of the parents, could no longer be sustained. The common good required that restrictions be imposed on citizen-children's right to family life and to their right to the 'company, care and parentage' of their parents within the state. At the time of the Supreme Court judgment, more than 11,500 applications for residence from parents with Irish-citizen children were pending.[37]

In June 2004, a referendum was held to amend the Constitution so as to restrict the entitlement to citizenship of children born to non-national parents. By a majority of almost four to one, the electorate voted to amend the Constitution, removing the right to citizenship from future generations of Irish-born children who could not demonstrate generations of belonging to the state. The outcome was that people born on the island of Ireland after the constitutional amendment took effect did not have a constitutional right to become Irish citizens, unless at the time of their birth one of their parents was an Irish citizen or was entitled to become an Irish citizen. Naturalisation criteria were set out under the Irish Nationality and Citizenship Act (2004).

On 15 January 2005 the Minister of Justice, Equality and Law Reform announced new procedures for the consideration of applications for leave to remaining the state from the non-Irish-citizen parents of Irish-born children (IBC) born in the Republic as distinct from the island of Ireland before that date. Prior to the closing date, 17,917 applications were received under the IBC/05 Scheme; of these, 16,693 were granted leave to remain. Some 59 percent of IBC/05 applicants were Nigerian, 16 percent Romanian, 10 percent Chinese, 9 percent Filipino and 6 percent Pakistani. Under the scheme, applicants had to provide evidence that their child had been born in the state and that the parent or parents had been continuously resident in the state in the period since the birth of their Irish-born child.[38] Successful IBC/05 applicants became eligible to apply for Irish citizenship from 1 January 2010.

The number of immigrants seeking naturalisation has risen year on year from a very low base since the 1990s. So too have the numbers granted Irish citizenship. Because of the time lag, the number of certificates of naturalisation granted in any given year is appropriately considered as a percentage of applications for citizenship made in earlier years. In 2008 some 10,885 applications for citizenship were received; decisions on these are likely to emerge in

2011 or 2012 on the basis of current processing times. In 2008, 3,117 certificates of naturalisation were issued; these most likely relate to applications submitted in 2005 by applicants who had at that time, as required by the 2004 Citizenship Act, five years of 'reckonable residence' in Ireland. Many of these are likely to have lived in Ireland for several years prior to that; time spent as an asylum seeker, in education or on some kinds of work permit does not count under the Act as reckonable residence. In most cases it takes more than a decade for an immigrant to become an Irish citizen.

Because of this time lag only a small percentage of Ireland's mostly recently arrived immigrant population are citizens. Most of those who naturalised between 2000 and 2004 were from outside the European Union; out of at total of just 5,387 who acquired Irish citizenship the largest cohorts were Pakistani (653), Bosnian (578), Indian (299), Somali (257), Iraqi (229) and Sudanese (200), reflecting the inflow of migrants some years earlier. The Pakistani and Indian Irish were most likely health professionals recruited into Ireland during the 1990s; the others were mostly refugees or asylum seekers.[39] The Bosnians were mostly Programme Refugees (entitled to refugee status on arrival) who arrived from 1992.[40] In more recent years naturalisation patterns have reflected the proportions of non-EU migrants who arrived in the later 1990s. For example, it can be anticipated that a high proportion

Figure 2 Naturalisation applications and refusals[a]

Year	Applications for naturalisation	Certificates issued	No of apps refused/ deemed ineligible[b]
1999	739	416	79
2000	1004	125	57
2001	1431	1048	8
2002	3574	1332	135
2003	3580	1664	179
2004	4074	1335	779
2005	4527	1451	2428
2006	6183	1390	2191
2007	7616	1501	1612
2008	10885	3117	2795

[a] Figures provided in response to a Dáil question asked by Aengus Ó Snodaigh TD, 7 April 2009: 'To ask the Minister of Justice, Equality and Law Reform the number of citizenship applications received each year for the last 10 years; the number processed in each of those years; the average waiting time for applicants; and the countries from which applicants are from originally'.
[b] Numbers of applications refused/deemed ineligible relate to applications for naturalisation submitted (2–3 years) earlier.

of those permitted to naturalise from 2009 will be families with Irish-born citizen children (born before 2004) and subsequent cohorts will include those granted residency under the IBC/05 scheme, eligible to apply for citizenship from 2010. Other means of naturalisation include applications from those married to Irish citizens; 10,312 post-nuptial certificates of naturalisation were issued between 2001 and 2005. Between 2001 and 2005 a further 6,794 other applications for naturalisation were accepted, bringing the total for this period to 17,106 (Figure 2).[41]

By international standards a very large percentage of applications for naturalisation from persons with residency status are refused. According to the Immigrant Council of Ireland some 47 percent of applications were refused, when comparable 2009 refusal rates for citizenship by naturalisation in other countries were less than 9 percent in the UK, less than 3 percent in Canada, 9 percent in Australia.[42] The high rates of refusal in the Irish case are partially explained by the absence of proactive measures to encourage immigrants to become citizens; many countries, such as the United Kingdom, have introduced pathways to naturalisation. Furthermore, Irish naturalisation application processing times are very slow by international standards. A comparison undertaken by the ICI in 2009 found that 95 percent of equivalent applications were processed in less than 6 months in the UK, identified an average processing time of 11.3 months in Canada, and found that 85 percent of applications were processed within 90 days in Australia, when 23 months was the average waiting time in Ireland.[43]

The Irish findings point to an influential anti-integrationist security-governance perspective centred institutionally within the DJELR. High 'failure' rates seem to have been designed into the administration of 2004 Citizenship Act and other pertinent legislation. The earlier Irish Citizenship Nationality Act (1956) provided that the Minister of Justice may 'at his absolute discretion' determine all applications to become a naturalised Irish citizen. In response to a parliamentary question in June 2009, the then Minister, Dermot Ahern, stated that in practice this discretion benefited applicants who would otherwise have been refused.[44] This claim has been contested in analyses of citizenship applications by the ICI and the Crosscare Migrant Project. ICI case studies highlight how ministerial discretion is sometimes used to impose exclusionary 'good character' criteria. Whilst these discretionary criteria are nowhere formally stated, they are alluded to on the government-run Citizens Information Board website:

> The requirement to be of good character – the Garda Síochána (Ireland's national police) will be asked to provide a report about your background. Any criminal record or ongoing proceedings will be taken into consideration by the Minister for Justice, Equality and Law Reform in deciding whether or not to grant naturalisation. Details of any proceedings, criminal or civil, in the State or elsewhere, should be disclosed in the application form.[45]

Many countries operate such criteria but, unlike the Irish case, these are transparently set down. Consider the clearly defined process set down in the Australian case:

> Good character is assumed unless there is evidence otherwise. A serious criminal record would be evidence that a candidate does not meet the good character requirement, however general conduct and associations can also be taken into account. As a result, an applicant with only minor criminal offending may be assessed as not meeting the good character requirement, particularly if the offending has been quite recent and there has not been sufficient time between the offending and the application for citizenship to establish that they are likely to reoffend. In the event that a decision is made to refuse an application for citizenship on these grounds, an opportunity to respond must be given to the applicant.[46]

In 2009 the ICI drew attention to a number of cases where citizenship applications were turned down on the basis of ministerial discretion for reasons that would not breach 'of good character' criteria in the cases of Canada or Australia. David arrived in Ireland in 1999; along with his wife, he was granted full residency rights in the state upon arrival. In 2000, while driving his wife's car, he was stopped by Gardai conducting routine checks on car insurance. David had a full licence but was unaware that his wife's insurance did not cover him. He was fined €100 and had his driving licence endorsed. This was his sole offence. He applied for citizenship 2005 and in 2008 was informed that the Minister had decided that the traffic offence, eight years previously, gave sufficient grounds to warrant his application for naturalisation being refused. He had no means of appealing this decision other than to submit a new application for naturalisation.[47]

Florence has been legally resident in Ireland in 2001. She worked full time but briefly became unemployed in 2004 and received social welfare assistance for six months (unemployment benefit, family income supplement and rent allowance). After this period she subsequently re-entered the workforce and has been in employment ever since. However, once her child was born she found, as a single parent that she could afford to work only part time, due to the high cost of childcare; she is still in receipt of family income supplement. She applied for citizenship in 2005 but was turned down in 2008 on the grounds that she was in receipt of social welfare assistance.[48] A somewhat similar example was highlighted by the Crosscare Migrant Project (CMP). George, an American citizen, had worked in the information technology sector since 2000 on an Employment Permit. In 2003 he had been made redundant but soon found a new job. In 2005 he applied for Irish citizenship. In 2007 he received a letter from the Immigration and Naturalisation Service (INIS) stating that he had been refused naturalisation. No reasons for this refusal were stated in the letter. After extended efforts to get written reasons from INIS he was informed that his application had been refused because he had accessed social welfare. George stated: 'I was absolutely dumbstruck when I read the reasons for refusal. It was not stated in the application criteria that I could be refused for this reason.'[49] These grounds are not specified in legislation but are, rather, an example of ministerial discretion. It would be highly unlikely that many of the persons whose case studies are cited in the previous chapter would be deemed on discretionary grounds to be entitled to Irish citizenship even if they satisfied mandatory criteria.

In another 2009 case reported by the *Irish Times* a 23-year-old Zimbabwean man challenged in the High Court the decision to refuse him Irish citizenship on the grounds that he was not of good character, arising from a conviction for drunk driving. Noel Dick arrived in Ireland as a 15-year-old asylum seeker. He was granted refugee status a few months after his arrival in July 2002; his defence stated that Mr Dick had never in fact been charged with the offence, and nor had he been convicted.[50] Under the provisions of the 1956 Act no appeal mechanism exists; the sole avenue for applicants who are refused citizenship (other than redress through the courts) is to reapply. A combination of ministerial discretion (effectively the administrative discretion of the DJELR) and the lack of a right to appeal arguably accounts for extremely high rates of refusal of applications for naturalisation in the Irish case, as compared to other countries.

The importance of administrative transparency in determining naturalisation outcomes should not be underestimated. Research conducted in 2007 on Irish Naturalisation and Immigration Service (INIS) customer and information services concluded, on the basis of an analysis of 1,207 client cases, that INIS did not provide a user-friendly service. Specifically, it stated that 'key information is unavailable (to clients) and it is leading to ill-informed migration decisions'; it described services as difficult to access and described a general lack of administrative transparency, as compared to the British case, where naturalisation application refusal rates were considerably lower (9 percent, as compared to 47 percent of DJELR rulings).[51] A 2009 report, also by the CMP, illustrated how a lack of transparency contributed to high refusal rates:

> CMP has had clients who satisfied all the stated requirements and yet were refused citizenship. Added to such decisions is that reasons for refusal are not always provided. When some reasons for refusal are given they relate to requirements that were not stated or available to the applicant prior to applying. Not only is this a waste of public resources it is a furtive and disingenuous approach to the applications process which effectively tells the applicant at the end of the process that there was a rule he/she was not told about that makes him/her ineligible.[52]

A further apparent obstacle to naturalisation has been the narrow definition of 'reckonable residence', the period of time a migrant is required to live in the state prior to being able to apply for asylum. The 2004 Act specifies that applicants for naturalisation must have a period of one year's continuous 'reckonable residence' in the state immediately before the date of their application for naturalisation and, during the eight years preceding that, have had a total reckonable residence in the state amounting to a further four years. Persons who have obtained refugee status are eligible to apply for citizenship. The Act specifies that certain periods of residence may be excluded from the reckoning when calculating periods of residence in the state. These include time as an undocumented migrant or periods covered by a permission to remain for study purposes (requiring a student visa) or while having a claim for asylum examined. Unlike criteria pertaining to 'good character', those for reckonable residence are set out in the Act. However, again these were, arguably, being interpreted restrictively by the DJELR.

The ways in which reckonable residence criteria imposed barriers to naturalisation were the focus of a Seanad debate on citizenship in October 2007. In a case highlighted by Senator David Norris, the child of resident migrants entitled to seek naturalisation was not deemed eligible to apply for citizenship because the time she had spent in third-level education was deemed not to count as reckonable residence. This, Norris argued was unfair to families who had put down genuine roots in Irish society:

> However once a person turns 19 and goes on to third level education, he or she is resident here on a student visa and such time is excluded from reckonable residence. The results of the exclusion of student visa time from the reckonable residence calculations are, first, that the person would need to stay up to eight or nine years before he or she could apply for citizenship. Then he or she would experience about a three-year delay before possibly getting citizenship. That means that a person would have to wait 11 to 13 years in total for citizenship. Second, after completing third level education, he or she would only be able to remain in Ireland on a work permit. There is no certainty that the person would get such a permit.[53]

Norris detailed the specific case of a South African man 'headhunted by the Government' in 2001 to work as a planning inspector for An Bord Pleanála; he arrived with his wife and daughter on a work visa. His daughter went straight into secondary school and completed her leaving certificate in 2004; she spent a year completing a post-leaving certificate course before starting a three-year veterinary nursing diploma at University College Dublin; she passed her second year and, as a requirement of the course, worked part-time in a veterinary practice. Having been in Ireland for five years, the family applied together for Irish citizenship in November 2006. The planning official experienced no difficultly with his application ('He is sailing through, if one could call it that, and is on the right track even though the procedure is extraordinarily slow … it will take the usual 30 months'). In his wife's case, the authorities discounted the nine months from the time when her family arrived until the time in 2002 when her passport was stolen ('it was perfectly well known that she was here with her husband as his wife and living in the family home, he having been recruited by the authorities in this land'); this meant she was considered not to have built up the required time to make an application. In their daughter's case, INIS discounted all the time since she had left secondary school from her period of reckonable residence. Furthermore, once she completed college, she would have to apply for a work visa and could conceivably be deported. A response on this case on behalf of the Minister of Justice, Equality and Law Reform stated that, upon review, the wife was deemed to have sufficient 'reckonable residency.' However, their daughter was deemed ineligible to apply for citizenship because she had been in education since her arrival in 2004. A blogged response to Senator Norris's online posting of the Seanad debate criticised the 'unnecessary administrative abuse' of applicants for citizenship.[54]

Challenges

The right to participate in local elections offers a crucial mechanism for integrating non-citizen immigrants into Irish society. It allows for immediate political participation, unimpeded by the time delays associated with the naturalisation process. However, the concern is that inclusive politics will stop at a local level and remain underdeveloped at a local level unless large numbers of immigrants naturalise. For example, research undertaken in the run-up to the 2007 general election noted a pragmatic indifference towards immigrants on the part of Irish political parties; immigrants were of little or no electoral significance. Yet in 2009 the responses of various political parties grappled with the inclusion of migrants within the Irish nation. Sinn Fein stated that 'a new Ireland needs an inclusive nationalism', without defining what this might mean. Fianna Fáil (in the quote that opens this chapter) identified the need to integrate immigrants into the Irish nation. Fine Gael stated that streamlining the process of achieving long-term residency and citizenship was vital.[55] If Ireland is serious about integration, proactive policies aimed at encouraging naturalisation need to be developed. Otherwise the cognitive distinctions between 'nationals' and 'non-nationals' that prevailed in 2004 are likely to persist within 'national' politics. The absence of a political impetus to engage with immigrants on an ongoing basis is likely to undermine an ongoing focus on integration. The alternative, witnessed in Ireland in the run-up to the 2004 Referendum on Citizenship, is a politicisation of immigration that does not include immigrants or a focus on integration.

The overwhelming majority of immigrants in the Republic of Ireland have not naturalised. At the time of writing many have not been resident in the country long enough to be eligible to apply for Irish citizenship, and of those who are so eligible a disconcertingly high percentage have had their applications refused. The experience of other EU member states suggests that many immigrants from them are unlikely to seek Irish citizenship because they do not need to do so in order to obtain employment and social entitlements. Yet the engagement of East European candidates in Irish local politics in 2009 highlights the potential of political integration. In the case of Polish immigrants, their right to vote in local elections prompted Irish political parties to engage with Ireland's largest immigrant community for the first time. Yet their future exclusion from mainstream electoral politics is of concern. Just half the Polish and other East European candidates interviewed in the 2009 MCRI study stated that they intended to naturalise. Polish nationals are not prevented from acquiring dual nationality.[56] Nor does naturalisation in the Irish case require a person to renounce citizenship of their country of origin. Lithuanians, on the other hand, cannot acquire dual nationality; for this reason one candidate stated that she did not intend to apply for Irish citizenship. All but two of the eighteen candidates interviewed in 2009 had children living with them in Ireland; this, to a considerable extent, explained their involvement in local politics: they had put down roots. Whilst African and East European candidates differed in some respects (see Chapter 4), they were similar in that their primary stated motivation for entering politics concerned local issues, services and facilities. As put by one Polish respondent: 'My baby is Irish so I want to be too.' Another Polish candidate stated: 'If I stay in Ireland and if I get the chance I will apply for Irish citizenship because I will never be an Irish person but I am part of Irish society and when you are a citizen you have full rights – referenda, parliamentary elections.' One African candidate reflected on the role of residency status in creating the conditions for immigrant civil and political participation:

> Often immigrants start out with immigrant-specific concerns (residency status, immigration issues, English language) but gradually move on to more mainstream concerns (childcare, housing, public transport etc). One of our Nigerian members described it as 'if you are thirsty you only care about getting water'. That's how it is with what is your immediate concern. If I need residency, I only care about that, not about public transport. But once I am settled and maybe get a job, I want to sort out how to get to work by public transport and I no longer care about residency but public transport.

All ten African interviewees had secure residency status and, having arrived in Ireland between 1999 and 2003, were comparatively long-standing immigrant members of Irish society. Just one of the ten African respondents was an Irish citizen, another was a citizen of another EU member state; with one exception, all the rest stated that they intended to naturalise.

The integration debate as presented by the EU Common Basic Principles on Integration and by Irish reports such as *Migration Nation* (see Chapter 2) depicts integration as an administrative or governance project rather than a political one. Governance approaches that build on good international practice and so on can work to further integration; Christian Joppke suggests that these presume to side-step nativist political populism that might work to veto integration.

Countries such as the UK, Canada and Australia have policies and procedures in place aimed at proactively turning migrants into citizens. In the Irish case the extremely high rate of refusal of naturalisation applications received from persons with established residency status works to undermine the political integration of immigrants. Such political integration is crucial to future social cohesion. For example, the proposition that the extremely high rates of marginalisation of African immigrants can be adequately addressed without the political participation of Africans is unsound. Africans in Ireland comprise one of Ireland's largest and longest-established immigrant communities. Of these, the predominant country of origin is Nigeria. Many have run a gauntlet of deliberate social exclusion as asylum seekers and racism; they became the racialised focus of the 2004 Referendum on Citizenship; many suffered extreme anxiety about their residency status in its aftermath; now, several years later, most have residency status and have made or are soon likely to make applications for citizenship. According to the DJELR in 2009 applications from Nigerians outnumbered those from any other country of origin. Nigerian applicants for Irish citizenship also experienced the highest refusal rates.[57] This refusal rate was presumably greater than the overall 47 percent of applications for naturalisation that were turned down.

Notes

1 The Republic of Ireland grants electoral rights to all non-Irish nationals in local elections (voting and standing), and has done so since 1972: Electoral Act 1992 s.10.

2 B. Fanning, *New Guests of the Irish Nation* (Dublin: Irish Academic Press, 2009), p. 2

3 R. Doyle 'The Local', *Metro Éireann*, 7 May 2009

4 'Iwodu gets a boost from FF minister', *Metro Éireann*, 7 May 2009

5 'Okafor Criticises Fine Gael Candidate's "False Promises" to Migrants', *Metro Éireann*, 7 May 2009

6 B. Fanning, F. Mutwarasibo and N. Chadamayo, *Positive Politics: Participation of Immigrants and Ethnic Minorities in the Electoral Process* (Dublin: Africa Solidarity Centre, 2003)

7 N. Chadmayo, B. Fanning and F. Mutwarasibo 'Breaking into Politics', in B. Fanning (ed.), *Immigration and Social Change in the Republic of Ireland* (Manchester: Manchester University Press, 2007), p. 189

8   The rule was changed by the party's National Executive at its meeting on 4 December 2003

9   Fianna Fáil, *Handbook for Local Election Candidates* (Dublin: Fianna Fáil, 2004)

10 B. Fanning, F. Mutwarasibo and N. Chadmayo, *Negative Politics, Positive Vision: Immigration and the 2004 Elections* (Dublin: Africa Solidarity Centre, 2004), pp. 10–11

11 Africa Centre, *Strategic Plan 2005–2008*, p. 7. Available at: www.africacentre.ie

12 T. Ejorh, *Inclusive Citizenship in 21st Century Ireland: What Prospects for the African Community?* (Dublin: Africa Centre, 2006)

13 A. Feldman, D. Ndakengerwa, A. Nolan and C. Fresse, *Diversity, Civil Society and Social Change in Ireland: A North-South Comparison of the Role of Immigrant/'New' Minority Ethnic-Led Community and Voluntary Sector Organisations* (Dublin: Migration and Citizenship Research Initiative, 2005), p. 10

14 'Ireland Looks beyond Race – Adebari', *Irish Times*, 6 July 2007

15 Government of Ireland, *Migration Nation: Statement on Integration Strategy and Diversity Management* (Dublin: Stationery Office, 2008), p. 44

16 Migrant Voter's Project, www.dublin.ie/arts-culture/migrant-voters-campaign.htm

17 As obtained from the Franchise Department of Dublin City Council, 19 March 2009

18 Ruadhan Mac Cormaic, 'Encouragement for Immigrants To Become Irish Urged', *Irish Times*, 27 April 2009

19 'Migrant Election Failures "Big Blow" Say Candidates', *Metro Éireann*, 11–17 June 2009

20 'Maphoso Unshaken by "Racist Attack"', *Metro Éireann*, 7 May 2009

21 'Nigerian Local Election Candidate Dismissed Web Track', *Leinster Leader*, 7 January 2009

22 'Migration Watch Webiste Shuts Down after Leinster Leader Story', *Leinster Leader*, 15 January 2009

23 Editorial, *Dundalk Leader*, 24 June 2009

24 The case study researched by Kevin Howard is set out in B. Fanning, K. Howard and N. O'Boyle, 'Immigrant Candidates and Politics in the Republic of Ireland: Racialization, Ethnic Nepotism or Localism?' *Nationalism and Ethnic Politics*, 2010, 16, 1–23

25 Ruadhan Mac Cormaic, 'Reality Check for Immigrant Hopefuls', *Irish Times*, 15 June 2009

26 Catherine Reilly, 'No Easy Answers', *Metro Éireann*, 18 June 2009

27 Mac Cormaic 'Reality Check'

28 *Ibid.*

29 One Drogheda candidate, Yinka Dixon (Green Party), organised a post-election meeting of African candidates to explore their options for the future. This led to a further in-camera event in 26 September 2009 (which I attended) organised by Integrating Ireland, where African, East European and other immigrant candidates frankly discussed their experiences.

30 B. Fanning, N. O'Boyle and J. Shaw, *New Irish Politics: Political Parties and Immigrants in 2009* (Dublin: Migration and Citizenship Research Initiative, 2009), p. 9.

31 *Ibid.*, p. 14

32 Article 3 of the 1922 Constitution stated that: 'Every person without distinction of sex, domiciled in the area of the jurisdiction of the Irish Free State (Saorstát Éireann) at the time of the coming into operation of this Constitution, who was born in Ireland or either of whose parents was born in Ireland, or who has been ordinarily resident in the area of the jurisdiction of the Irish Free State (Saorstát Éireann) for not less than seven years, is a citizen of the Irish Free State (Saorstát Éireann) and shall within the limits of the jurisdiction of the Irish Free State (Saorstát Éireann) enjoy the privileges and be subject to the obligations of such citizenship.'

33 Documents on Irish Foreign Policy, No. 400 UDCA P80/603, Letter from John J. Hearne, Department of External Affairs, to Stephen A. Roche, Assistant Secretary, Department of Justice, 21 August 1930. www.difp.ie

34 See Twenty-Seventh Amendment of the Constitution Act, 2004 (Irish Citizenship of Children of Non-National Parents), The Referendum Commission, www.refcom.ie/pastreferendums/Irish citizenship

35 The Fajujonus, a Moroccan and Nigerian married couple with two Irish-born children, had successfully contested a deportation order under the Aliens Order (1946) on the basis that their children were Irish citizens. The Fajujonus argued successfully that their children, as Irish citizens, had a right to family life, in accordance with the rights of the child under the Irish constitution. Article 40 of the Irish Constitution sets out the personal rights of citizens. Article 41 sets out the rights of the family (notably 41.1.1. 'The state recognises the family as the natural primary and fundamental unit group of society, and as a moral institution possessing inalienable … rights, antecedent and superior to all positive law.'). Article 42 refers to the right (and duties) of parents to provide for the religious and moral, intellectual, physical and social education of their children.

36 The L. and O. cases involved two families of Czech Roma and Nigerian origin, each with Irish citizen children. Deportation proceedings were commenced against L. and O. following the failure of their asylum applications. Seeking a judicial review of the deportation orders, L. and O. both asserted a right to exercise a choice of residence on behalf of their citizen children, and on behalf of their children claimed the right to the company, care and parentage of their parents within the state. The majority of the Supreme Court distinguished the Fajujonu case on the basis of the length of time the parents had lived within the state and the changing context of immigration in Ireland since then. See S. Mullally, 'Children, Citizenship and Constitutional Change', in B. Fanning (ed.), *Immigration and Social Change in the Republic of Ireland* (Manchester; Manchester University Press, 2007), pp. 32–33

37 S. Mullally, 'Children, citizenship and constitutional change'

38 Immigration and Naturalisation Service, www.inis.gov.ie/en/Inis/Pages/WP07000030 scheme

39 Data from Department of Justice, Equality and Law Reform cited in National Economic and Social Council, *Managing Migration in Ireland: A Social and Economic Analysis* (Dublin: Stationery Office, 2005), p. 37

40 M. Haliloviv-Pastuovic, 'The Bosnian Project in Ireland: A Vision of Divisions in B. Fanning (ed.), *Immigration and Social Change in the Republic of Ireland* (Manchester: Manchester University Press, 2007), p. 153

41 Response to a Dáil Question to the Minister of Justice, Equality and Law Reform 'To ask the Minister of Justice, Equality and Law Reform the steps he is taking to address the long waiting lists for citizenship and residency applications,' by Caoimhghín Ó Caoláin TD, 21 February 2006.

42 Immigrant Council of Ireland, 'Citizen Processes in Need of Overhaul', press release, 7 May 2009

43 *Ibid.*

44 Dermot Ahern, Minister of Justice, Equality and Law Reform, in response to a Dáil question on citizenship applications, 6 June 2009, Question No. 409

45 Citizens Information Board www.citizensinformation.ie/categories/moving-country/irish-citizenship

46 Legal Services Commission of Southern Australia. Information last revised 23 February 2009, www.lawhandbook.sa.giv.au

47 Immigrant Council of Ireland, 'Citizen Processes', www.ici.ie

48 *Ibid.*

49 Crosscare Migrant Project, *Invisible Pathways: A Critique of the Irish Immigration System and How It Can Contribute to People Becoming Undocumented* (Dublin: Crosscare Migrant Project, 2009), p. 91

50 'Zimbabwean Challenges Refusal of Citizenship', *Irish Times*, 2 July 2009

51 Crosscare Migrant Project, *Analysis of the Irish Naturalisation and Immigration Service Customer and Information Provision Services* (Dublin: Crosscare Migrant Project, 2007), p. 2

52 Crosscare Migrant Project, *Invisible Pathways*, p. 90

53 Senator David Norris, Seanad, vol. 137, 31 October 2007

54 www.senatordavidnorrisie/blogger/2007/11/adjournment-debate-on-issue-of.html

55 Fanning *et al.*, *New Irish Politics*, p. 14

56 Polish nationality law is based on the principle of *jus sanguine*. Polish law does not allow the government to revoke a person's citizenship. It is legally difficult for a person to renounce their Polish citizenship. In effect, Polish law tolerates dual citizenship. www.polishcitizenship.co

57 'Nigerians Top of the List Seeking Irish Citizenship', *Metro Éireann*, 5 November 2009

9

Some challenges

Integration can occur as the often-unintended cumulative by-product of choices made by individuals to improve their social situation. If integration is – in this sense – a kind of market process there is on the other side a political process that sets conditions and gives incentives for individual choices and decisions: integration politics. (Friedrich Heckmann)[1]

In December 2007 the unemployment live register stood at 173,200; a year later it had risen to 293,000; by December 2009 some 423,400 persons were registered as unemployed. It may seem that the depths of an economic recession is hardly the optimum time to invest in integration, but there is no better one to focus on questions of social inclusion and social cohesion that affect immigrants and Irish citizens alike. Much of the information and research on which this book was built slightly predates the economic crisis of 2009. Immigration in the Irish case was driven by economic growth and, like other post-boom challenges being reckoned with in hard times, the integration of immigrants cannot be deferred without imposing considerable future social costs upon Irish society. In hard times the political appetite for integration programmes may be slight. But there was also, for different reasons, little commitment to integration in boom times. When it comes to leadership on integration and social cohesion issues, the biggest policy barriers arguably remain cognitive ones rather than economic ones.

Governments sometimes frame integration initiatives in debates about national identity, asking what does it mean to be British or French? In the French case, in 2009 the government established a website on 'le grand débat sur l'identité nationale' where luminaries from French public life and ordinary citizens could express their views on the meaning of Frenchness in a context where 'identity has become the master noun of the media cycle'. Writing about this, Ruadhán Mac Cormaic commented that in the Irish case one of the surest ways to ensure that a debate never happens is to call for one.[2] In a context where the media cycle or even the Irish political system tends to process one issue at a time there are always other issues to deal with. The chances are that integration will not become *the* national issue until or unless some crisis invokes deliberate reflection. There are benefits as well as problems with such reticence.

The Irish non-debate about integration has coincided with a general unwillingness amongst Irish politicians to pollute the public sphere with anti-immigrant populism. Despite the depths of Ireland's economic crisis at the time of writing, in 2010 no major Irish political figure has explicitly called for Irish jobs for Irish people. No Irish political party (except Libertas, and with little success) has invested in overt anti-immigrant populism; by European standards, this is unusual.

However, there are major problems with benign tolerance and its flipside, benign indifference. The first of these, discussed in the first chapter, is that such tolerance amounts to benign neglect. The Dutch abandoned what they thought was multiculturalism but really was a form of liberalism indifferent to the social and economic exclusions experienced by some immigrants. Similar critiques of multiculturalism have emerged in Britain. Western debates about integration have been to some extent dominated by symbolic politics whereby immigrants are to demonstrate fealty towards liberalism as a value culture. But this is mostly taken to mean negative freedoms ideologically conducive to an idealised, frictionless public sphere rather than positive freedoms under-stood in terms of the means to participate in some specific actual society. In summary, the first problem with benign tolerance is that it neglects the barriers to integration that some immigrants inevitably experience. Some of the case studies in earlier chapters have highlighted levels of exclusion already being experienced by some immigrants that may prove difficult to recover from. For some, the seeds of intergenerational exclusion may already have been sown.

The second problem with benign tolerance in politics is that it coexists with malign intolerance in the governance of immigration. A security immigration-governance perspective described in Chapter 3 has come to dominate integra-tion policy in the Irish case. This is no lazy, left-field academic claim. The previous chapter demonstrated considerable political openness to immigrants, tempered always by electoral pragmatism, but openness nevertheless, limited only by the fact that relatively few immigrants have yet become Irish citizens.

The first major integration challenge is to move from begrudging to proactive integration through citizenship. Clearly, not all immigrants want to become Irish citizens. Irish naturalisation figures reveal that those consist-ently most likely to naturalise are long-established immigrants from non-EU countries, with Africans currently at the head of the queue. It must be acknowl-edged that proactively turning long-standing immigrants into Irish citizens will not automatically ensure their integration. Marginalised citizen black and ethnicity minority populations are to be found in many other European countries. However, impeding the naturalisation of immigrants will stack the odds against their successful integration.

In the Irish case, majority-group ethnic identity and national identity remain apparently synonymous. The implicit Irish version of *le grand débat*, the 2004 Referendum on Citizenship, pitted Irish nationals against 'non-nationals'. Irish citizens voted by a four to one majority to remove the birthright to Irish citizenship from the Irish-born children of immigrants. Low levels of naturalisation constitute the single largest potential barrier to political integration. As the study of immigrants in Irish politics in the previous chapter illustrated, immigrants are much more likely to be taken seriously when they have a vote; where they do not, they remain politically irrelevant. Citizens, on the other hand, retain a political veto on any measures that might promote the integration of non-citizen immigrants.

In a previous book, *New Guests of the Irish Nation* (2009), I emphasised the limits of empathy and solidarity that needed to be treated realistically in debates about integration. *New Guests* focused extensively on the risks of ethnic nepotism, an ongoing 'us' versus 'them' solidarity with co-ethnic fellow citizens, as a barrier to integration.[3] In this book I have foregrounded barriers imposed by security-governance perspective that, in defending Irish sovereignty, defends 'nationals' from 'non-nationals'. It is unfortunate, then, but unsurprising, a social fact of Irish sovereignty, that security-governance perspectives have so much influence in immigration and integration policy decision making. These seem more adept at imposing internal borders than at proactively fostering integration.

A specific challenge, then, is to overcome institutional obstacles to citizenship. The mission of the Immigration and Naturalisation Service should be to proactively turn immigrants into Irish citizens. By international standards (compared to the United Kingdom, Australia and Canada), Irish naturalisation rates are exceedingly low. The shift that is required is from apparent bureaucratic intransigence (rules and procedures that screen out almost half of all applicants) to good-practice pathways to citizenship programmes with transparent decision-making processes and goals of educating and mentoring applicants towards meeting the criteria for naturalisation. High rates of refusal in the Irish case have nothing to do with immigrant quality. The immigrants up for naturalisation at the time of writing are ones identified by OECD comparisons (see Chapter 4) as having higher levels of education than are found in the Australian and British cases. Immigrants in Canada were marginally better educated than those in Ireland for 2001, although Ireland's immigrant population enjoyed a higher educational advantage over the host population than did those in the Canadian case. In the Irish case, many refusals may be for reasons covered by ministerial discretion (such as those due to minor driving offences, or because the applicant at some time claimed benefits to which they were entitled) or due to opaque administrative processes that compare unfavourably with international good practice.

One way to defuse the interlocking exclusionary pressures of ethnic nepotism and security governance is to turn enough non-citizens into Irish nationals so as to sunder the automatic cognitive link between Irish nationality and mono-ethnic Irish identity. Such inclusive naturalisation, a policy of turning 'strangers into citizens', would create further knock-on incentives for political integration. This potential can be seen in the pragmatic responsiveness of Irish political parties towards immigrants in the run-up to local government elections, where there are migrant votes to be won.

The second major integration challenge is to recognise that integration is best addressed through social policy rather than by means of security policy. In the current economic climate funding barriers to social policy measures that include immigrants are likely to persist, but what is crucially needed is the cognitive shift that recognises the relationship between social inclusion for citizens and integration of immigrants. The underlying rationale for both social inclusion and integration is the same: combating poverty and waste of human potential, promoting social cohesion and economic growth. What is known about what works to further social inclusion also constitutes our knowledge and expertise base for furthering integration. The need for a strong evidence base for integration as social inclusion is emphasised in Chapter 4.

Systematically disaggregated data are crucial in understanding the inevitably different needs and barriers experienced by different immigrant groups. Two specific capacity-building needs are emphasised. Firstly, the need for comprehensively disaggregated data on the experiences of different immigrant communities are needed to inform targeted policy. Clearly, not all immigrant communities have the same needs. There is an urgent need to develop research capacity in response to recent large-scale immigration; relatively little is known about the experiences of some of Ireland's largest immigrant communities. Secondly, there is a need to focus data analysis on specific geographical areas. There is also an urgent need to promote a longitudinal analysis of census and survey data capable of tracking the distinct experiences and circumstances of diverse immigrant communities.

Available census and survey data reveal crisis levels of social exclusion experienced by some black immigrants. Africans, for example, experience disproportionately high rates of unemployment. The 2006 Census found an unemployment rate of 50 percent amongst Nigerians even though 41 percent were educated to degree levels or higher. Explanations for this include the absence of a right to work for asylum seekers and a linked prohibition on access to employment training and state-funded English-language education; under such conditions the capability deficits that impede integration are very much the product of institutional failure. Many African migrants experienced several years of deliberate social exclusion alongside racism and discrimination in domains in which they had rights. A decade after Ireland declared an asylum crisis, it is faced with having to undo a legacy of damaging exclusions that have undermined the capabilities of many to participate in Irish society. Applications for Irish citizenship from the comparatively long-standing African immigrant communities now outnumber those from other communities of origin, even if they experience apparently disproportionate rates of refusal from the state.

For all this, African immigrants seem 'hungry to participate' in civil society because of, rather than in spite of, their experiences of insecurity. As a relatively established (pre-2004) immigrant cohort, Africans have been at the forefront of bottom-up immigrant political participation. About half the immigrant candidates who stood in the 2009 local government elections were African. Behind them exists a discernable African civil society. African immigrants are clearly here to stay but experience institutional barriers to integration as well as racism in society. Whilst writing this book during 2009, particularly in the aftermath of the 2009 local government elections, I encountered increasing frustration, anger and despondency amongst African immigrants about the scale of such barriers and the lack of commitment by Irish politicians and the Irish state more generally to their integration. If the focus on Africans in this book seems disproportionate, as compared to other immigrant groups considered here, this is because research on the experiences of many of these, notably the Chinese but also various Eastern European communities, remains woefully inadequate.

The third major integration challenge, then, is to invest in the capabilities of immigrants no less than in those of Irish citizens. Research on immigrant participation in the labour market consistently emphasises an immigrant penalty whereby immigrant human capital is underused in the Irish labour market. The value of the capability approach drawn on in some chapters is that it offers a means of analysing how and why such under-utilisation occurs; even skilled migrants may possess capability deficits which impede their ability to realise their potential. Arguably, investment in immigrant capabilities might realise a good economic return as well as an integration dividend. Immigration provides host countries with human capital that they did not have to invest, in just as emigration deprives the country of origin of the human capital of those who leave. But high levels of immigrant human capital do not on their own secure integration; nor do they automatically benefit the host economy. The corollary of life-long learning is a sustained investment in integration. Any new, twenty-first-century nation-building settlement must reckon with the social costs of both migrant and citizen social exclusion. All the arguments against wasting human potential apply no less to immigrants than to citizens.

Whilst immigrants require some culturally specific capabilities to integrate within Irish society, it has also been argued that Irish society needs to invest in capabilities that will enable its citizens to function in the new global economy. The 2008 *Smart Economy* report emphasised the ongoing expansion of human, social and knowledge capital as a means of securing Ireland's economic future.[4] Part of its emphasis is upon the need for outwardly focused capabilities. For example, *Smart Economy* emphasised investing in cultural and economic relationships with China. Specifically, it advocated expansion of the teaching of Mandarin.[5] If Ireland is to trade successfully within the world's largest economy it needs to invest in linguistic capabilities. Yet, unknown thousands of migrants living in Ireland already speak Mandarin. In such a context the invisibility of Ireland's Chinese community to statisticians, social researchers and policy makers seems negligent.[6] Some skills and capabilities possessed by migrants, such as fluency in the languages of their countries of origin, may not count as capabilities when it comes to integrating into Ireland, but they are nevertheless resources of considerable value to Irish society in its engagement with the wider world. Part of the case for a proactive approach to integration is that the skills and abilities of immigrants may be of considerable economic benefit to the Irish economy. The 'elusive knowledge economy', as Constantin Gurdgiev describes it, is one that requires more people with cultural and linguistic skills and other skill sets not characteristic of unemployed Irish citizens.[7]

Integration occurs (or not) within a range of domains, each of which brings its own challenges. Those focused upon in this book include the labour market, education and specific geographical areas where risks of socio-spatial segregation need to be addressed. The Irish version of benign neglect has included the presumption – credible perhaps in the boom years, that most credulous of times – that participation in the labour market means integration. Vulnerable migrant workers tend to be overlooked in debates about integration. They are perceived as temporary sojourners; indeed, many such migrants see themselves in such terms. However, because many stay on, it is important to invest in their integration. In a 2005 speech the then Minister of Justice, Equality and Law Reform, Michael McDowell, acknowledged the argument, distilled from the experiences of other countries, that allowing the exploitation of immigrant workers served to undermine future social cohesion:

> Migrant workers in Ireland are welcome, are positive and are essential for the economic development and social prosperity of this country … We will need to set standards for the treatment of immigrants now so that we will not see in 10 or 15 years time scenes like those unfolding in Paris.[8]

Such acknowledgements by government ministers about the stakes in failing to integrate vulnerable immigrants have, to date, been rare. All migrant workers have rights under employment equality legislation but the case studies examined in Chapter 5 illustrate how the most vulnerable have little meaningful access to such rights. Improvement in the lives of such vulnerable migrants depends on two sets of factors. The first of these are structural; there is a need to persistently address the licence to exploit, effectively given by the state to employers and traffickers; a holistic approach to the welfare of vulnerable migrants is needed. One of the main threats levied by employers against vulnerable migrants is the threat of sanctions by the Irish state. Here the balance of power needs to be shifted; what the MRCI describes as the sustainable integration of third-country nationals is required.[9] The MRCI advocates 'combating undeclared work and reducing the informal economy with a view to developing a broad mix of sanctions and preventative measures to translate undeclared work into regular employment'.[10] The state needs to do more to protect and empower vulnerable migrants, and more to punish their exploiters. Employers could, for example, be required to enrol and fund non-English-speaking employees in English-language courses.[11]

The same MRCI case studies also reveal the need to address the complicity of the current regulatory system in the exploitation of migrants threatened with becoming undocumented. In effect, what is needed is greater access by vulnerable migrants currently living in Ireland to long-term work permits. Documented migrants who have lived and worked in Ireland for five years receive long-term residency rights without having to apply for further permits. Those who become undocumented through no fault of their own need protection. The challenges here should not be underestimated. Economic downturn resulted in the imposition of new prohibitions on the renewal of work permits in June 2009; this made many vulnerable migrants even more vulnerable to exploitation. Migrants from outside the European Economic Area (EEA), which includes the EU, Norway, Iceland, Lichtenstein and Switzerland, who lost their jobs were given only three months to find alternative employment or leave the country. These restrictions were relaxed somewhat in August 2009. The Minister of Justice, Equality and Law Reform announced that migrant workers who had held an employment permit for less than five years would now be able to stay for up to six months after losing their jobs.[12] Such workers could only apply for jobs that could not be filled from within the EEA; the effective choice for many was to leave to the country or become undocumented. For all that, the experiences of other countries and available evidence in the Irish case suggest that Ireland will continue to have a population of vulnerable migrants, some documented, others not. As in the case of the naturalisation process, a proactive goal of regularising existing immigrants who are long-term residents is needed.

Authoritative research, considered in Chapter 6, suggests the need for a specific focus on how the education system is responding to black children; the issues here are well rehearsed in other Western countries that have failed black children; the dangers that Ireland will replicate intergenerational patterns of educational disadvantage on the basis of race are real in the Irish case.

Research on educational disadvantage emphasises how factors outside the school, such as parental social exclusion, contribute to educational inequalities. The findings of research examined in Chapter 6 suggest the need for some specific holistic, area-based programmes that address immigrant educational needs alongside wider social inclusion and integration issues.

A fourth major integration challenge relates to the inclusion of immigrants in decision making in the various domains within which integration occurs. The more involved immigrants can become in the design and delivery of integration initiatives, the better. But this is easier said than done. While the health services depend on immigrant doctors and other health workers, immigrants are very much under-represented across much of the public sector, and also within the NGO and community sector. There is a clear strategic need to invest in capacity building through investment in immigrant-led organisations. Those in existence have crucial on-the-ground expertise and have been responsible, along with the wider NGO sector engaged in migrant advocacy, for much of the research on immigration and integration in the Republic of Ireland.

Much of what might be described as integration occurs through the efforts of immigrants themselves to build lives in Ireland. In considering the contexts within which such efforts occur, emphasis has been placed on the role of capabilities, social capital and cultural capital as resources that contribute to integration. Capabilities are to be understood in terms of individual attributes but they also depend on the wider context of barriers and opportunities presented by the host society. In theory, capabilities beneficial to life in a specific society equip individuals with the means to integrate. Yet capabilities cannot be understood as a means to some externally decided end, such as integration goals and parameters set by policy makers. Yet, as emphasised in Chapter 1 and Chapter 5, attributes and dispositions understood variously as individual capabilities, individual social capital and individual cultural capital delineate the contexts within which integration occurs. From these, some rules of thumb that address concerns about immigrant cultural barriers to integration, highlighted by critics of multiculturalism, might be proposed. From the available evidence considered in Chapter 5 the following integration hypothesis is suggested.

The integration of immigrants is likely to be furthered by thick bonds with co-ethnics (bonding social capital) when individuals within such communities possess the capabilities to engage independently with the host society. Thick bonds with co-ethnics and familial supports can work to enable the functional integration of migrants. As defined in Chapter 5, functional integration means that migrants have achieved their own economic and social goals, not necessarily those of the host society. Functional integration is of obvious benefit to migrants themselves (their sojourn in Ireland is successful), even if it falls short of what the host society has in mind. Dysfunctional integration (examples given include migrants who experience serious exploitation at the hands of co-ethnics) benefits nobody. Cultural bonds between immigrants are less likely to impede immigration where individuals have the capabilities to participate economically and socially in the wider community and where the host society does not impose its own barriers to participation. Human capital alone may not benefit immigrants unless they also possess culturally specific capabilities. English-language capability deficits impose formidable barriers to integration. One of the fundamental ways through which integration into market relations is secured is through the possession of good negotiation skills and adequate information about the market-place.[13] Without language competency, it is difficult to maximise such potential. Language capability deficits undermine the usefulness of other kinds of capabilities.

Various forms of education play an important role in engendering capabilities. But there is more to empowerment than self-belief or forms of individualised knowledge that foster some new sense of agency and possibility; many of the barriers to integration that immigrants must reckon with are those either imposed deliberately or permitted by the host society.

Notes

1 F. Heckmann, 'From Ethnic Nation to Universal Immigrant Nation', in F. Heckmann and D. Schnaper (eds), *The Integration of Immigrants in European Societies: National Differences and Trends of Convergence* (Stuttgart: Lucius and Lucius, 2003), p. 46

2 R. Mac Cormaic, 'Identity Debate Rouses Passions of French Public Life', *Irish Times*, 12 November 2009

3 B. Fanning, *New Guests of the Irish Nation* (Dublin: Irish Academic Press, 2009), pp. 181–187

4 Department of the Taoiseach, *Building Ireland's Smart Economy: A Framework for Sustainable Economic Renewal* (Dublin: Stationery Office, 2008), p. 32

5 *Building Ireland's Smart Economy*, p. 16. Also see reports published by the Confucius Institute at University College Dublin on the business case for teaching Mandarin as part of the secondary curriculum. www.confuciusinstitute.ie

6 See studies published by the Confucius Institute at University College Dublin on the business case for teaching Mandarin as part of the secondary curriculum. www.confuciusinstitute.ie

7 Constantin Gurdgiev, 'Refusal To Listen Caused Year of Pain', *Sunday Times*, 27 December 2009

8 Cited in Migrant Rights Centre Ireland, *Realising Integration: Creating the Conditions for the Economic, Social, Political and cultural Inclusion of Migrant Workers and their Families in Ireland* (Dublin: MRCI, 2006), p. 47

9 *Ibid.*, p. 47

10 *Ibid.*, p. 42

11 A study of barriers to employment and education in Cork by the NASC immigrant support centre recommended the need to investigate ways in which employers can provide English-language classes to their staff members; employees were more likely to avail themselves of classes during working hours; there should be incentives for migrants to improve their English. Overall this research emphasised that there was an inadequate strategic focus on English-language training and that many migrants found it difficult to access such training. P. Dunbar, *Evaluating the Barriers to Employment and Education in Cork* (Cork: NASC, 2008), p. 7

12 'Rules for Jobless Migrants Eased', *Irish Times*, 28 August 2009

13 W. Reimer, 'Social Exclusion in a Comparative Context', *Socologia Ruralis*, 44.2 (2004), 76–94

Select bibliography

Adams, M., 'The Reflexive Self and Culture: A Critique' *British Journal of Sociology*, 54.2 (June 2003), 221–238

Adams, M., 'Hybridizing Habitus and Reflexivity: Towards an Understanding of Contemporary Identity?' *Sociology* 40.3 (2006), 511–528

Adkins, A., *Revisions: Gender and Sexuality in Late Modernity* (Buckingham: Open University Press, 2002)

Alibhai-Brown, Y., *After Multiculturalism* (London: The Foreign Policy Centre, 2000)

Atkinson, T., Cantillon, B., Marlier, E. and Nolan, B., *Social Indicators: The EU and Social Inclusion* (Oxford: Oxford University Press, 2002)

Barrett, A.S., McGuinness, S. and O'Brien, M. (2008), *The Immigrant Earnings Disadvantage across the Earnings and Skills Distributions: The Case of Immigrants from the EU's New Member States in Ireland*, Working Paper No. 236 (Dublin: Economic and Social Research Institute, 2008)

Barros, W. and Manfli, G., 'Approaching Migrant Youth Marginalisation through the Capabilities Approach: Methodological Proposals', *Social Work and Society*, 7.1 (2009), 7–24

Baumgartner, M., *The Moral Order and the Suburbs* (Oxford: Oxford University Press, 1988)

Beck, U., *Risk Society: Towards a New Modernity* (London: Sage, 1992)

Beck, U., Giddens, A. and Lash, S., *Reflexive Modernization* (Cambridge: Polity Press, 1994)

Begley, M., Garavan, K.C., Condon, M., Kelly, I., Holland, K. and Staines, A., *Asylum in Ireland: A Public Health Perspective* (Dublin: Department of Public Health Medicine and Epidemiology, 1999)

Berlin, I., 'Two Concepts of Liberty', in H. Hardy and R. Hausheer (eds), *The Proper Study of Mankind: An Anthology of Essays* (London: Pimlico, 1998)

Bhreatnach, A., *Becoming Conspicuous: Irish Travellers, Society and the State 1912–70* (Dublin: University College Dublin, 2007)

Bielenberg, A. (ed.), *The Irish Diaspora* (Harlow: Pearson, 2000)

Boucher, G., 'Ireland's Lack of a Coherent Integration Policy', *Translocations: Migration and Social Change* 3.1 (2007), 5–28

Bourdieu, P., 'The Social Space and the Genesis of Groups' *Theory and Society* 14.6 (1985), 723–744

Bourdieu, P., 'The Forms of Capital', in J.G. Richardson (ed.), *The Handbook of Theory and Research for the Sociology of Education* (New York: Greenwood, 1986), p. 249

Bourdieu, P. and Passeron, J.C., *Reproduction in Education, Society and Culture* (London: Sage, 1977)

Bourdieu, P. et al., *The Weight of the World: Social Suffering in Contemporary Society* (Cambridge: Polity Press, 1999)

Brandom, R.B. (ed.), *Rorty and His Critics* (London: Blackwell, 2002)

Brubaker, R., 'The Return of Assimilation? Changing Perspectives on Immigration and Its Sequels in France, Germany, and the United States', *Ethnic and Racial Studies* 24.4 (2001), 531–548

Cabinet Office, *Minority Ethnic Issues in Social Exclusion and Neighbourhood Renewal* (London: HMSO, 2000)

Cheong, P., Edwards, R., Goulbourne, H. and Solomos, J., 'Immigration, Social Cohesion and Social Capital: A Critical Review', *Critical Social Policy* 27.1 (2007), 24–49

Coakley, L., *The Challenges and Obstacles Facing Refugees, Persons with Leave to Remain and Persons Granted Subsidiary Protection, as they Seek To Access Post-second Level Education in Ireland* (Dublin: Refugee Information Service, 2009)

Connolly, P. and Troyna, B. (eds), *Researching Racism in Education: Politics, Theory and Practice* (Buckingham: Open University Press, 1998)

Conroy, P., *Trafficking in Unaccompanied Minors in Dublin* (Dublin: International Organisation of Migration, 2003)

Corkery, D., *The Hidden Ireland: A Study of Gaelic Munster in the Eighteenth Century* (Dublin: Gill and Macmillan, 1970)

Cox, R., *The Servant Problem: Domestic Employment in the Global Economy* (London: I.B. Tauris, 2006)

Crosscare Migrant Project, *Analysis of the Irish Naturalisation and Immigration Service Customer and Information Provision Services* (Dublin: Crosscare Migrant Project, 2007)

Crosscare Migrant Project, *Invisible Pathways: A Critique of the Irish immigration System and How It Can Contribute to People Becoming Undocumented* (Dublin: Crosscare Migrant Project, 2009)

Crotty, R., *Ireland in Crisis: A Study in Capitalist Colonial Underdevelopment* (Dingle: Brandon, 1986)

Department of the Taoiseach, *Building Ireland's Smart Economy: A Framework for Sustainable Economic Renewal* (Dublin: Stationery Office, 2008)

Devine, D., 'Welcome to the Celtic Tiger? Teacher Responses to Immigration and Increasing Diversity in Irish Schools', *International Studies in Sociology of Education* 15 (2005), 49–70

Drinkwater, S., Eade, J. and Garapich, M., *Poles Apart? EU Enlargement and the Labour Market Outcomes of Immigrants in the UK*, Institute for the Study of Labor (IZA): Discussion Paper No. 2410

Duleep, H.O. and Rogers, M.C., *The Elusive Concept of Immigrant Quality: Evidence from 1970–1990* (Bonn: Forshunginstitut zur Zukunft der Arbeit/Institute for the Study of Labour, 2000)

Dunbar, P., *Evaluating the Barriers to Employment and Education in Cork* (Cork: NASC, 2008)

Durkheim, E., *The Rules of Sociological Method* (New York: Free Press, 1938)

Durkheim, E., *Suicide: A Study in Sociology* (New York: Free Press, 1951)

Durkheim, E., *The Division of Labour in Society* (London: Macmillan, 1984)

Economic and Social Research Institute, *Adapting to Diversity: Irish Schools and Newcomer Students* (Dublin: ESRI, 2009)

Ehrenreich, B. and Russell Hochschild, A. (eds), *Global Woman: Nannies, Maids and Sex Workers in the New Economy* (London: Granta, 2003)

Ejorh, T., *Inclusive Citizenship in 21st Century Ireland: What Prospects for the African Community?* (Dublin: Africa Centre, 2006)

Entzinger, H. and Biezeveld, R., *Benchmarking in Immigrant Integration, Report written for the European Commission, European Research Centre on Migration and Ethnic Relations* (Rotterdam: ERCOMER, 2003)

Erne, R., 'A Contentious Consensus', in T. Schulten, R. Bispinck and C. Schäfer (eds), *Minimum Wages in Europe* (Brussels: ETUI, 2006)

Erne, R., *European Unions: Labour's Quest for Transnational Democracy* (Ithaca, NY: Cornell University Press, 2008)

Fahey, T. and Fanning, B., 'Immigration and Social Spatial Segregation in Dublin', *Urban Studies* 47.8 (2010), 1625–1642

Fanning, B., *Racism and Social Change in the Republic of Ireland* (Manchester: Manchester University Press, 2002)

Fanning, B., 'Asylum-seeker Children in Ireland: Racism, Institutional Racism and Social Work', in D. Hayes and B. Humphries (eds), *Social Work, Immigration and Asylum: Debates, Dilemmas and Ethical Issues for Social Work and Social Care Practice* (London: Jessica Kingsley Press, 2004)

Fanning, B. (ed.), *Immigration and Social Change in the Republic of Ireland* (Manchester: Manchester University Press, 2007)

Fanning, B., *The Quest for Modern Ireland: The Battle of Ideas 1912–1986* (Dublin: Irish Academic Press, 2008)

Fanning, B., *New Guests of the Irish Nation* (Dublin: Irish Academic Press, 2009)

Fanning, B. and Mooney, T., 'Pragmatism and Intolerance: Nietzsche and Rorty', *Philosophy and Social Criticism* 36 (2010), 735–755

Fanning, B. and Mutwarasibo, F., 'Nationals/Non-nationals: Immigration, Citizenship and Politics in the Republic of Ireland', *Ethnic and Racial Studies* 30.3 (2007), 439–460

Fanning, B. and Veale, A., 'Child Poverty as Public Policy: Direct Provision and Asylum Seeking Children in the Republic of Ireland', *Child Care in Practice* 10.3 (2004), 241–252

Fanning, B., Hasse, T. and O'Boyle, N., 'Well-being, Cultural Capital and Social Inclusion: Immigrants in the Republic of Ireland', *Journal of Immigration and Integration* (forthcoming)

Fanning, B., Howard, K. and O'Boyle, N., 'Immigrant Candidates and Politics in the Republic of Ireland: Racialization, Ethnic Nepotism or Localism?' *Nationalism and Ethnic Politics* (2010), 16, 1–23

Fanning, B., Loyal, S. and Staunton, C., *Asylum Seekers and the Right to Work in Ireland* (Dublin: Irish Refugee Council, 2000)

Fanning, B., Mutwarasibo, F. and Chadamayo, N., *Positive Politics: Participation of Immigrants and Ethnic Minorities in the Electoral Process* (Dublin: Africa Solidarity Centre, 2003)

Fanning, B., O'Boyle, N. and Shaw, J., *New Irish Politics: Political Parties and Immigrants in 2009* (Dublin: Migration and Citizenship Research Initiative, 2009)

Fanning, B., Veale, A. and O'Connor, D., *Beyond the Pale: Asylum Seeking Children and Social Exclusion in Ireland* (Dublin: Irish Refugee Council, 2001)

Farrell, C., 'Thinking Critically about Social Capital', *Irish Journal of Sociology* 16.2 (2007), 27–49

Feldman, A., Gilmartin, M., Loyal, S. and Migge, B., *Getting On: From Migration to Integration, Chinese, Indian, Lithuanian and Nigerian Migrants' Experiences in Ireland* (Dublin: Immigrant Council of Ireland, 2008)

Feldman, A., Ndakengerwa, D., Nolan, A. and Fresse, C., *Diversity, Civil Society and Social Change in Ireland: A North-South Comparison of the Role of Immigrant/'New' Minority Ethnic-Led Community and Voluntary Sector Organisations* (Dublin: Migration and Citizenship Research Initiative, 2005)

Flynn, K., 'Understanding Islam in Ireland', *Islam and Christian-Muslim Relations* 17. 2 (2006), 223–238

Forrest, R. and Kearns, A., 'Social Cohesion, Social Capital and the Neighbourhood', *Urban Studies* 38 (2001), 2125–2143

Frost, C., 'Is Post-nationalism or Liberal-culturalism behind the Transformation of Irish Nationalism?' *Irish Political Studies* 21.3 (2006), 277–295

Fundamental Rights Agency, *European Union Minorities and Discrimination Survey* (2009). Available at: http:///fra.europa.eu/eu-midis/

Garvin, T., *Preventing the Future: Why Was Ireland so Poor for so Long?* (Dublin: Gill and Macmillan, 2004)

Gellner, E., *Culture, Identity and Politics* (Cambridge: Cambridge University Press, 1987)

George Boyce, D. and O'Day, A., *The Making of Modern Irish History: Revisionism and the Revisionist Controversy* (London: Routledge, 1996)

Gesthuizen, M., van der Meer, T. and Scheepers, P., 'Ethnic Diversity and Social Capital in Europe: Tests of Putnam's Thesis in European Countries', *Scandinavian Political Studies* 32.2 (2009), 121–142

Giddens, A., *The Transformation of Intimacy* (Cambridge: Polity, 1992)

Giddens, A., *The Third Way: The Renewal of Social Democracy* (Cambridge: Polity, 1998)

Government of Ireland, *Economic Development* (Dublin: Stationery Office, 1958)

Government of Ireland, *Report of the Commission on Itinerancy* (Dublin: Stationery Office, 1963)

Government of Ireland, *Investment in Education* (Dublin: Stationery Office, 1966)

Government of Ireland (1997) *Sharing in Progress: The National Anti-Poverty Strategy* (Dublin: Official Publications)

Government of Ireland, *Integration: A Two Way Process* (Dublin: Stationery Office, 2000)

Government of Ireland, *Revised Anti-Poverty Strategy* (Dublin: Stationery Office, 2002)

Government of Ireland, *Migration Nation; Statement on Integration Strategy and Diversity Management* (Dublin: Stationery Office, 2008)

Government of Ireland, *The National Report for Ireland on Strategies for Social Protection and Social Inclusion 2008–2010* (Dublin Stationery Office, 2008)

Gray, B., 'Migrant Integration Policy: A Nationalist Fantasy of Management and Control', *Translocations* 1.1 (2006), 118–138

Haase, T. and Byrne, K., *Divided City: The Changing Face of Dublin's Inner City* (Dublin: DICP, 2007)

Haase, T. and Pratschke, J., *New Measures of Deprivation for the Republic of Ireland* (Dublin: Pobal, 2008)

Health Service Executive, *Ireland's National Plan of Action to Address Female Genital Mutilation* (Dublin: Health Service Executive, 2008)

Healy, C., 'Carnaval Do Galway: The Brazilian Community in Gort, 1999–2006', *Irish Migration Studies in Latin America* 4.3 (2006), 150–153

Heckmann, F. and Schnaper, D. (eds), *The Integration of Immigrants in European Societies: National Differences and Trends of Convergence* (Stuttgart: Lucius and Lucius, 2003)

Held, D., *Democracy and the Global Order: From the Modern State to Cosmopolitan Governance* (London: Polity, 1995)

Hickman, M., Crowley, H. and Mai, N., *Immigration and Social Cohesion in the UK* (York: Joseph Rowntree Foundation, 2008)

Immigrant Council of Ireland, *Globalisation, Sex Trafficking and Prostitution: The Experiences of Migrant Women in Ireland* (Dublin: Immigrant Council of Ireland, 2009)

Jones-Correa, M. and Leal, D.L., 'Political Participation: Does Religion Matter?' *Political Research Quarterly* 54.4 (December 2001), 751–770

Joppke, C., 'Why Liberal States Accept Unwanted Immigration', *World Politics* 50 (1998), 226–293

Joppke, C., *Selecting by Origin: Ethnic Migration in the Liberal State* (Cambridge, MA: Harvard University Press, 2005)

Joppke, C., 'Transformation of Immigration: Civic Integration and Antidiscrimination in the Netherlands, France, and Germany', *World Politics* 59 (January 2007), 243–273

Kelly, D., 'Dublin's Spatial Narrative – the Transition from Essentially Monocultural Place to Polycultural Spaces', *Irish Geography* 28.2 (2005), 209–224

Keogh, D., *Jews in Twentieth Century Ireland* (Cork: Cork University Press, 1999)

Kinsella, A., 'Welfare Rights and the Risks of Poverty for Immigrants in Ireland: Stratification and Access Barriers', MPhil thesis (Dublin: University College Dublin, 2009)

Kirby, P., 'Tom Garvin and the Causes of Irish Underdevelopment', *Administration*, 54.3 (2006), 55–67

Kropiewiec, K. and King O'Riain, R., *Polish Migrant Workers in Ireland* (Dublin: NCCRI, 2006)

Kymlicka, W., *Politics in the Vernacular* (Oxford: Oxford University Press, 2001)

Lee, J.J., *Ireland 1912–1985: Politics and Society* (Cambridge: Cambridge University Press, 1989)

Leighley, H.E. and Vedlitz, A., 'Race, Ethnicity and Political Participation: Competing Models and Contrasting Explanations', *The Journal of Politics* 61.4 (1999), 1092–1114

Lentin, A. and Titley, G., *Questioning the European 'Crisis of Multiculturalism'* (2009). Available at: http://multiculturality wordpress.com/about

Li, A., 'Social Capital and Economic Outcomes for Immigrants and Ethnic Minorities',
    Journal of International Migration and Integration 5.1 (2004), 171–190
Lively, A., *Masks: Blackness, Race and the Imagination* (London: Chatto and Windus,
    1998)
Lukes, S., *Power: A Radical View* (London: Macmillan, 1974)
Mac an Ghaill, M., *Young, Gifted and Black: Student–Teacher Relations in Schooling
    Black Youth* (Milton Keynes: Open University Press, 1988)
McCarthy, C., *Modernisation: Crisis and Culture 1969–1992* (Dublin: Four Courts
    Press, 2000)
McGinnity, F., O'Connell, P.J., Quinn, E. and Williams, J., *Migrants' Experience of
    Racism and Discrimination in Ireland: Results of a Survey Conducted by the Economic
    and Social Research Institute for the European Union Monitoring Centre on Racism
    and Xenophobia* (Dublin: ESRI, 2006)
McGorman, E. and Sugrue, C., *Intercultural Education: Primary Challenges in Dublin
    15* (Dublin: Department of Education and Science, 2007)
McGrath, B. and Murray, F., 'Brazilian Migrants in Ireland, Emergent Themes from
    Research and Practice on the Significance of Social Networks and Social Capital',
    Translocations: Migration and Social Change 5.1 (2009), 1–20
Macpherson, W., *The Stephen Lawrence Inquiry: Report of an Inquiry by Sir William
    Macpherson of Cluny* (London: HMSO, 1999)
Manandhar, M., Share, S., Friel, O., Walsh, O. and Hardy, F., *Food, Nutrition and
    Poverty amongst Asylum Seekers in North-West Ireland*, Combat Poverty Agency
    Working Paper Series 06/01 (Dublin: Combat Poverty Agency, 2006)
Mann, M., 'Social Cohesion and Liberal Democracy', *American Sociological Review* 35
    (1970), 423–439
Massey, D. and Sánchez, M., *Restrictive Immigration Policies and Latino Immigrant
    Identity in the United States*, United Nations Development Programme Research
    Paper 2009/43
Massey, D.S. and Denton, N., *American Apartheid: Segregation and the Making of the
    Underclass* (Cambridge, MA: Harvard University Press, 1993)
Migrant Rights Centre Ireland, *Private Homes: A Public Concern* (Dublin: Migrant
    Rights Centre Ireland, 2004)
Migrant Rights Centre Ireland, *Social Protection Denied: The Impact of the Habitual
    Residency Condition on Migrant Workers* (Dublin: MRCI, 2005)
Migrant Rights Centre Ireland, *Realising Integration: Creating the Conditions for the
    Economic, Social, Political and Cultural Inclusion of Migrant Workers and Their
    Families in Ireland* (Dublin: MRCI, 2006)
Migrant Rights Centre Ireland, *Exploitation in Ireland's Restaurant Industry* (Dublin:
    MRCI, 2008)
Mills, C.W., *The Sociological Imagination* (Harmondsworth: Penguin, 1959)
Modood, T., Berthood, R., Lakey, J., Nazroo, J., Patten, S., Virdee, S. and Beishon, S.,
    Ethnic Minorities in Britain (London: Policy Studies Institute, 1997)
Mushroom Workers Support Group, *Harvesting Justice: Mushroom Workers Call for
    Change* (Dublin: Migrant Rights Centre Ireland, 2006)
National Economic and Social Council, *The Developmental Welfare State* (Dublin:
    Stationery Office, 2005)

National Economic and Social Council, *Managing Migration in Ireland: A Social and Economic Analysis* (Dublin: Stationery Office, 2005)

Ní Laoire, C., Bushin, N., Carpena-Méndez, F. and White, A., *Tell Me about Yourself: Migrant Children's Experiences of Moving to and Living in Ireland* (Cork: University College Cork, 2009)

Nolan, B., *Child Poverty in Ireland* (Dublin: Oak Tree Press, 2000)

Nolan, B., 'Promoting the Well-being of Immigrant Youth', in A. Masten, D. Hernandez and K. Liebkind (eds), *Capitalizing on Migration: The Potential of Immigrant Youth* (Oxford: Oxford University Press, forthcoming)

Noll, H.H., 'Towards a European System of Social Indicators: Theoretical Framework and System Architecture', *Social Indicators Research* 58.1–3 (2002), 47–87

Nowlan, E., 'Underneath the Band-Aid: Supporting Bilingual Students in Irish Schools', *Irish Educational Studies* 27.3 (2008), 253–266

O'Boyle, N., 'Integration and Political Participation: Immigrants and the 2009 Local Elections in Ireland', *Studies* 95.389 (2009), pp. 59–70

O'Boyle, N. and Fanning, B., 'Immigration, Integration and the Risks of Social Exclusion: The Social Policy Case for Disaggregated Data in the Republic of Ireland', *Irish Geography* 42.2 (2009), 145–164

Ó'Brian, E., *Towards an Integrated Community: A Survey of Minority Ethnic Communities in Fingal* (Dublin: Fingal Development Board and Fingal County Council, 2009)

O'Connell, D. and Smith, C., 'Citizenship and the Irish Constitution', in U. Fraser and C. Harvey (eds), *Sanctuary in Ireland: Perspectives on Asylum Law and Policy* (Dublin: Institute of Public Administration, 2003)

O'Connell, P. and McGinnity, F., *Immigrants at Work: Ethnicity and Nationality in the Irish Labour Market* (Dublin: ESRI, 2008)

O'Donnell, I., 'Imprisonment and Penal Policy in Ireland', *The Howard Journal* 43.1 (2004), 253–266

O'Donnell, I., 'Crime and Justice in the Republic of Ireland', *European Journal of Criminology* 2.1 (2005), 99–131

O'Faolain, S., *King of the Beggars: A Life of Daniel O'Connell, the Irish Liberator, in a Study of the Rise of Modern Irish Democracy* (Dublin: Poolbeg, 1980)

O'Grada, C. and O'Rourke, K., 'Economic growth since 1945', in N. Crafts and G. Toniolo (eds), *Economic Growth in Europe since 1945* (Cambridge: Cambridge University Press, 1996)

O'Riain, S., 'Social Partnership as a Mode of Governance', *The Economic and Social Review* 37 (Winter 2006), 311–318

O'Sullivan, D., *Cultural Politics and Irish Education since the 1950s: Policies, Paradigms and Power* (Dublin: Institute of Public Administration, 2005)

OECD, *Where Immigrant Students Succeed: A Comparative Review of Performance and Engagement in PISA 2003* (Paris: OECD, 2006)

OECD, *International Migration Outlook* (Paris: OECD, 2007)

Olson, M., *The Logic of Collective Action* (Cambridge, MA: Harvard University Press, 1967)

Olson, M., 'Response to Lessons from Ireland', *Journal of Economic Perspectives* 12.1 (1998), 241–242

Peach, C., 'Does Britain Have Ghettos?' *Transactions of the Institute of British Geographers* 21 (1996), 216–235

Peach, C., 'Sleepwalking into Ghettoisation? The British Debate over Segregation', in K. Schönwälder (ed.), *Residential Segregation and the Integration of Immigrants: Britain, the Netherlands and Sweden*, Discussion Paper Nr. SP IV 2007–602 (Berlin: Wissenschaftszentrum Berlin für Sozialforschung gGmbH, Social Science Research Centre Berlin, 2007). Available at: www.wzb.eu

Peach, C., 'Slippery Segregation: Discovering or Manufacturing Ghettos', University of Manchester Institute for Social Change, Working Paper (2007)

Peach, C., Robinson, V. and Smith, S., *Segregation in Cities* (London: Croom Helm, 1981)

Peach, C. and Glazer, N., 'London and New York: Contrasts in British and American Models of Segregation', *International Journal of Political Geography* 5 (1999), 319–351

Penninx, R., *Integration: The Role of Communities, Institutions, and the State* (2003), Available at: www.migrationinformation.org

Picot, G., Hou, F. and Columbe, S., 'Poverty Dynamics among Recent Immigrants to Canada', *International Migration Review*, 42.2 (2008), 393–424

Portes, R.D. and Landolt, P., 'The Downside of Social Capital', *American Prospect* 26 (1996), 18–21

Putnam, R.D., *Bowling Alone: The Collapse and Revival of American Community* (New York: Simon and Schuster, 2000)

Putnam, R.D., '*E Pluribus Unum:* Diversity and Community in the Twenty-first Century', *Scandinavian Political Studies* 30.2 (2006) 137–174

Reimer, W., 'Social Exclusion in a Comparative Context', *Socologia Ruralis* 44.2 (2004), 76–94

Rhodes, R.A.W., 'The New Governance: Governing without Government', *Political Studies* 44 (1996), 652–667

Robinson, D. and Reeve, K., *Experiences of New Immigration at Neighbourhood Level* (York: Joseph Rowntree Foundation, 2006)

Roche, M., *Comparative Social Inclusion Policies and Citizenship in Europe: Towards a New European Social Model*, Targeted Socio-Economic Research (TSER) SOE2-CT97-3059 (Brussels: European Commission, 2003)

Rorty, R., *Philosophy and the Mirror of Nature* (Princeton, NJ: Princeton University Press, 1979)

Rorty, R., *Objectivism, Relativism and Truth* (New York: Cambridge, 1991) p. 2

Rorty, R., *Philosophy and Social Hope* (London: Penguin, 1999) p. xxiv

Rottman, D. and O'Connell, P., 'The Changing Social Structure', in B. Fanning and T. MacNamara (eds), *Ireland Develops: Administration and Social Policy 1953–2003* (Dublin: IPA, 2003)

Ryan, C., *Socio Economic Profile of Blanchardstown, Blanchardstown Area Partnership* (Dublin: Blancharstown Area Partnership, 2008)

Ryan, L., 'Social Dynamite: A Study of Early School Leavers', *Christus Rex* 21.1 (1967), 7–44

Samers, M., 'Immigration and the Global City Hypothesis: Towards an Alternative Research Agenda', *International Journal of Urban and Regional Research* 26.2 (2002), 398–402

Sampson, R., 'Disparity and Diversity in the Contemporary City: Social (Dis)order Revisited', *British Journal of Sociology* 60.1 (2009), 1–31

Sen, A., 'Capability and Well-being', in M. Nussbaum and A. Sen (eds), *The Quality of Life* (Oxford: Clarendon Press, 1993)

Sen, A., 'Editorial: Human Capital and Human Capability', *World Development* 25.12 (1997), 1959–1961

Sen, A., *Identity and Violence: The Illusion of Destiny* (London: Penguin, 2006)

Sharpe, A. and Banting, K. (eds), *The Review of Economic Performance and Social Performance: The Longest Decade: Canada in the 1990s* (Ottawa: Centre for the Study of Living Standards and The Institute for Research on Public Policy, 2001)

Smith, E., Darmody, M., McGinnity, F. and Byrne, D., *What Do We Know about Large Scale Immigraion and Irish Schools?* ESRI Research Bulletin 2009/2/6 (Dublin: Economic and Social Research Institute, 2009)

Strand, S., *Minority Ethnic Pupils in the Longitudinal Study of Young People in England*, DCSF-RR029 (Warwick: University of Warwick, Institute of Education/Department for Children, Schools and Families, 2007)

Sweetman, P., 'Twenty-first Century Dis-casc? Habitual Reflexivity and Reflexive Habitus', *Sociological Review* 51.4 (2003), 528–549

Tam Cho, W., 'Naturalisation, Socialization, Participation: Immigrants and Non-Voting', *The Journal of Politics* 61.4 (1999), 1140–1158

Terray, E., 'Headscarf Hysteria', *New Left Review* (March 2004), 118–127

Theiler, T., 'Societal Security', in M. Dunn and V. Mauer (eds), *The Routledge Handbook of Security Studies* (London: Routledge, 2009)

Titley, G., 'Pleasing the Crisis: Anxiety and Recited Multiculturalism in European Communicative Space', in I.S. Moring (ed.), *Manufacturing Europe: Spaces of Democracy, Diversity and Communication* (Goteborg: Nordicom, 2010)

Tönnies, F., *Community and Civil Society* (Cambridge: Cambridge University Press, 2001)

Turner, B.S., 'Citizenship and the Crisis of Multiculturalism', *Citizenship Studies* 10.5 (2006), 607–618

Ugba, A., 'African Pentecostals in Twenty-first Century Ireland: Identity and Integration', in B. Fanning (ed.), *Immigration and Social Change in the Republic of Ireland* (Manchester: Manchester University Press, 2007)

Van Kempen, R., 'Divided Cities in the 21st Century: Challenging the Importance of Globalisation', *Journal of Housing Built Environment* 22 (2007), 13–31

Verba, S., Lehman-Schlozman, K. and Brady, H., *Voice and Equality, Civic Voluntarism in American Politics* (Cambridge, MA: Harvard University Press, 1995)

Wang, Y.Y. and King-O'Riain, R., *Chinese Students in Ireland* (Dublin: NCCRI, 2006)

Ward, E., '"A Big Show-off to Show What We Could Do": Ireland and the Hungarian Refugee Crisis of 1956', *Irish Studies in International Affairs* 8 (1996), 131–141

Whitaker, T.K., *Interests* (Dublin: Institute of Public Administration, 1983)

White, R., 'Liberalism and Multiculturalism: The Case of Mill', *The Journal of Value Inquiry*, 2003, 37: 205–216

Wylie, G. and McRedmond, O. (eds), *Human Trafficking in Europe: Character, causes, consequences* (Basingstoke: Palgrave, 2010)

Index